THE PRICE OF PARADISE

Volume II

THE PRICE OF PARADISE

Volume II

EDITOR
RANDALL W. ROTH

MUTUAL PUBLISHING

Design
Michael Horton Design
Graphics
Bryant Fukutomi, Kevin Hand, and Rob Dudley
Cover layout
John Roth

First Printing 1993
9 8 7 6 5 4 3 2

ISBN 1-56647-042-0

Mutual Publishing
1127 11th Avenue
Honolulu, Hawaii 96816
Telephone (808) 732-1709
Fax (808) 734-4094

Printed in Australia

CONTENTS

*Communities that engage in lively, informed dialogue
will deal with their challenges more effectively.*

INTRODUCTION

Every community has its challenges. Some are big, others small. Some are solvable, others will never be resolved—at least not completely. Some are easily recognized, others require careful research.

Occasionally, there will be clear consensus within a community as to the best way to deal with a particular challenge, but usually not. In fact, disagreement and contention are to be expected, especially when the stakes are high.

The seventy-nine people who contributed to one or both volumes of *The Price of Paradise* share a love of Hawai'i. To us, this requires that we not only appreciate and celebrate this home we call paradise but also do what we can to preserve and enhance it for future generations.

Guiding principles. Because seventy-nine individuals are unlikely to agree on any one issue, and certain not to agree on every issue, we had to begin by defining our common bond—the "glue" that would hold us together. The following guiding principles were the result of that process:

1. Communities must take an honest look at the problems they face if they hope to do anything about them.

2. Communities that engage in lively, informed dialogue will deal with their challenges more effectively.

3. Communities have a moral obligation to keep the interests of future generations in mind when dealing with current challenges.

The title. Thomas Jefferson once wrote, "The price of freedom is eternal vigilance." His point, I think, was that something as precious as freedom should not be taken for granted. In somewhat the same vein, the price of paradise is eternal vigilance.

A friend who was kind enough to read a first draft of this volume called it depressing and wanted to know why these books weren't more uplifting. Specifically, he said, "Everybody knows things are screwed up. . . . we want you to tell us what to do about it."

To me, it just doesn't work that way. As painful as it may be to focus on problems, that's a first step that simply can't be skipped. The next, equally essential steps are for the community to discuss these problems, and then focus on possible solutions.

Elected officials can only do so much. It's *our* community and *we* have to be a part of any lasting solution. It would be tragic if the first step represented by the *Price of Paradise* books were not followed by additional steps toward specific solutions.

Struck a nerve. If book sales, media coverage, and speaking invitations from community groups are accurate indicators, our first volume struck a nerve in the community: readers purchased 20,000 copies in less than a year; 26 of its 38 chapters were reprinted in a wide variety of local and national publications; the book received generous coverage in the newspapers and on TV and radio; the authors made more than two hundred presentations to numerous community groups; and Hawai'i Public Radio started a weekly "Price of Paradise" talk show.

Perhaps even more exciting is that over a hundred community-minded individuals and businesses paid for a special printing of an additional 10,000 copies for classroom use by high school seniors. That increased the total number of books in circulation to 30,000 and put many of them into the hands of Hawai'i's future leaders. This is the intellectual equivalent of planting trees.

Diverse group. Most of the chapters in Volume I were written by economists and, naturally enough, focused on economic analysis. The contributors to Volume II are a more diverse group, and so the range of perspectives is noticeably wider. For example, readers will find more than a few chapters in this volume that focus on sociological and political analysis. *Vive la différence!*

The Democratic party in Hawai'i takes a few hits in this volume, some of them pretty hard. For what it's worth, that's not necessarily because we think other political parties have more to offer. If Republican officeholders weren't so rare in Hawai'i, I'm sure they would take a few shots, too. Anyone who thinks Hawai'i's challenges will go away if only we oust the Democrats had better think again. What this book is all about transcends party lines.

Each chapter is short and was written for nonexperts. As a result, the explanations are less technical and less complete than the authors would prefer. One of my jobs, as editor, was to convince them that you, the reader, would take that into account.

We have taken this step toward lively, informed dialogue as a service to the community. No author, cartoonist, graphic artist, advisor, or editor will receive monetary compensation. As with Volume I, all royalties will go to local charities.

The price. I believe all of us are lucky to be living in Hawai'i. But without effort on our part, future generations will not be so lucky. Paradise has its price, and in our case it's measured as much in vigilance as in dollars.

Randall W. Roth, Editor
September 1993

Communities have a moral obligation to keep the interests of future generations in mind when dealing with current challenges.

*Communities must take an honest look at the problems
they face if they hope to do anything about them.*

High School Seniors Comment on The Price of Paradise, Volume I

"Reading *The Price of Paradise* has proved to be awakening and informative. I found it to be very interesting because it dealt with very local and real concerns."

"The chapters were short and the comics added a sort of spunk that kept my attention span."

"I am definitely not a person who keeps up with the news or economics of our time, but what I was reading on politics, housing, sewers, tourists, education, etc., was really interesting! It was an eye opener, and a definite pleasure to read (once I got through the tax section)."

"It was easy to read and the cartoons helped a lot in explaining the concepts."

"Personally, I liked the book because of the wide range of topics covered. From Hawaiian Sovereignty to the capabilities of the University of Hawai'i; it was all good."

"It was tough reading for me. . . . I admit, though, that the information in the book was interesting, often surprising."

"I especially loved the cartoons that beautifully understated the points of each chapter. I feel that this book should be required in this course, and also think that all Hawai'i citizens should read it."

"Personally, I feel that *The Price of Paradise* is a really important book to read. . . . I've lived in Hawai'i all of my life for 17 years. Many of the terms explained in the book, like leasehold conversion and pollution, seemed to be of little importance to me. Through reading the book, I became more aware of the problems in Hawai'i."

CHAPTER 1

PETER S. ADLER
Executive Director
Hawai'i Bar Foundation

NORALYNNE PINAO
Attorney at Law
Amano & Pinao

"Are we losing our aloha spirit?"

There is a certain abiding spirit of community that we tend to associate with insular places. It has to do with the gift of giving, with reciprocity, and with interdependence. While little gestures and conventions speak to this, each community's "habits of the heart" are unique.

In many small towns, some folks always seem to know the names and genealogies of the families that live there and all the other ties that bind people together and to that place. They will share their stories with you if you ask them nicely and, often as not, will tell you all about that ineffable "something" that happens when people in their community interact.

In other locales—places where people farm and ranch, for example—it is still customary for people to gather to raise a barn or rebuild a house that has burned. Everyone comes from far away. Everyone pitches in, even people who don't like each other very much.

Even in a few hard-core city neighborhoods, this same attitude surfaces when neighbors bring each other welcoming gifts or stop to inquire about each other's health in barbershops and supermarkets. Wherever it occurs, it seems to have something to do with intimacy, caring, and the imparting of friendship to others.

Aloha spirit. In Hawai'i, we call all these things "aloha spirit," and it is part of what makes us special. It's part of who we are and why Hawai'i is different from Los Angeles, Wichita, Lexington, Philadelphia, and every other place. Here, the word "aloha" is used to convey love, to express compassion, to show mercy or sympathy, to describe charity and kindness, and to say hello, goodbye, farewell, and alas.

Despite its many uses, or maybe because of them, there is little agreement about what aloha means. George Kanahele, scholar, businessman, and civic leader, says, "It is hard to think of another word that over so many decades has aroused more public attention, even controversy among Hawaiians and non-Hawaiians, than aloha." What we can say, though, is that all its meanings—from compassion to charity, to simple greetings of kindred human beings—are essential to a caring and humane society.

Tourists and malihini. Are we losing our aloha spirit? The question is asked repeatedly, but the answer seems to depend on your perspective and who you define as "we." If you are a tourist or *malihini*, a comparative newcomer, Hawai'i probably looks considerably better than the place you've come from. The climate is temperate, the landscape is magnificent, beauty surrounds you on a daily basis, and Hawai'i's thriving local cultures offer endless diversity in food, art, dance, literature, music, and perspective. Along with these things are simple, everyday acts of friendliness that somehow didn't happen in that place you just left, or that happened with much less frequency: the touch of a smile from a stranger, a flower lei given, a helping hand, a kind word offered when none was needed or foreseen.

People from elsewhere—the occasional visitor, the repeat tourist, the recent transplant—notice these things right away. Aloha spirit, says King Intermediate School seventh-grader Joel H. K. Nakila, Jr., winner of an essay contest sponsored by Thomas Cook Currency Services, "is what people come to Hawai'i for. It's caring for people without expecting something in return." Perhaps because this caring is rare in the places they come from, or because it takes a more hospitable and amiable form here, *malihini* accumulate these experiences. They treasure them, remember them, and come back (or stay) because of them.

Depending on your tolerance for generalization, however, there are at least two other groups of people who might disagree strongly.

Kama'aina. If you are a certain kind of longtime resident of Hawai'i but not originally from here, some of this aloha spirit may look frayed and worn around the edges. Some might list it as an endangered species. A few say it's completely dead. What many kama'aina see these days is the crowding, congestion, and upraised middle-finger protestations that seem to come with urbanization. Looking around, you note the loss of little Mom and Pop stores in neighborhoods, the influx of chains with fancy French names at Ala Moana shopping center, the advent of warehouse discounters, crowds of tourists on formerly remote beaches, traffic jams, and a general decline in civility compared to life here ten, twenty, or thirty years ago.

Nostalgia plays a part no doubt, and, interestingly, many kama'aina date the decline in aloha from about the time they themselves arrived. Perhaps there is a cause-and-effect relationship. Nonetheless, there are other indicators that also may tell part of the story. Remember when front doors didn't have locks? Today, Hawai'i suffers from the "break-in blues": $10.3 million in cash and goods stolen during 5,718 burglaries in 1992. Or take traffic. There was a time—not so very long ago, in fact—when people still waved at each other from their cars. Nobody honked. Nobody cut in. Auto theft was completely unknown. Or even a little thing like fruit trees. Many kama'aina can still remember bags of mangos left on front porches. Today it's more likely your fruit tree will be stripped clean if nobody is looking.

Does this mean that aloha spirit has really deteriorated significantly? Andrew Lind, a renowned sociologist from the University of Hawai'i, thought so back in 1972. He believed that beneficence, consideration for others, and hospitality inherently decline when communities lose their intimacy.

Loss of familiarity, in turn, is in great measure a function of population increase and technology. It's harder to maintain that unique feeling of interconnectedness when the medium of exchange is a computer, a modem, a conference call, or a fax machine instead of a face-to-face smile. The reality today is that people on O'ahu, where the majority of Hawai'i's population reside, no longer can know and interact with everyone else as if Honolulu were a small community. Increasingly, our day-to-day associations take place with strangers.

Hawaiians. There is a third view that comes from people indigenous to this place, most of whom are resurgent with cultural pride, many of them politically astute and assertive. Some call themselves *kanaka maoli*, "true people." The aloha spirit, say some of these folks, isn't an elusive concept and it isn't dead. It's just gone underground for awhile. Why? Because it's been exploited.

Aloha spirit is a special blessing, intimately tied to Hawaiian culture. Because of this, it is vulnerable. It is easily captured by others and transformed by image-makers and marketeers into something designed to sell vacations to people from Japan, Germany, and Canada. Like the aloha shirt—which was "invented," patented, and then turned into an industry that primarily benefited people from elsewhere—there is a risk that the phrase "aloha spirit" could become a cynical commercial contrivance.

For this reason, many Hawaiians want to reclaim the phrase from non-Hawaiians entirely. "Aloha spirit," says Mahealani Kamau'u, executive director of the Native Hawaiian Legal Corporation, "is based on unconditional giving and sharing. Ironically, the very people who have the least to give materially—Hawaiians—are now being called on to share their aloha spirit in the greatest proportions. We see that the phrase has been expropriated by the tourism industry and turned into a call to self-interest. We should be nice because it's good for business. We reject that view." In fact, for Hawaiians, retaining the phrase "aloha spirit" as a unique cultural property may prove critical to coalescing the many diverse views Hawaiians have regarding sovereignty.

Shared sentiments. Many non-Hawaiians, including *kama'aina* and *malihini*, share those sentiments. Holly Henderson, a friend who cares deeply about such issues, puts it this way: "The dilemma of aloha is that it is possible to take it for granted, accept it as your due, love it, revel in it, luxuriate in it, take from it—and never reciprocate, never give anything back, and maybe never even know that if you don't, you destroy the balance that enables it to uplift community." Said differently, aloha spirit is not an abstract intellectual idea. It is a life form which must be nurtured and practiced if it is to survive.

Given the pace of demographic, economic, and political change in Hawai'i, this may become progressively more difficult. It is easier to reduce the notion of aloha spirit to a bundle of interpersonal codes than it is to infuse the "spirit" half of the equation into everyday affairs. But for some people, aloha spirit ultimately means just that. It is the divine breath that gives all of us a sense of humility, balance, and grace.

An individual thing. Perhaps it all comes down to individuals and their sometimes complicated relationships with each other and with the land that grounds and surrounds them. There are Hawaiians who don't have much aloha spirit for other people or for Hawai'i itself. Conversely, there are some non-Hawaiians who seem to have been born with aloha spirit. They give to others and to the place with no thought of receiving anything back. There are non-Hawaiians who have lived here for generations and have lost that spirit (or never had it in the first place), and people just arriving on United Airlines Flight 107 from Los Angeles who have more than their share of aloha but have never before heard the word spoken.

Love, affection, compassion, mercy, pity, and kindness—the things Mary Pukui and Samuel Elbert in their Hawaiian dictionary tell us make up aloha—transcend and cut across cultures. No cultural or ethnic group owns these things exclusively. If they are in decline, let's not forget that they seem to be in decline everywhere as we skate to the close of this difficult, extraordinary century.

In Hawai'i, however, these essential qualities of life—community caring, community giving, and community feeling—have a better-than-even chance of enduring because they spring so brightly from the land and its first people.

So long as these two things persist, so too will aloha spirit.

CHAPTER 2

CITIZEN RESPONSIBILITY

NANCY J. O'MALLEY
Foster Parent/Advocate

MICHAEL J. O'MALLEY
Attorney at Law
Goodsill Anderson Quinn & Stifel

"Does a citizen's responsibility to help the helpless end with the payment of taxes?"

The answer to this question is no, primarily because government agencies function properly only when held accountable for their actions. If the community-at-large doesn't show interest in the circumstances of abused and neglected children, for example, many such children will not be helped.

"Throw-away kids." The number of drug babies, battered children, sexually abused boys and girls, and other "throw-away kids" is shockingly high. The public seldom wonders about the well-being of these children once they have been taken into "protective custody" (i.e., removed from their own homes); people just assume that some government agency will take good care of these helpless victims. But it often doesn't work out that way. All too often, these children are further victimized by a dysfunctional system. They generally don't have family or friends who are willing and able to advocate on their behalf, and so they are totally dependent upon a bureaucracy called the Department of Human Services (DHS).

We will share information about the DHS which should concern and may even shock you. To be honest, that's our goal. We see helpless children falling through gaping cracks in this bureaucracy and want to do what we can to catch them.

Our report is based on data from a 1990 audit by the National Child Welfare Resource Center and information obtained directly from the DHS, plus numerous contacts with DHS social workers and administrators, court-appointed attorneys, foster children, and foster parents. You may find some of our statements hard to believe—at least our editor did until he checked them out.

Responsibility and performance. It's the DHS's responsibility to investigate reports of child abuse and neglect and to manage almost all of the 1,400 foster children in the state. When this agency is granted legal custody of a child, the state essentially becomes that child's legal parent, assuming the numerous responsibilities of that role. The child is then placed in the care of foster parents who receive compensation from the DHS for their services in caring for the child. How good is the DHS at "parenting"? Consider its record:

• Persistent high caseworker turnover results in workers frequently having little or no personal knowledge of the children they serve. In fact, 36 percent of the DHS caseworkers surveyed during the audit had held their position for less than one year. Although there are many qualified, committed caseworkers within the ranks of the DHS, too often these individuals get fed up and leave. Survey respondents cited problems with DHS management, policies, and bureaucracy among the major reasons to leave, ahead of low pay, stress, or burn-out. According to the audit report, DHS attempts to stem the tide have been "short-term and piecemeal."

• DHS caseworkers are legally required to maintain regular contact. Yet it's not unusual for caseworkers to go several months without seeing or even speaking to the children or their caregivers.

• At the time of initial placement into foster care, an extremely traumatic time in the life of a child, many DHS practices add to the pain of removal. For example, children are frequently taken to police stations before being placed in a home. Ever been to a police station? It can be a terrifying experience, even for adults. Children are often dropped off at a home or shelter with few or none of their belongings

and only the clothes they're wearing. Siblings have been separated abruptly, sometimes for years, with little opportunity for contact with each other.

• Children are frequently placed in "temporary" emergency shelters where they may languish for months. There used to be a 30-day maximum stay, but this rule was more often breached than observed and was discarded by the DHS. The living conditions in some of these shelters are substandard, if not deplorable. In violation of the DHS's own administrative rules, the children are often overcrowded, with no personal freedom to use the telephone or see friends. In one case, a child was kept in such a shelter for fourteen months, free to do nothing but go to school and watch television. Hawai'i has four times more children living in emergency shelters than the national average.

• Children in Hawai'i experience a substantially higher number of placements than the national average. Over 25 percent of teenage foster children, many of whom have been raised in the system, have had more than four placements; over 10 percent have experienced more than ten placements. Children are traumatized over and over, once by removal from their family, and again and again by DHS staff who shuffle them from placement to placement and from school to school.

• The DHS has a poor record of finding permanent homes for children. Federal money is available to subsidize the adoption of special-needs children, but as of the end of 1989 only twenty-four children statewide had received such assistance. The audit report concluded that the DHS had not diligently claimed federal funds to which it could be entitled, "resulting in loss of millions of dollars throughout the 1980s." The situation has not improved appreciably since then.

• Although federal law requires services designed to prepare older children for independence, Hawai'i's response has been disappointing, or, in the words of the audit report, "slow to non-existent." Thus, at age 18, many foster children are discharged into the adult world ill equipped to become self-supporting members of the community.

• The DHS often fails to obtain needed services for foster children. For example, Hawai'i has a well-funded program for infants and toddlers up to three years of age with special needs, and yet there are DHS workers who are unaware of this or simply fail to complete the paperwork required for participation. Further, mental health services so desperately needed by many foster children either are unavailable or are obtained only after lengthy delays.

Hard to be a foster parent. Consider what foster parents face:

• DHS workers often fail to inform them of, and even withhold information about, their rights as foster parents. For example, foster parents are legally entitled to attend court review cases pertaining to their child. Yet prior to the passage of 1993 legislation requiring the DHS to give notice of such hearings to foster parents, the majority of such parents didn't know that this right existed.

• Foster parents have a right to utilize a grievance procedure against the DHS when the department's actions violate administrative rules. But the process is incredibly intimidating for foster parents, who face DHS attorneys and numerous DHS staff in a courtlike setting one door from the DHS director's office, with no one to represent their interests unless they can afford a private attorney. Also, the objectivity of the "judges" is suspect, since they are deciding cases involving their co-workers and employer.

• There have been cases in which foster parents who questioned DHS workers or otherwise advocated for their children were explicitly threatened by caseworkers with removal of their child. This fear inhibits foster parents from voicing their concerns, no matter how legitimate. As hard as it may be to believe, the DHS seems to prefer dealing with profit-seeking people who are willing to quietly "ware-house" children and not make waves for the DHS.

• The audit report noted that fewer than half the responding foster parents thought the agency demonstrated a positive attitude toward them, and it quoted a particular foster parent who complained of the DHS's "vindictive attitude towards parents who ask questions."

The DHS response. The DHS director declined an invitation to meet with our editor to discuss a draft of this chapter. One of her assistants, upon being told that the chapter would be highly critical of the DHS, said, "foster care doesn't work well anywhere. . . . it's no different in Hawai'i." She went on to describe a new emphasis on not taking the children from their homes in the first place. From what we have seen, this may lighten the burden on the DHS—but only at the expense of the children.

The bigger lesson. Are you shocked by what you have just read? If so, do you want someone to blame? Many who work for and with the DHS, including caseworkers, judges, and attorneys, believe the endemic problems are due in large part to one or more of the following factors: poor management, an inert bureaucracy, institutional arrogance, and practices that result in little or no accountability. But we don't think the blame should stop there. Have you ever heard the expression, "When I point one finger at someone else, there are three pointed at me"?

Citizens who think their personal responsibility to help the helpless is extinguished by their payment of taxes had better think again. Government can do great things, but only if it is accountable, and that happens only when citizens insist upon it. Like it or not, the price of paradise includes getting informed and involved—about the work of the Hawai'i Department of Human Services as well as many other matters of great importance.

Call to action. Our hope is that some readers will decide to "do something." Perhaps they will volunteer to be foster parents, or maybe they'll provide financial support to the various local charities doing what they can to provide a safety net for children who are at risk, or maybe they will support efforts to prevent the violence and substance abuse that cause so many children to be taken into protective custody in the first place. Still others may take it upon themselves to be advocates for the helpless in general and foster children in particular. This last group might begin by insisting that their duly elected representatives pay more attention. It's not enough to just fund an agency; the legislature has to insist on reasonable results.

The hallmark of any caring community is the way it helps its members who cannot help themselves. By allowing children who already have been victimized to languish in a system that isn't working, the community victimizes them again. Besides the immediate and tragic human loss, there is the inevitable expense to society. A community that treats young victims like "throw-away kids" should start building more prisons and mental hospitals now because it's just a matter of time before they are needed.

"HEY, DON'T BLAME THE UNIONS FOR THE FILM INDUSTRY WOES—IT'S THE HIGH PRICES..."

CHAPTER 3

LABOR UNIONS

DAVID McCLAIN

Henry A. Walker, Jr. Distinguished Professor of Business
Enterprise and Financial Economics & Institutions
College of Business Administration, University of Hawai'i

ROBERT M. REES

Producer and Host of KFVE's "Island Issues"
Instructor of Business and American Studies
University of Hawai'i

CHARLES H. TURNER

Freelance Writer

"Have labor unions outlived their usefulness in Hawai'i?"

The answer to this question is no, but with one important qualification: some of Hawai'i's unions have become part of the establishment they used to counterbalance. These unions have lost the "fire in the belly" that got them started, and to that degree they now stand in the way of progress.

Background. For many people, contemporary images of unions go back to the bitter struggles that came to a head in 1946 when Hawai'i endured its first industry-wide strike. Five large companies (the Big Five) had controlled the sugar and pineapple laborers up until 1944, but between 1944 and 1947 the International Longshoremen's and Warehousemen's Union (ILWU) successfully organized those workers and the waterfront as well. The result was that Hawai'i quickly went from one of the lowest to one of the highest agricultural wage levels in the world.

Others remember the sugar strike of 1958. It lasted four months. Says one sugar industry executive, "Both sides of the table were shocked by the enormity of the '58 strike and I think both were resolved never to let such a thing happen again." What labor and management in Hawai'i learned was that sometimes it's better to share the wealth with each other and pass along any additional costs to the consumers.

The idea of unions in Hawai'i is symbolized for some by the recent struggle between rival factions of labor for control of film industry crews. There were whispers that this jurisdictional conflict culminated in arson and, ever since, Hollywood has been wary of Hawai'i. Some see this episode as a microcosm of all that's wrong with our unions; others see it as one unsubstantiated incident not indicative of anything.

Early struggles for reform. The more extreme views of unions overlook the courageous early struggles of organized labor. It was through these efforts that unions became an integral part of the American idea of reform and progress.

On the mainland, the United Auto Workers in Detroit had to physically defend themselves against violent attacks until General

Motors and Ford finally came to an agreement with them in the 1930s. Harry Bridges, the leader of longshoremen on the West Coast, forced so many reforms that he was branded a Communist by the House Committee on Un-American Activities.

The early union people in Hawai'i, determined to break the stranglehold of the Big Five, suffered similar hardships. As former ILWU union activist Ah Quon McElrath points out, it was a case of the "unions versus colonialism." McElrath also notes that the plantation workers in Hawai'i after World War II were fighting for "real wages— not wages that went for food at the company stores."

Union leaders often experienced personal attacks of one sort or another. Teamster and Hotel Worker president Arthur Rutledge was nearly deported during the 1950s on the charge of entering the United States illegally while still a child. Jack Hall, the leader of the Hawai'i ILWU, was convicted of Communist conspiracy under the Smith Act, but never served time because that act was struck down by the U.S. Supreme Court.

The struggle in Hawai'i was a struggle of working men and women against the establishment. The unions were the champions of the poor and the powerless. Their efforts were long and hard, but eventually they succeeded in providing dignity and financial reward to their members.

Recent developments. Union strength in America has declined in recent years. Unions have become less important and therefore less powerful as labor-intensive manufacturing has declined and service industries have grown.

The unions have also lost the advantage of good economic times. It used to be that management would meet almost any union demand to avoid interrupting the flow of commerce. Wage increases could be passed along as price increases. But those days of sharing the wealth and sticking it to consumers are gone, both on the mainland and in Hawai'i.

Some unions—in labor's version of the wisdom of Saint Theresa that the only thing worse than unanswered prayers is answered prayers— have learned that it is possible to demand and get too much. The Big Three automobile companies met so many union demands during the boom years of the 1950s and 1960s that they soon found themselves with commitments that were almost impossible to meet and still be competitive. Similarly, sugar and pineapple growers in Hawai'i, though they are the most productive in the world, have found it difficult to compete globally with companies whose workers earn in a day what Hawai'i's union members earn in an hour.

As a result of these global economic factors, the "hard work" industries of America have suffered and union strength has ebbed. Membership on the mainland is now only 16 percent of the workforce. And many of those unions that are surviving have had to abandon a strategy of confrontation and instead work *with* management to create a high-performance, globally competitive workplace.

Different in Hawai'i. The specter of the unions' waning power on the mainland combined with the continued decline of Hawai'i's agricultural workforce has led many here to conclude that organized labor in Hawai'i has outlived its usefulness and is on the verge of decline. Yet the union's part of our total workforce has not declined and remains at about 30 percent, nearly twice that of the mainland. This is partly because Hawai'i had relatively few manufacturing jobs in the first place.

The disparity in union strength between the mainland and Hawai'i is also influenced by the continuing importance of unions to our huge tourist industry and the growth of governmental unions—Hawai'i Government Employees Association, Hawai'i State Teachers Association, University of Hawai'i Professional Assembly, and United Public Workers—during a period of governmental workforce expansion.

In the tourist industry, Hawai'i's hotel worker and other tourist-related unions continue to represent the interests of workers, some of whom are relatively unskilled, who would otherwise be powerless. In that regard, these unions continue to make a substantial and relevant contribution to fairness and progress. In government, however, union organizations seem to have succumbed to the natural tendency of any bureaucracy toward survival and self-aggrandizement. This is the portion of the labor movement that often seems to oppose change and reform.

Symbiotic relationship. The government unions have become part of the Democratic party's grip on Hawai'i: the two enjoy a symbiotic relationship in maintaining the status quo. Unlike private businesses, which are limited in their ability to pass higher costs on to others, the government in Hawai'i has been willing and able to raise taxes to meet union demands for higher wages and better benefits in exchange for political support. The government unions prosper, the politicians get reelected, and it's all paid for by the taxpayers.

The leadership of the Hawai'i State Teachers Association (HSTA) provides a perfect example. This group has successfully opposed any meaningful attempt to evaluate the performance of its members despite community-wide concerns about teacher competence. Former HSTA president John Radcliffe once boasted, "No HSTA member was ever fired on my watch." In that spirit, the HSTA became one of the harshest critics of the findings of the lieutenant governor's Task Force on Educational Governance and has opposed local hiring and firing and lump-sum budgeting because these educational changes would invite schools to evaluate their teachers. Meanwhile, the HSTA is one

"GIVE 'ER THE CHECK..."

of the largest political contributors in the state. Even the principals of our public schools belong to a union and are given tenure not only as teachers but as administrators. They thus have little incentive to change anything, let alone to evaluate teachers.

Another government union, the University of Hawai'i Professional Assembly (UHPA), is the largest financial contributor to political campaigns in the state. The UHPA also spent almost $40,000 in 1992 just to promote itself on television during the legislative session.

The Hawai'i Government Employees Association (HGEA), once a progressive force that worked hard for the 1970 collective bargaining reforms, now seems to have as its primary mission the protection of a bloated public payroll of 50,000 employees. The HGEA has only the vaguest inkling of the trend on the mainland toward downsizing and "reinventing government."

The HGEA is also well known for providing legions of volunteers to political campaigns. During the 1993 session of the 17th Legislature—while budgets were being cut for programs for public school students, the mentally ill, and the poor—the HGEA was being assured that its members would receive a pay increase.

The conventional wisdom about organized labor—that it is in decline and is being forced by global competitive pressures to work more closely with management to improve productivity—certainly doesn't apply to Hawai'i's government unions. These unions have become part of the establishment and an extension of the Democratic party. They now use their clout not so much for reform but to protect a comfortable and contented status quo. It is this portion of the labor movement, the portion without "fire in its belly," that has outlived its usefulness and now stands in the way of the streamlining of government that is so sorely needed in these difficult budgetary times.

CHAPTER 4

PUBLIC SCHOOLS

RODERICK F. McPHEE
President
Punahou School

"Are Hawai'i's public schools likely to improve?"

I initially declined an invitation to write this chapter, thinking some readers would be turned off by the thought of a private school president evaluating the job being done in the public schools. But two things caused me to change my mind: I have been a public school superintendent and know what public schools can be, and it has become increasingly clear that people inside Hawai'i's public school system are reluctant to "tell it like it is" because they have to work daily with elements that are part of the problem. I have the luxury of not having to worry about upsetting the legislature, teachers union, school board, or whatever.

Running a well-funded private school is relatively easy. The people who run Hawai'i's public schools face an almost impossible task because of social realities beyond their control: about one-third of Hawai'i's preschool children are already headed for failure because of poverty, sickness, and other handicapping conditions, coupled with a lack of adult protection and nurturance. Private schools can dismiss students whose behavior disrupts the learning environment; public schools don't have that option. They have to do the best they can with everyone who shows up at their doorstep. There are, however, several areas in which improvement is necessary and could be achieved.

Political leadership. George Orwell would undoubtedly have had some incisive comments concerning the "double-speak" we receive from our elected officials about education. Governor Waihee, for example, has stated repeatedly that he wants public education in Hawai'i "second to none." But the only area I can find where Hawai'i leads the nation is in the 47 percent of the kindergarten children who are not ready to attend school when they arrive. It seems money is always tight when it comes time to actually provide more funds to the schools rather than just talk about providing them.

Modern parenting. A major part of the problem is the way the American parent brings up the American child. I offer this not as an excuse but as a simple observation. I agree with the following comments of psychologist John Rosemond, which appeared in the *Honolulu Advertiser*.

> In order to be educable a child must pay attention in class, accept personal responsibility for assignments given him by his teachers, and be determined to hang in there when the academic going gets rough. Almost without exception, teachers tell me that today's typical child does not pay attention, makes every attempt to avoid responsibility, and gives up at the first twinge of frustration.
>
> The connection between this and what is happening, or not happening, in the American family is as clear as the grass is green. This generation of American parents acts as if it's more their responsibility to pay attention to their children than it is their children's responsibility to pay attention to them. This generation of American parents believes it is their utmost duty to shield their children from frustration and failure, and rescue them if need be.

A related problem is the pervasive influence of television on young people. I believe this to be far worse than most people recognize, both in terms of the values children acquire during the incredible number of hours they watch, and in terms of what they are *not* doing—like reading and using their imaginations—while they sit as passive observers.

Average viewing for elementary students is about 25 hours a week, and for high schoolers, 28 hours a week. This is approximately six times the hours spent doing homework. "Sesame Street and the Death of

Reading," a chapter in Jane Healy's *Endangered Minds*, should be read by every parent. The implications are frightening.

"NOW I'M WORRIED — I UNPLUGGED THE THING AN HOUR AGO..."

Teachers aren't appreciated. What really matters in our schools are people: how well teachers teach and how well children learn. One problem is that the best students in our schools are not interested in going into teaching. This is not too surprising, since the incentives aren't there and since they read (when they do read) about the problems facing our schools, and about the blame attributed to the teachers for the problems of young people. Who needs that?

No revolution will ever occur in the schools unless it is focused primarily on what teachers do in the classroom with their students.

Adding to my concerns about schooling in Hawai'i is a statement made in 1992 by the president of the Hawai'i State Teacher's Association (HSTA) that 80 percent of the math teachers in Hawai'i are not certified to teach math.

Unsatisfactory governance. Clearly, governance of education in Hawai'i is not satisfactory at present. The Department of Education (DOE) is too centralized, with many layers of bureaucracy that slow normal activities and stifle innovation, and the governor, legislature, and State Board of Education are all involved in the decision-making process. Too many decisions are decreed by administrators at the top rather than by teachers and principals in the field. No institution can prosper with a system like that. The question of who is in charge here is a real one.

The task force on educational governance provided a litany of horror stories about our public schools. A teacher at Hau'ula Elementary School told of using her own money to buy school supplies needed by her students. Another teacher described a special education class on the Big Island being taught in a converted boys restroom, and a Farrington High School teacher reported serious problems in the storing and disposing of hazardous chemicals at the schools.

Unions erect barriers. My own belief is that the rise of unions in public education is a major problem. What I would label the "tyranny of collective bargaining" makes it difficult, if not impossible, for any school reform effort to succeed.

In 1961 the teachers of New York voted to unionize, in 1962 they won their first major collective bargaining agreement after a one-day strike, and in 1963 College Board scores in that state began to decline. This may be a mere coincidence, but I am convinced that the trade union mind-set that has dominated the teaching profession over the past twenty-five years is a major part of what has gone wrong in education.

Along those same lines, I can't reconcile the concept of tenure with the concept of professionalism. Teachers can't have it both ways, and Hawai'i provides an unfortunate example of why this is so. To my knowledge, very few teachers, no matter how incompetent, have been released in recent years. Most teachers in Hawai'i are competent and dedicated, but there obviously are some who should not be in the classroom. There seems, however, to be no effective mechanism to remove them.

Union members sometimes put their personal finances ahead of the welfare of their students. For example, in a recent teachers' job action in Montgomery County, Maryland, NEA-affiliated teachers refused to write letters of recommendation for college-bound seniors unless those same students wrote letters to legislators encouraging them to increase teachers' salaries. In Hawaiʻi, despite an acute shortage of teachers for special education, the HSTA has opposed higher pay for these people, retreating to their litany of higher pay for all teachers.

School community-based management (SCBM). Much is written about SCBM in Hawaiʻi. But, as long as our principals are unionized, and the union must approve actions involving the principals, little change should be expected. A few schools are making progress on SCBM, but they are the exception.

Nonprofit schools spend far less for results than governments spend for failures. The cost per pupil in the New York archdioceses' parochial schools—70 percent of whose students stay in school, stay off the streets, and graduate with high literacy and saleable skills—is about half that in New York City's failing public schools.

Recent research has isolated several characteristics of private schools which may make them more effective than public schools. Some of these traits could well be emulated by public schools: an emphasis on values; high expectations for students; an orderly learning environment; clear sense of institutional direction; vigorous team spirit; and adroit instructional leadership. Such characteristics are possible only when responsibility and authority are in place at the local school level. Lump-sum budgeting on a per pupil basis to each of our schools, with decisions about how to allocate these funds made by the people in each school, would ease the way to this kind of growth.

Another suggestion is to modify the method of selecting members of the school board so that a majority of them are appointed by the governor, with some elected by the people. This might increase accountability and could be a step in the right direction.

Clearly, school repairs must be removed from the Department of Accounting and General Services and put closer to the schools; our present system is inefficient, ineffective, and indefensible.

Some way must be found to reduce the bureaucracy and influence of the DOE on a teacher's actions in the classroom. A way of bringing important decisions down to the level of the school must be found, and teachers must be involved in the process or it is doomed to fail.

There should be much more choice in the public sector; competition in that sector would be advantageous to all concerned. Within the public schools, parents should be free to choose where their children attend.

Misplaced priorities. In a state where teachers need to use their own money to buy school supplies, a bookkeeping error meant an extra $32 million for a sports arena at the University of Hawai'i.

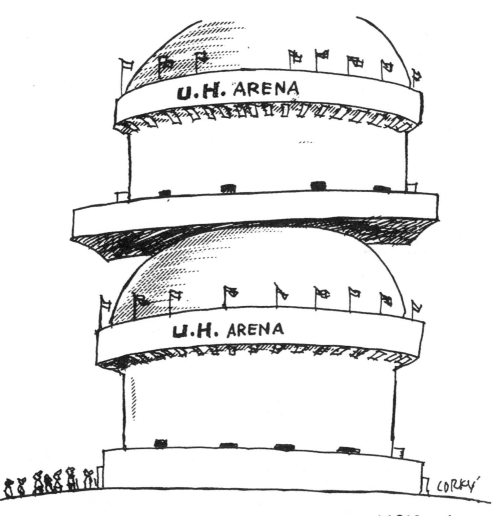

"WELL, IT SEEMS THE STATE BUDGET AND SUPPORTING BILLS HAD SOME TYPOS EVERYONE IGNORED..."

The renovation of the State Capitol should be further evidence to the public school teachers of Hawai'i that their importance to the state is not very impressive to those who control state finances.

Are our public schools likely to improve? I would like to be hopeful, but I don't see too many signs pointing in the right direction. Hawai'i's teachers and administrators face many obstacles, and our political leadership doesn't appear to be giving them much help.

"WE REALLY DON'T WANT A RUN-DOWN SYMBOL."
— A senator

"IT'S THE KID'S SAT SCORES; HERE, I CAN'T MAKE HEADS OR TAILS OF IT..."

CHAPTER 5

INVESTIGATIVE REPORTING

JAMES DOOLEY
Staff Writer
Honolulu Advertiser

"Why isn't there more investigative reporting in Hawai'i?"

All reporting is investigative. So-called investigative reporters do the same things all other reporters do. They collect information and write it into stories.

There are no special techniques. You don't have to wear a raincoat or exchange code words with golden sources. The only time I do things like that is to satisfy the expectations of people who have information I want. They've seen *All the President's Men* and want to rendezvous in underground garages. That kind of thing is fun once in a while, but not as a steady diet.

A matter of time. The only true distinction between investigative and standard reporting is time. The investigative reporter gets more time to work on stories, which means greater latitude in picking subjects to cover. How to use that luxury of time—choosing good subjects—is the single most important aspect of investigative reporting and the most difficult to execute.

Investigative Reporters and Editors, a national organization established after a reporter for the *Arizona Republic* was murdered in 1976, defines investigative reporting as independent work that leads to meaningful social change. It sounds high-flown, but I suppose this is as good a definition as any.

What it really means is that you don't scrounge around the police station or U.S. attorney's office trying to get details on the latest criminal investigation. You do your own work on a subject that hasn't been covered before and that badly needs exposure. All it requires is luck, timing, good editors, patience, and a thick hide.

There are some misses along the way: you know a story is true but you can't document it; or you finally realize a story is not true. But that's okay. Save the research; it will come in handy someday, probably in an unexpected way, but eventually it *will* connect to something else.

Stories are everywhere. An old television show about journalism, *Lou Grant*, once had an episode in which a reporter and editor were walking down the street, arguing the proposition that everyone they passed on the sidewalk was a potential Pulitzer Prize news story. I agree with that proposition, but I would take it a couple of steps farther. The story possibilities weren't just in everyone they passed, but in every thing. From the sidewalk under their feet (who laid it? how much did it cost? how'd they get the work?), to the food in their stomachs (where'd it come from? who shipped it? is it nutritious?), to the sky above them, they were surrounded by potentially great news stories. That's the wonderful thing about journalism. It's everything: life and death, mundane and magnificent. The ability of a reporter and editor to realize the news potential of a subject is a key to their success. Too often in this business we pay too much attention to the immediate and lose sight of, not just the future, but the past as well. There has to be time for it all.

Another thing I would add to the curbside discussion of the investigative reporter and editor is that all stories are related. Somehow or other, sooner or later, you will find that the most disparate of subjects are connected in unforeseen ways.

Hawai'i has taught me this. It is a journalism laboratory, rich and fertile. Most stories can't run away. Those that try can now be tracked down with the help of newsroom computers.

Hawai'i has a good public records law and a civil service that is, with a few notable exceptions, honest and hardworking. Some of my best stories have come from bureaucrats so sorely offended by waste or abuse that they just couldn't keep quiet about it any longer.

And in Hawai'i, more so perhaps than in other places, one story leads to another. Pull one out of the ground, follow its roots, and you've got a million more. We have a joke in the newsroom that the staff is really working on just one big story . . . we just don't know what it is yet. Someday it will all come together.

One big story. I'll cite one story and list some of the peripheral stories that are connected in one way or another to it—just some of them because I don't have nearly enough room here for all. Plus, I don't know them all.

I did a series of stories back in the early 1980s about secret land partnerships here, commonly known as "huis," that included influential public officials as investors.

One of the partnerships I discovered had quietly bought and sold a piece of property at Nukoli'i on Kaua'i several years earlier, turning a $4 million profit. The land itself turned out to be the subject of an intense antidevelopment campaign raging on the Garden Isle just at the time I discovered the hui. Luck and timing.

Investors in the Nukoli'i hui, I learned, included a state supreme court justice, the son and daughter of former governor John Burns, and John E. S. Kim, a convicted tax evader and former lobbyist for Amfac (the state's largest corporation at that time). Amfac had sold Nukoli'i to the hui. A key Amfac executive later turned up as a hui investor.

Another investor was Edwin Honda, a state circuit judge who earlier had been director of the State Department of Regulatory Affairs (DRA), the agency that is supposed to oversee public registration of business partnerships.

I asked Honda if he thought the hui should have been registered. He told me the question had never come up when he was the boss of the DRA (which was when the Nukoli'i hui was formed). So I addressed the question to DRA official Russel Nagata, who later became state comptroller. Nagata told me the hui probably should have been registered, but later he changed his position when interviewed by George Cooper, coauthor with Gavan Daws of *Land and Power*.

Years later, I accidentally discovered that Nagata, while serving as state comptroller, had doctored a copy of a state record before giving it to me. He had carefully excised a portion of the memo which concerned state protocol spending, to make it look like I had received a complete document. The missing paragraph concerned Bank of Hawaii vice president Dolly Ching's role in providing credit cards to state officials for their use in charging protocol expense. At the time, Ching was a member of the Judicial Selection Commission, which later selected Russel Nagata to be a state district judge.

All related. Are you getting the picture here? The original Nukoli'i story, written in 1981, was connected to the doctored documents story written in 1992, which was connected to the Judicial Selection Commission story, which was connected to other Dolly Ching stories I then wrote.

Back to Nukoli'i now. Another investor was a little known state bureaucrat named Yukio Takemoto, later plucked from relative obscurity to become director of the Department of Budget and Finance in the Waihee administration. Takemoto became a central figure in a later series of stories I wrote on non-bid and sole-source state purchasing. My starting place for that series was not Takemoto's department but the purchasing division in the Department of Accounting and General Services, headed by . . . Russel Nagata. That department maintained a list of non-bid contracts awarded by most, but not all, departments of the executive branch. The list was a gold mine of stories.

One of the first nuggets concerned a non-bid contract awarded by Takemoto to GTE Hawaiian Tel to supply a new telephone system for the executive branch. The $1 million contract later grew into a $3 million job. It was awarded on a non-bid basis in part because of the phone company's monopoly position in Hawai'i telecommunications, which in turn is regulated by the Public Utilities Commission (PUC).

In 1992, I wrote a story about how members of the PUC, along with Takemoto and assorted other officials, were the phone company's guests at a week-long social bash and professional golf tournament at the Royal Ka'anapali golf courses on Maui.

Those courses were built by Amfac (a familiar name) with the invaluable political assistance of Masaru "Pundy" Yokouchi, a Maui power broker and developer who had organized . . . the Nukoli'i hui.

The same Ka'anapali golf courses also served as collateral for a $60 million operating loan granted Amfac in 1991 by the State Employees' Retirement System, the $5 billion public pension fund operated out of Yukio Takemoto's budget department.

Now are you getting the picture?

This is not a conspiracy theory. Many of the connections and relationships recited here may be accidental or incidental results of life in an island state. But they are connections nevertheless, part of what I increasingly perceive to be one huge, organic News Story.

Connecting dots. That's really what the news business is: exploring, chronicling, and investigating life. Everything is connected in one fashion or another, whether by accident or design.

The work is not costly, expense account-wise. You do run up some legal bills, but so does every other line of work these days. I have never been sued for a story I've written. There have been threatened lawsuits—the only kind of threat editors take seriously—but no actual suits. And to a great degree, the work gets easier as you go along. You build up files, develop a network of sources, and start connecting dots.

Why the field has been left largely to me in the past decade or so by local news organizations is something I can't answer. Certainly there have been occasional and quite successful efforts by other local reporters—but no sustained commitment, as far as I can see, by any medium except the *Advertiser*.

CHAPTER 6

TELECOMMUNICATIONS

GEORGE DARBY
Attorney at Law

MEHEROO JUSSAWALLA
Senior Fellow/Economist
East-West Center

"Why hasn't the state been able to attract high-tech companies?"

State officials have spent tens of millions of dollars trying to diversify Hawai'i's economy and attract higher-paying jobs. The rhetoric has been especially fierce with respect to high-tech possibilities. Like their counterparts in other states, our elected officials see high-tech as *the* industry of the future. It is relatively friendly to the environment, provides high-paying jobs, and seems certain to grow.

To pursue this high-tech vision, the state government has created, staffed, and funded the High Technology Development Corporation, the Hawai'i Information Network Corporation, the Office of Space Industry, the Hawai'i Innovation Development Program, the Hawai'i Strategic Development Corporation, the Research and Development Industry Promotion Program, and many other programs and agencies.

Hawai'i's advantages. Multinational corporations have made it clear that Hawai'i has the potential to be the most attractive place for their telecommunications-intensive operations in the Asia-Pacific region. At the top of their list of reasons is Hawai'i's location. They know that many of the new, high-powered telecommunications satellites will be "invisible" and of limited benefit to earth stations on the U.S. mainland. That makes Hawai'i the best state in which to put a state-of-the-art teleport to access the new satellites *as well as* existing transpacific fiber optic cables. (A teleport is like an airport, except that messages, rather than airplanes, come and go.)

Compared with non-U.S. locations in the Asia-Pacific region, Hawai'i has the advantages of political stability, inexpensive telecommunications to the U.S. mainland, and better legal protection of trade secrets and software. And Hawai'i is a beautiful place with a rich history and diversified population, all of which add to its charm and appeal.

Total failure. Despite these advantages, the state has yet to attract *even one* sizable company. In fact, Hawai'i is losing, not gaining, high-tech jobs. VeriFone, Inc. and Intelect, Inc., two high-technology companies that started in Hawai'i, have relocated significant portions of their businesses out of Hawai'i. Sadly, Hawai'i finds itself on the "trailing edge" of telecommunications-oriented high-tech. Anyone concerned about the future of Hawai'i has got to be wondering why.

Some of the factors (e.g., high cost of living, inadequate public school system, and unfriendly business environment) are discussed in *The Price of Paradise*, Volume I, and elsewhere in this volume. But to us, the single biggest reason for Hawai'i's dismal failure in this area is that it doesn't have a competitive telecommunications environment. This, in turn, is the result of actions (and inactions) by a highly politicized Public Utilities Commission (PUC) and surprisingly effective lobbying by GTE Hawaiian Telephone Company (Hawaiian Tel) to preserve its monopoly.

Monopolies and regulatory commissions. The PUC is charged with regulating certain types of utility companies, such as motor carriers, water carriers, electrical utilities, and telecommunications utilities. The regulatory task of the PUC is based in economic theory: states should permit "natural monopolies" to hold franchises for exclusive service and, in return, accept government regulation of their prices and conditions of service.

Prior to the 1980s, many of the PUC commissioners were experts who thoroughly understood the industries they were regulating. But more recently PUC commissioners typically have been career state government employees, ex-legislators, or other politically connected persons.

Most mainland experts now recognize that the regulatory treatment of telephone companies as natural monopolies outlived its usefulness some years ago. It benefited the old Bell System by ensuring profits without the rigors of competition. And it was advantageous to elected officials because a monopoly can subsidize local service by charging more for toll service. That generally pleased residential subscribers (also known as constituents) who didn't understand that the long-term effect of no competition was higher costs for *both* local and long-distance service.

The federal government, recognizing it was time for a new approach, broke up the Bell System in 1984. The benefits with respect to interstate telecommunications are already apparent: greater variety of service options; increased quality and efficiency; more rapid introduction of innovation; and, perhaps most important to most people, lower prices—much lower prices.

A growing number of mainland states have followed the federal government's example by deregulating intrastate telecommunications (calls within one state). Those states—such as California, New York, Illinois, and Georgia—tend to be the homes of most of the country's new telecom-intensive businesses and jobs.

Continuing monopoly in Hawai'i. Do you realize that a one-minute, daytime call from Honolulu to Kahului costs forty cents, while the same call to New York City costs thirty cents? In a nutshell, the reason is that the federal government has deregulated calls from one state to another, but our elected officials have chosen *not* to deregulate intrastate calls.

You've got to be wondering why. We believe it primarily has to do with Hawaiian Tel's effectiveness in lobbying for protection from competition. And make no mistake, it does not want to compete.

The following story is instructive: a subsidiary of Hawaiian Tel's parent corporation used to be in the business of providing something called a central office switch. In the middle and late 1980s, this switch—known by technocrats worldwide as the GTD-5—was "leap-frogged" by those of other companies such as AT&T and Northern Telecom. Within a relatively short time, a growing number of experts had concluded that the GTD-5 was no match in price, performance, or upgradability. Consequently, it became increasingly difficult (eventually impossible) for Hawaiian Tel's sister company to sell GTD-5 switches on the mainland where telephone company procurement had been made competitive. But because there were no requirements for competitive procurement here, Hawaiian Tel was allowed to buy the outdated GTD-5 switches.

Thanks to its monopoly, Hawaiian Tel has been in no hurry to buy and install modern switches. The last batch of GTD-5s bought by Hawaiian Tel was obsolescent when purchased. Tragically, the GTD-5 was then and forever will remain technically incapable of providing something called Integrated Service Digital Network (ISDN). We don't want to bore you with the details, so we'll cut to the bottom line: ISDN has become the nervous system of modern interstate and international business. Without it, we can forget about attracting much in the way of high-tech business. Only one other state, Alaska, is equally backward when it comes to modern switching.

Modern technologies. Simply to get into the game of trying to attract new high-tech businesses (not to mention retaining the few already here), Hawai'i must get ISDN and other modern technologies which the GTD-5 is incapable of providing. But in order for that to happen, Hawaiian Tel must face the expensive and time-consuming task of installing a second, non-obsolete switch in each central office—and it has not even *begun* that process.

Surely you're wondering why Hawaiian Tel has been allowed to do this. We believe the answer has to do with politics. Hawaiian Tel has successfully used lobbying and other activities to defend its monopoly powers: every attempt to introduce meaningful intrastate competition in telecommunications has been killed in the legislature or vetoed by the governor.

We don't blame Hawaiian Tel for its effective lobbying or its self-interest. It pretty much has behaved the way profit-seeking companies are expected to behave. The failure is that of politicians who don't understand that Hawaiian Tel's best interests and those of the state are on two separate paths.

Not so local. We are not in favor of labeling businesses as "local" and "nonlocal." There's been too much of that in recent years, often as a pretext for cronyism, protectionism, or corruption. But with a name like *Hawaiian* Tel and an annual report that tries hard to make it look ... well, Hawaiian, it should be noted that its chief executive officer and five out of the eight directors listed in its 1992 annual report do not live in Hawai'i and, presumably, have no intention of ever doing so.

Bud Smyser pointed out in the first volume of *The Price of Paradise* that nonresident owners lack "the commitment that comes from knowing their children and grandchildren will grow up here." He also noted: "To assure that [future-shaping decisions] are of our people, by our people and for our people, we will have to look more to our elected state and local governments."

Until our elected officials recognize that Hawaiian Tel's best interests and those of the state are on different paths, Hawai'i will remain a "digital backwater" that trails other states and nations. Our children and their children may be able to find jobs changing bed sheets, but they can forget about designing spreadsheets.

© 1993 JOHN S. PRITCHETT

CHAPTER 7

INTERNATIONAL ROLE

A. A. "BUD" SMYSER
Contributing Editor
Honolulu Star-Bulletin

"Is Hawai'i's location an economic plus or minus?"

A friend of mine phrases the question this way: "Are we in the center of the Pacific or the middle of nowhere?" However the question is phrased, the answer is anything but easy and, frankly, not a lot of fun. You see, at one time I was considered by many the head cheerleader for Hawai'i's international role (other than just as a tourist destination). Some commentators have credited me with expressions like "Capital of the Pacific" and "Geneva of the Pacific." I even researched and wrote an East-West Center report in 1988 on Hawai'i's future in the Pacific.

I had my doubts, but basically I was optimistic. I even compared Hawai'i's level of international economic activity (an estimated 3 percent of gross state product) to that of pre-statehood tourism. I never thought international economic activity would supplant tourism as the engine that drives Hawai'i's economy, but I did feel it could be a strong diversifying element.

Sadly, I'm not nearly so optimistic these days.

Office of International Relations. When the state Office of International Relations (OIR) was created in 1990, Governor Waihee said he hoped it would be his strong left arm in the international arena just as his Office of State Planning has been his strong right arm in state affairs. It hasn't been, for several reasons.

First, it has had three different directors in three years, and a recommendation that it have a strong community-wide international advisory board was never implemented.

Second, for much of its short life OIR has fought just to preserve its existence. It now exists under a law that will sunset June 30, 1995.

Third, OIR is saddled with fifteen separate functions, none particularly burdensome by itself, but with a collective weight that ties down its staff the way Gulliver was tied down by the tiny Lilliputians. There is little wiggle room and no escape from paperwork or the threat of political reprisal if something is left undone.

Other problems. We have gone backward as a transportation center. Available airline seats to the U.S. mainland are down 30 percent since 1991, and low seat occupancy seems sure to diminish international flight schedules. United and Continental no longer offer direct connections from Hawai'i to New Zealand and Australia. Singapore Airlines and All Nippon Airways no longer serve Hawai'i at all. And if airport landing fees have to go up significantly to fund our planned $2.5 billion expansion project, even more international carriers may choose to overfly Hawai'i.

As discussed in the preceding chapter, Hawai'i would be at the top of the list of places to locate the telecommunications-intensive operations of multinational corporations if only we had a competitive telecommunications environment. But we don't, and we aren't likely to, given the protectionist practices of our Public Utilities Commission and state legislature.

We now know beyond doubt that Hawai'i will never be an international Silicon Valley; dreams of an international stock exchange located in Honolulu have been dashed; and plans for the building of a Pacific Nations Center in downtown Honolulu have been set aside, perhaps permanently.

What went wrong? New technology increased the airlines' ability to overfly us. That development could be countered only by strongly increased demand on the ground, and that hasn't happened.

Our visitor industry may be losing its lustre. The aloha spirit, difficult though it may be to measure, clearly has eroded. We've enjoyed heady economic growth, but we didn't do a good job of getting everyone into the act. Those excluded are angry and increasingly likely to show it. Overcrowding and crass commercialism surely are a part of this as well. Too many tourists head home feeling used and abused. A growing number of residents feel the same.

We also must face up to a business climate that has been damaged by government intrusion and excessive regulation; widespread cronyism in government; emotional resentment against outsiders as evidenced in the flare-ups against Japanese investment overall and against golf courses in particular; and a disappointing public education system that doesn't seem to be getting any better.

Outsiders also have been repelled by our protectiveness. They may understand it in sugar, our fading number-one agricultural crop, and maybe even in the way we protect our banks from outside competition—after all, the banks have repeatedly proven themselves to be public-spirited leaders in the community. But outsiders cannot understand or readily accept ad hoc actions like those of Senator Inouye and Governor Waihee when United Airlines tried to expand its interisland flight schedule. Telling United to take a hike surely offended that company, but the bigger problem is the message that kind of tactic sends to others thinking of doing or expanding business activity in Hawai'i. They've got to want to come here pretty badly to subject themselves to the unpredictability of ad hoc protectionism.

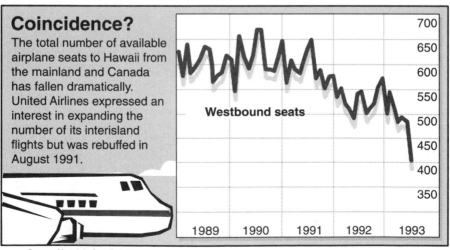

Coincidence?

The total number of available airplane seats to Hawaii from the mainland and Canada has fallen dramatically. United Airlines expressed an interest in expanding the number of its interisland flights but was rebuffed in August 1991.

Westbound seats

700
650
600
550
500
450
400
350

1989   1990   1991   1992   1993

Source: Honolulu Star-Bulletin

Fall from the sky? Our political and business leaders seem to be waiting for Hawai'i's international role to define itself and fall from the sky. Not long ago, the Bank of Hawaii sent out a map of certain Pacific and Asian countries after deleting the names of eighteen countries (Australia, Cambodia, China, Hong Kong, Indonesia, Japan, Laos, Malaysia, Myanmar, New Zealand, North Korea, Papua New Guinea, Philippines, Singapore, South Korea, Taiwan, Thailand, and Vietnam). The Bank asked a group of community leaders to label each of those eighteen countries and give its approximate population, capital city, and current leader.

If each participant had been able to supply just one of these four items about each of the eighteen countries, they would have scored a combined 810 points (one item, times eighteen countries, times forty-five participants). In the aggregate, they scored only 485 and would have done worse except for three or four standout individuals.

"We all have to start doing our homework," the Bank report concluded, "or any claim to a special role in the Pacific may soon have to be abandoned." I'll be the first to say it will take more than a geography lesson to make things happen. But the results of this quiz

make it look as though the participants, at least, think Hawai'i is indeed in the middle of nowhere.

What will it take? It is truly unfortunate that United Airlines' 1991 attempt to increase its investment in Hawai'i was so rudely rebuffed. Instead of a financial incentive to fly more people to Hawai'i, United was given reasons to cut back on flights.

Protectionism may keep special interests happy for a while, but it tends to leave everyone that much less able to compete. It's easy with hindsight to blame Senator Inouye and Governor Waihee, but their kneejerk protectionism was probably a mere reflection of an Island-wide, inward-looking mentality stemming from what the late Governor John A. Burns used to call a "subtle sense of inferiority." We can't be inward-looking, and we certainly can't doubt our ability to go head-to-head with others, if we are to increase our role in the international arena.

And we cannot continue to take tourism for granted. As an industry, tourism may have its shortcomings, but it has never been fully appreciated for having single-handedly raised the standard of living of *most* residents of Hawai'i. We must treasure and nurture it more. The place to begin is with tourism industry people who don't understand and appreciate what makes Hawai'i Hawai'i.

To the extent possible, all tourism should revolve around the Hawaiian culture—not to exploit it, but to celebrate it! Let's slow down a bit on the glitz and invest more in the education and inculturalization of the workers, many of whom currently know nothing of Hawaiian history, language, or culture. Aloha spirit would replenish, travelers would want to return (maybe to do business), and those who have been most left out of the economic good times—native Hawaiians—would find their services in especially high demand.

We must demand better government. A good start would be to insist that candidates not only tell us what they *will* give us but also what they *won't*. It's the hard choices they're prepared to make that define each candidate. Roadside waving and "second to none" rhetoric tell voters nothing about hard choices.

We must recognize areas where unions are holding us back and make changes accordingly. There are constructive ways to deal with difficult labor issues. For example, the International Longshoremen's and Warehousemen's Union has shown that flexibility and reasonableness can be effective in getting what its members need, if not what they want. Similarly, the International Typographical Union has led by example by allowing unnecessary jobs to be phased out, as long as affected workers are compensated, retired, or given a chance to retrain for another position. Unfortunately, too many unions insist on inflexible work rules and unproductive positions, evidently without realizing that every employer has to be competitive to survive in the long run.

Special environment. We must recognize and take advantage of our strengths. Our ethnic and cultural diversity is more than just unique, it is inspiring. By showing the world that many different races can maintain ethnic pride and heritage and yet work and play and raise families side by side, we attract public-spirited employers who want to provide that kind of special environment for themselves and their workers.

Education should be our calling card. From preschool to postgraduate work, Hawai'i should be in the running as a place to get educated. I'm especially hopeful with respect to our community colleges. It's tough for UH to compete with Harvard, Stanford, and the like. But our community colleges could be a major provider of international training.

Our educational system will not be what we want it to be until the state Department of Education develops and articulates a clear mission the community can support. The desire for change and a readiness to act are there, waiting for leadership. I'm for a voucher system that would give parents more of a choice about where to send their kids. The department would *have* to compete. Unfortunately, it will probably take that kind of "nuclear" jolt to force meaningful change.

Finally, all of us must be more outward-looking. It's folly to think of ourselves as being in the center of anything until we pay more attention to what's going on elsewhere. That will involve more than a geography quiz, but we've got to start someplace. See how well you do identifying the eighteen Pacific and Asian countries that I listed on page 54 and a few things about them. These are countries, by the way, that are growing daily in importance. If most readers do poorly, perhaps that means that, at least for now, Hawai'i is in the middle of nowhere.

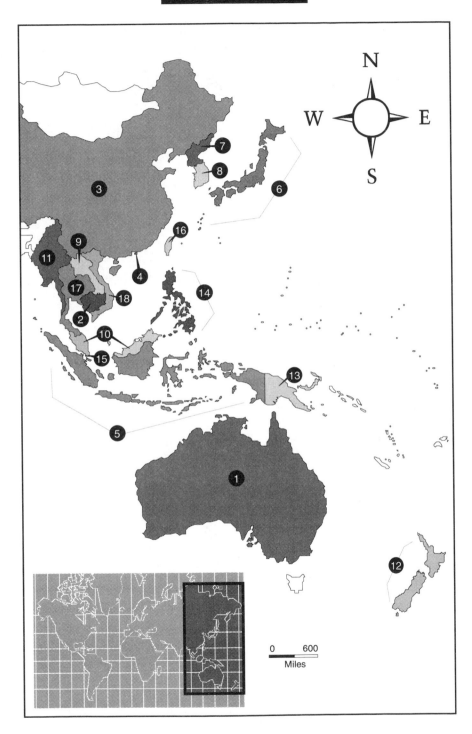

Country	Capital	Population	Political or National Leader
1. Australia	Canberra	17,000,000	Paul Keating
2. Cambodia	Phnom Penh	7,000,000	Hun Sen
3. China	Beijing	1,200,000,000	Jiang Zemin, Li Peng
4. Hong Kong	—	6,000,000	Chris Patten
5. Indonesia	Jakarta	180,000,000	Suharto
6. Japan	Tokyo	123,000,000	Morihiro Hosokawa
7. North Korea	Pyongyang	22,000,000	Kim Il Sung
8. South Korea	Seoul	44,000,000	Young Sam Kim
9. Laos	Vientiane	4,000,000	Nousak Phoumsavan
10. Malaysia	Kuala Lumpur	18,000,000	Datuk Seri Mahathir Mohamad
11. Myanmar	Rangoon	42,000,000	Dhan Shwe
12. New Zealand	Wellington	3,400,000	Jim Bolger
13. Papua New Guinea	Port Moresby	4,000,000	Paias Wingti
14. Philippines	Manila	65,000,000	Fidel Ramos
15. Singapore	—	2,700,000	Goh, Chok Tong
16. Taiwan	Taipei	20,000,000	Lee Tung-hui
17. Thailand	Bangkok	56,000,000	Chitichai Choonhavan Chuan Leekpai
18. Vietnam	Hanoi	67,000,000	Le Puc Anh

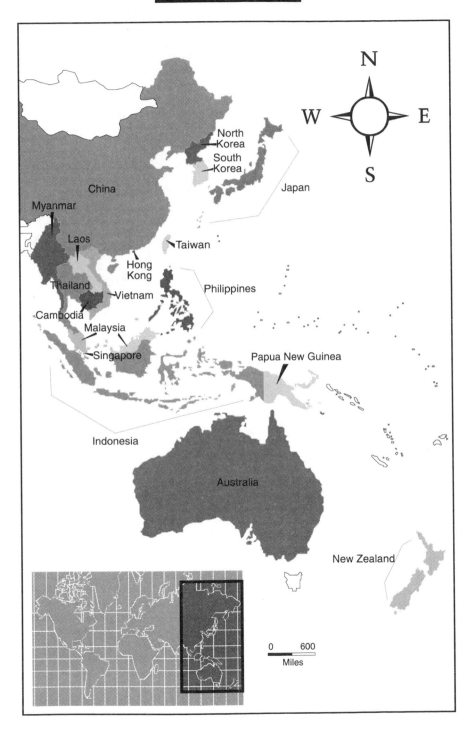

CHAPTER 8

PRIVATIZATION

GEORGE MASON
Editorial Page Editor and Publisher Emeritus
Pacific Business News

"Should government privatize some of its functions?"

"Privatization" is a relatively new word one hears more and more. It describes the shift of functions from the public sector (government) to the private sector (profit-seeking businesses). The shift may be in the form of a sale or long-term lease of a government-owned facility; a franchise to finance, develop, own, and operate a new facility; a short-term contract to manage a facility or provide services; or issuance of vouchers that can be used by the public to pay for privately produced goods and services.

Examples outside Hawai'i. The concept has caught on rather quickly. For example, no one imagined in 1980 that prisons could or would ever be owned or run by private companies. But by the end of 1992 there were fifty-five privately run facilities across the country, with an inmate population of 18,808 and a capacity of 20,867. Experts estimate that another seven or eight prisons will be privatized by the end of 1993.

Many small airports are already under private management or ownership, and serious negotiations are under way to privatize Baltimore, La Guardia, Los Angeles, and other major airports. London's Heathrow is one of seven British airports that went private in 1987.

Tucson, Arizona's fire department is privately run. So is its garbage collection. Private toll roads are quite common, especially in the

Northeast. And in recent years, the private sector has virtually taken over package delivery from the U.S. Postal Service—and nipped off a chunk of its letter mail service as well.

Hawai'i examples. A tiny fraction of Honolulu's bus system went private in 1993, with four Grayline buses being put into rush-hour express service, no standing permitted. This could be the forerunner of a plan called BusPlus in which a consortium of tour bus operators would put dozens of buses on the road during critical rush hours.

A private company, Waste Management, Inc., was hired by the Big Island mayor and county council in 1993 to operate a new landfill in North Kona.

But these examples illustrate the exception rather than the rule. In fact, Hawai'i might even be described as the only state moving *away* from privatization. For example, the state and counties have more or less gotten into the housing development business, competing with private companies in the process. Also, the state displaced some private after-school child-care providers when it adopted the A+ program, and traffic helicopter businesses when it made Captain Irwin a state employee.

Reasons to privatize. The private sector tends to be much more efficient than government when it comes to providing goods and services. Government generally doesn't know its cost of providing specific goods and services, and doesn't have a strong incentive to minimize such costs. Private businesses must watch costs like a hawk. If a company's costs get higher than necessary, profits fall, and if adjustments aren't made, it's just a matter of time before that company can't keep up with competitors who have kept costs in check.

The mayor of Indianapolis, Steve Goldsmith, wanting to improve city services while holding the line on taxes, decided to put a pencil to his costs. What he found was that tremendous amounts of taxpayer dollars could be saved by privatizing many services traditionally provided by the city.

When he said pothole repair work would be put out to bid, the ninety-two affected city workers refused to believe that a private company could do their work for a lot less. What they didn't realize (but soon learned) was that the cost of road work includes more than just the wages of the folks actually repairing potholes. In this case, there were thirty-two supervisors whose salaries and overhead had to be included.

Once enlightened to the basics of cost accounting, the workers made the mayor an offer: "Keep just four of those thirty-two managers and put five of us (rather than four) on each truck, thus eliminating the need for five vehicles." The mayor's accountant ran the numbers and said it all made sense. For everyone except the twenty-eight managers who had to find more productive things to do with their time, it was a story with a happy ending. The city crew won the contract against private bidders.

Worker resistance. Workers tend to view privatization as a negative process, one that results in lost jobs. But they are beginning to realize that the lost jobs are mostly those of unproductive management. The Indianapolis case is a perfect example of that.

Government workers worldwide have a well-deserved reputation for inefficiency. But it's wrong to blame them. Workers in Russia, for example, are not lazy. And yet, Western observers marvel at how unproductive they have become. Their inability to compete in a global economy, or even provide themselves with a decent standard of living, is a *system* problem, not a *people* problem.

The bigger problem is resistance from union leadership, even though privatization doesn't mean decertification of the union. For example, the United Public Workers already has filed a lawsuit to stop the attempt to privatize the new landfill in North Kona, even though the private contractor is willing to deal with that union. If nothing else, this action might discourage future privatization efforts.

Ironically, one of the reasons for contracting with the private company was a desire to shift legal liability from the county to the operator. This can be a significant benefit to taxpayers in an increasingly litigious society.

Accountability. Privatization does *not* mean that government simply walks away and trusts that the lowest qualified bidder will do a good job. Accountability is the hallmark of privatization, and it requires government involvement.

Government must set standards and then hold the contracting party to those standards; it has to continue steering the boat now being paddled by the private sector. If left to steer on its own, the private sector will invariably choose a direction based on its self-interest. For example, a private garbage collection company would love to drop customers located in difficult-to-serve areas. But, if public policy dictates that everyone should be served, the contract can so provide and any failure to do so will subject the company to liability. Similarly, if private companies were to run the libraries and the cost of staying open evenings and weekends cut profits too much, an unregulated company would simply eliminate those hours of operation. But they can't do that if government does its job of setting clear standards and conditions and then holds companies to them.

Those who feel threatened by privatization say it leads to hanky panky (better known as corruption). This is always a possibility, but less so than the alternative, where decisions are based more on politics than efficiency. Without privatization, government is accountable to no one except an electorate that usually doesn't have a clear view of the hanky panky meter.

Successful privatization requires that both government and citizen watchdogs remain alert. All interested parties should know exactly what the private provider is contractually obligated to do. Imagine a private operator telling us he wanted to cut back on library hours evenings and weekends simply because his workers preferred a regular 9 to 5 work week. The community would raise cain!

Different with government. Bureaucrats almost never calculate the cost of providing goods or services. And when they try (usually for political reasons), cost accountants generally snicker. For example, the State of Hawai'i does not know the cost of the housing units it has provided. Sometimes direct costs are mentioned, but that's just the beginning—the high cost of street repair in Indianapolis was almost totally the result of excess management, not high direct costs. Similarly, if the cost of an inefficient bureaucracy were taken into consideration, the cost of state-provided housing would be shockingly high.

Perhaps you're thinking, "Yes, but at least they got some housing built!" If so, ask yourself if you would feel differently knowing that the cost of providing each $100,000 housing unit was, say, $300,000. We do know the cost of recently built prisons in Hawai'i, and at $520,000 per bed they are well beyond the national average of $40,000 to $100,000.

Privatization would not adversely affect the quality of trash collection, library services, prison construction and operation, housing construction, child care, road maintenance, airport management (to name a few of the possible areas); it *would* result in more efficiency. This, in turn, would allow our elected officials to reduce taxes or use the freed-up resources to improve the quality of those or other services.

Those of you who have been frustrated in your attempts to get more resources for your favorite area (mine is education) now know where to find them—it's called PRIVATIZATION.

"GEE, I KNEW YOU WHEN YOU WERE...UH, JUST THIS HIGH...."

CHAPTER 9

GOVERNMENT EFFICIENCY

DOLORES FOLEY
Assistant Professor of Public Administration
University of Hawai'i

"Are we getting our money's worth from government in Hawai'i?"

Hawai'i is a high-tax, big-government state. We paid 14.1 percent of our personal income in state and local taxes in 1990, well above the national average of 11.5 percent. Not too surprisingly, we also had above-average government expenditures that year: $626 more per man, woman, and child than the national average. And while everyone expects the number of government workers to increase as a state grows, from 1980 to 1991 the number of government workers in Hawai'i increased about 10 percent faster than did the state's population. In other words, the trend is toward even bigger government and higher taxes. Perhaps this helps explain why we increasingly hear phrases like "tax hell," "paradise tax," and "bloated bureaucracies."

Money's worth? If we were to ask the community-at-large if it's getting its money's worth from government in Hawai'i, is there any doubt that the resounding answer would be no?

But I'm not sure that would be fair. Government grows partly because we allow it—but mostly because we demand it. The size and growth rate of government are directly related to what we ask it to do. Through our duly elected officials, we increasingly have asked government to be responsive to our needs, to ensure fairness for all, and to protect us from an expanding range of possible misfortunes. In short, we have insisted that government take on more and more services and problems, most of which used to be left to the private sector. Examples include everything from housing the homeless to giving middle-income residents a chance (literally) to own a home.

We demand that criminals be locked up longer ("throw away the key") but insist that expensive due process be provided for anyone who's been accused of a crime ("make *sure* you got the right person"). We want convention centers and more promotion of tourism and better highways. Then there's the occasional bailout (Thrift Guaranty Corporation, Hamakua Sugar, Hilo Coast Processing, Hawaiian Airlines) and the taking over of failing and sound businesses alike (Hawaiian Insurance Group, after-school child care). The list is long and growing.

I wonder, are the people who complain about high taxes and big government the same people who asked for all the above?

Government doesn't know. We really can't determine if we're getting our money's worth from government until we know what it has accomplished (called "outputs"). This is difficult since government itself seldom knows.

Governments generally focus exclusively on the level of resources needed for each particular activity (called "inputs"). For example, the Department of Human Services can tell you how many social workers it has and how many people are on welfare at any given time (inputs) but not how well its workers did their jobs or how many individuals managed to get off welfare during any particular year (outputs). Similarly, the Department of Education asks for funding each year based on the number of teachers and other resources needed to get a certain number of students through the year (inputs) rather than on how well those teachers taught or what the students actually learned or were trained to do (outputs).

Unfortunately for the citizenry, the problem of focusing only on inputs is widespread throughout all levels of government. Nationally, the failure of the Department of Housing and Urban Development's policy to promote housing through loans to developers has been linked to a focus on how many loans were made (inputs) rather than on how many houses were built (outputs). Incredibly, no one realized that little housing was actually being provided or that large numbers of developers were defaulting on their loans. The success of the program was measured by the number of loans made rather than houses built.

"WITH THE BUDGET SQUEEZE, IT CAME TO A CHOICE BETWEEN SAVING THE PAYROLL OR THE SERVICES..."

Procurement input. In Hawai'i, the recent attention given to procurement policies has focused on inputs. That has put undue emphasis on procedure. Whether the best product was received for the best price has pretty much been ignored.

Out of the fear of corruption (or, worse yet, bad press), increased controls are likely to be placed on procurement inputs. We can only hope that the legislature won't choose to handcuff *all* government workers (figuratively speaking) because of the small percentage who might be willing to do something illegal or unethical. Increased diligence, stiffer sanctions, and protection for whistle-blowers might provide the necessary controls and still allow emphasis on outputs.

The current backward approach is perhaps most obvious when one reviews year-end spending. Managers who do not get their entire budget (inputs) spent by the stroke of midnight on the last day of each fiscal year not only lose the unspent funds forever but probably get a reduced budget the next year. Is it any surprise that even normally frugal bureaucrats spend like frenzied shoppers at a day-after-Christmas sale?

Another example of backward thinking is the focus on line items (i.e., the breakdown of how certain funds are supposed to be spent). This fiscal straightjacket prevents managers from being creative or taking advantage of unexpected opportunities. It is terribly frustrating for government workers to see a crying need for something on line 1 (school books) when the only available funds are on line 2 (a school bus).

It doesn't have to be this way. Government can be more effective, responsive, and efficient. Just because something needs to be done doesn't necessarily mean government should be the one to do it. Many activities are best done by the private sector. The authors of *Reinventing Government* use the image of a boat (we'll make that an outrigger canoe): government should be steering but not paddling. Social policy, politics, and a whole bunch of other factors should be looked to by government as it charts a course and keeps us pointed in the right direction.

The real issue. Getting the private sector to do the paddling involves privatization, but that's only one of many possible mechanisms. The real issue isn't privatization, it's government reform. Privatization can introduce efficiencies, but that's secondary to government's need to chart a better course.

We need to decentralize. Hawai'i is currently the most centralized state in the union and is pulling away from the pack. In 1980, 75 percent of state and local government workers in Hawai'i worked for the state. By 1991, that was up to 80 percent. The trend should be reversed, with more responsibility in local jurisdictions, partly to get more workers thinking about outputs, but mostly just to get them thinking.

A highly centralized bureaucratic hierarchy encourages workers to operate on automatic pilot, to just push paper and go through motions. Why think when you have no flexibility or authority? Decentralization gets decision-making pushed out to the periphery, into the hands (and minds) of folks who are on the front lines and in the trenches. These are the people who can see what's happening, who can focus on outputs. Give them more decision-making authority and, virtually overnight, their agencies will become more flexible, innovative, and productive.

Citizen involvement. Effective, responsive government requires informed and involved citizens. Democracy means paying attention.

Decentralization of government implies giving decision-making back to the citizens, too. The idea is to create community-owned government. In this model, citizens are empowered to have control over services and make decisions about resources. Hawai'i's School Community-Based Management is a good example of a government agency trying to give more control to the local community by involving schools boards, community groups, and teachers in decision-making at their schools.

Rather than allocate funds to agencies and then *hope* something worthwhile comes of it, government needs to set realistic standards and then *know* they are met. It needs a system of accountability that focuses less on "what you received and whether you spent it" and more on "what you expected to accomplish and whether you did so." You know, outputs over inputs.

We need to insist that government set priorities that require tough decisions about the allocation of limited resources. It is through such decisions that we establish and live by our community values.

Output with a twist. A lowering of taxes and reduction in the size of government will not reduce our frustrations or lead us to believe we're finally getting our money's worth. We must recognize that there will never be enough funds for government to do everything. We must articulate and debate our needs. Then we must insist that candidates for office state clearly their vision for the future of Hawai'i and how they propose to get us there. Finally, we too need to focus more on "outputs," but with a twist: elected officials who haven't lived up to the rhetoric of past campaigns need to be "put out" of office.

"IF YOU ASK ME, IT'S GETTING TOO CROWDED HERE..."

CHAPTER 10

ISLAND ISOLATION

JOHN GRIFFIN
Columnist
Honolulu Advertiser

"Is Hawai'i unique?"

Former vice president Dan Quayle took a lot of flak after he proclaimed to gathered journalists on a Honolulu stopover in 1989 that Hawai'i "is in the Pacific. It is part of the United States that is an island that is right here."

In 1992, he added more perspective: "Hawai'i is a unique state. It is a state that is by itself. It is a—it is different from the other forty-nine states. Well, all states are different, but it's got a particularly unique situation."

To be fair, on the last occasion Quayle was answering a campaign question and seeking to minimize the potential national applications of Hawai'i's universal health care system. The Republican Bush-Quayle administration never found much inspiration in Democratic Hawai'i.

Looking east. Still, in his stumbling, accidental way Dan Quayle showed more perspective about Hawai'i than do many people who live here but don't appreciate that we are on a group of islands over two thousand miles from the U.S. mainland and almost halfway across the ocean to Asia. Some of these people I call Kansas City Kids, because they came from the mainland and mentally never left home. Even those who have been here a long time display attitudes that are more middle American than mid-Pacific. Their idea—in sports, business ties, media coverage, education, and even most social events—is most often to make Hawai'i like the rest of the country. For example, many such people would think it much more natural and desirable for Hawai'i to get a North American hockey franchise than to try to develop a local soccer team to play in international competition.

We also have a good share of Kaimuki Kids, local folks of all races who don't appreciate where Hawai'i is and how that affects our thinking. For many in this group, we might as well be a suburb of Los Angeles. They may eat rice, but the horizon they scan is more east toward Las Vegas than toward the Far East. Many seem little interested in visiting their ancestral homelands in Asia, much less in seeing another group of Pacific islands.

Of course, it seems natural, even patriotic, for older generations of Asians here to look toward the mainland and want to "make it" in the American way. Hawai'i's Asians won respect for their World War II service and eventually that helped gain statehood. But now a half century later youngsters at the University of Hawai'i still aren't interested much in international careers. Maybe that news can be tempered by the thoughts that those most interested go to mainland universities and that student disinterest in overseas careers is evident all across the country. It's just that you would hope for more in a mid-Pacific state.

Hawai'i's insularity can be appalling at a time when the Asia-Pacific region is humming with possibilities. Part of our challenge is to reduce some of that island provincialism, and its associated protectionism, while keeping the best of island attitudes. That difficult achievement calls for better understanding of the problem and education—starting right at the top of our society with political and business leaders.

Are islands special? Much poetic writing says so, even though you can argue that isolated pockets on land masses sometimes behave like islands. Few have been more glowing on the subject than James Michener. He termed himself and others like him "nesomaniacs," creatures who are mad about islands.

Columnist-author Bob Krauss has mused much about the physical joys, restraints, and mental attitudes (such as less cutthroat competition, more courtesy and tolerance of different races, religions, and customs) that come with living on islands of limited space and frequent contact. In one of his books he noted that Hawai'i's nickname, "The Aloha State," makes it the only state "named after an attitude. This complicated state of mind sometimes baffles new arrivals."

Similarly, Jocelyn Fujii's new book about living in Hawai'i, *Under the Hula Moon*, is full of insights on the Hawaiian, missionary, plantation, and other heritages that influence our lifestyles. She notes: "Whether newcomer, kamaaina, easterner, westerner, urbanite, country folk, young or old, those who have made Hawai'i their home share a common isolation. . . . The ocean is the womb and the horizon a reminder of their self-chosen exile."

Author Paul Theroux, a part-time Hawai'i resident, has written that the ocean, seemingly nothing but water, can be everything, a highway. In one of his better speeches here, President Bush referred to the Pacific Ocean area as an "aquatic continent."

So much for the poetry—and perhaps for the counterthought that the jet age, affluence, and new communications have shrunk our old physical isolation while not expanding our mental horizons enough. Satellite television adds to the illusion-becoming-reality that we are just another part of the United States.

A harder look. Stories about our higher cost of living—more than a third above the national average—have long been a staple example of the "practical" and often negative aspects of Hawai'i as an isolated island group. Identified villains include shipping costs (not as guilty as many think), high taxes, the need to warehouse more inventory, our small and isolated market, and the high costs of construction and land.

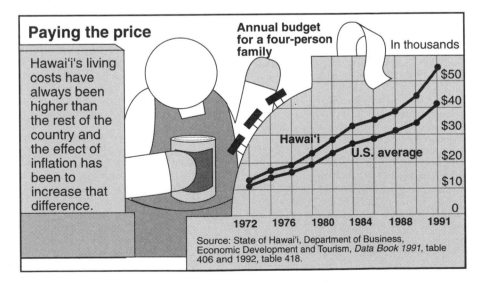

Paying the price

Hawai'i's living costs have always been higher than the rest of the country and the effect of inflation has been to increase that difference.

Annual budget for a four-person family

In thousands

Hawai'i

U.S. average

$50
$40
$30
$20
$10
0

1972   1976   1980   1984   1988   1991

Source: State of Hawai'i, Department of Business, Economic Development and Tourism, *Data Book 1991*, table 406 and 1992, table 418.

In Volume I of *The Price of Paradise*, economist Leroy Laney cited housing costs (based in part on our limited land supply) as the key factor in Hawai'i's high cost of living. Laney also made a point many complainers don't seem to appreciate: "High prices ration this favorable environment to those willing to pay those prices. In doing so, they preserve it."

Our situation is unfortunate in that many poorer Hawai'i folks who must or want to stay here are hit hardest by our combination of high living costs and lower wages. But there's no denying that a lower cost of living would mean more people, cars, and other strains on our limited resources. Our challenge is to make the price of paradise worth more for everyone. That doesn't mean just more social equality programs dear to the hearts of us liberals; it also means more imaginative political and business leadership in creating better jobs.

Hawai'i's highly centralized government system is another well-defined heritage of being an island group with an unusual political history. That includes the monarchy last century, the plantation system, our former territorial (some would say colonial) status, and the failure of our dominant Democrats to carry out their now-faded home rule promises.

Nor is Hawai'i unique in island centralization. On a Fulbright fellowship in Southeast Asia in the late 1970s, *Advertiser* editorial page editor Jerry Burris studied how being on an island affected attitudes toward growth in Hawai'i, Singapore, Penang, and Bali. He found different attitudes (e.g., Singapore gung ho, Hawai'i getting cautious), but the common denominator was centralized control and paternalism. Being on small islands makes such things easier; what counts is what you do with the power at the top.

Some conclusions.

• Hawai'i is still the most isolated archipelago in the world, and that is compounded by our fragmented islands. This naturally makes for insular attitudes that coexist with too much tunnel vision focused toward the mainland.

• Hawai'i has had it too easy compared to many other places. Tourism and investment flooded in with statehood, the jet age, and the more recent Japanese influx. Leaders and the people didn't see a need for diversifying industrially, looking out to Asia, or dumping a political machine that presided over the growing economic pie. Now times are changing.

• Our island location is both a blessing and a challenge. Outside forces have often shaped our community, but we are not powerless. Two strong but contradictory trends are at work in the world—one toward globalization, which we can see in telecommunications and trade, the other toward nationalism or tribalization, which at best is East European freedom and at worst ethnic war in Lebanon or Yugoslavia. The world has to live with these trends for now, so Hawai'i must balance insularism and outreach, getting the best from both. People on islands must see that they are both in "a special place" and part of a changing whole. We must learn to think locally and act globally as much as vice versa.

• We should be hard on ourselves but not consider our situation hopeless. Hawai'i has one of the oldest and most exotic political machines in the country, and it needs cleaning up. But it is not that different from other machines that have been reformed or dumped. Other chapters in this book clearly reflect the impact, good and less so, of Hawai'i as an island. And, on the plus side, there are signs that people here are not as insular as we critics claim. Some progress has been made, and maybe the recession will stir leaders to go beyond lip service in talking about Asia-Pacific opportunities. I even find hope in the growing interest in sumo, although that's been helped by stars from Hawai'i.

• My fear remains, however: we are not doing enough fast enough. Our attitudes toward life, and toward our real possibilities in the world, are being changed like indoor-outdoor housing is being replaced by air-conditioned mansions that reach the lot line and shut out the trade winds—and even the sound of the ocean that makes us an island. We are doing such things to ourselves, and too often we don't see anything wrong.

It's an island . . . Bill Clinton got elected president in part by concentrating on a slogan like this: "It's the economy, stupid." We might prosper by paraphrasing Quayle: "Hawai'i is an island right here in the middle of the Pacific."

Think about that, and maybe also about the deeper meaning of the word "aloha." Then you will know where you are—or at least could be.

CHAPTER 11

KEY INSTITUTIONS

CHUCK FREEDMAN
Vice President of Corporate Relations
Hawaiian Electric Company

"Can you name the Big Five?"

Most of us would have an easier time naming the Fabulous Five, that great UH basketball team. Long gone are the days when five large businesses monopolized the marketplace and exerted collective clout over everything else.

It's harder than ever to put your finger on what has replaced Hawai'i's oligarchy. At the same time, power abhors a vacuum. Private sector institutions *are* shaking and moving their way into the picture. They are diverse, constantly changing, and they seldom take action hand-in-hand. They're here, just harder to find.

So name your Big Five. Remember, they have to be private sector institutions with political know-how, an information network, and the ability to shape public opinion. Here are my nominees for today's Big Five:

The big banks. Almost by default. They know money and marketing. Walter Dods at First Hawaiian Bank is a marketing whiz who has lent his talents to many winning political campaigns. Dolly Ching at Bank of Hawaii possesses an extraordinary political eye. Officers from financial institutions serve on scores of voluntary boards and commissions and are among the state's leading corporate citizens.

Some critics would say that our banks get a return on their investment. For example, according to a Bureau of National Affairs banking report, Hawai'i is the only state in America without an interstate banking law (Montana, the next-to-last holdout, enacted a

79

law in 1993). Does this mean Hawai'i's banks are unduly protected from outside competition?

Let's take a look. On the mainland, a bank may be headquartered in one state, with operations in surrounding states. The arguments *for* interstate banking are that it serves customers who cross state lines, consolidates operations, and reduces administrative expenses and other costs. Risk is also spread around: if a bank from one region is doing badly, it can utilize funds from a sister bank of another region.

Hawai'i bankers argue that their customers don't regularly cross state lines and that home-based banks can best understand Island uniqueness. They remind us that when Hawai'i Kai was flooded, local banks immediately stepped forward with low-interest loans, with no mainland clearances required. On the issue of spreading risk they ask, why should Hawai'i's strong banks be the deep pockets for a weaker mainland institution?

Legendary bank robber Willie Sutton once was asked why he robbed banks. Without a moment's hesitation he replied, "Because that's where the money is." Sounds easy. But Hawai'i's big banks didn't make my list of key institutions just because of the money they control. They're there because they haven't hesitated to use the power money provides *and* because they've readily accepted the role of community leader. Bank of Hawaii's Howard Stephenson and First Hawaiian's Walter Dods, for example, have insisted that their respective institutions "give back" to the community. As long as they and their successors do that, their spot on my list is secure.

Bishop Estate. What we have here is an institution with lofty, charitable ends and a developer's means. The estate's critical mass (of land and wealth), more than its schizophrenic constitution, is enough to make it a major player in the Islands. It makes decisions on whether to invest funds in Hawai'i or elsewhere, what business and housing projects to develop, and how much rent to charge leaseholders. Any way you cut it, when the estate shakes, the marketplace moves.

Ten years ago Bishop Estate was not the visible player it is today. The politicizing of the leasehold question and the push for land use initiatives changed all that. So did the selection of activist trustees like Henry Peters, Oswald Stender, Dickie Wong, and Lokelani Lindsay.

Bishop Estate has always needed a strong and steady revenue stream for the education of Hawaiian children. What's new is that the estate has decided to establish a visible political presence. It has the leaders and the "people network" to sustain it. The question now is, what will the estate do with it?

Labor unions. The unions face a changing economy, a changing workforce, and changing values. Ah, for the good old days when the biggest enemy was management.

"FELLAS, FELLAS—THIS IS A LABOR DAY UNITY PICNIC, FOR HEAVENSSAKE!..."

For a half century, union power was personified by the International Longshoremen's and Warehousemen's Union (ILWU). The ILWU represented workers from the agrarian industries that built modern Hawai'i. It used its neighbor island presence to leverage power at the state legislature.

With the decline of Hamakua Sugar, we are seeing the end of more than an industry. We are bidding aloha to a political power base spawned by the labor movement and rooted in a way of life. Hawai'i will never be the same, and neither will the power structure within the state legislature.

But don't blink. Hawai'i's still a "labor" state, and its unions still have some degree of political clout, especially the Hawai'i Government Employees Association and the United Public Workers. The unions' greatest strength is their numbers and the message that, "If you do it to one of mine, you do it to me." In the right circumstances, that credo builds armies.

News media. It's ironic that the least "covered" of the agenda-setting institutions are the news media themselves. After all, these folks define reality on a daily basis.

Everyone knows that TV leaves lasting impressions and, more than any other single entity, shapes public opinion. The untold story with local TV stations is that there is seldom a political bias in their news reporting. Their flaws instead come from time constraints, the psychology of sound bites, the if-it-bleeds-it-leads mentality, and a news anchorperson having a bad hair day.

Most significant, TV news is undergoing fundamental change for two basic reasons: first, deregulation of the airwaves, more competition, and eroding audience shares; second, higher costs to run a station and produce news.

No one knows where local broadcast news is going. Joe Moore for free at six o'clock may soon be another TV memory, replaced by pay-as-you-use, round-the-clock news services. Because TV understands the increasingly segmented market it serves, its services will become more tailored to types of customers and their information needs. There are good TV journalists who worry about the Orwellian implications of this change. Stay tuned.

The Honolulu daily newspapers are a new pair of shoes, having undergone extraordinary ownership changes, with Gannett, the largest newspaper company in America, selling the *Honolulu Star-Bulletin* and buying the locally owned *Advertiser*.

Based on past performance, you should be able to count on the *Advertiser* and editor Gerry Keir to drive an agenda. Keir brought us Hawai'i's first published political polls and championed the cause of education reform with news coverage and editorials. Internally he'll have some hard choices. He faces the problems of a shrinking news section, an 18- to 30-year-old population that doesn't read newspapers, and nonlocal ownership. This shoe could be a tight fit.

Less predictable is the *Star-Bulletin*. Its newsroom is still overcoming a massive anxiety attack following the paper's sale. The *Bulletin* may be shedding its traditions as a more conservative and conventional newspaper, which old-timers will miss. Editor-publisher John Flanagan has made a long-term commitment to an evening paper. The hiring of political reporter Ian Lind and business *akamai* Diane Chang as editorial page editor are hints of change. This shoe isn't out of the box yet.

Sadly, as the news media move through a time of rapid change in which their own existence is threatened, no one analyzes and reports this important story. Not since Bob Dye stopped writing for *Honolulu Magazine* have we seen a solid piece on the subject. News reporting isn't newsworthy, it seems.

The anti-establishment establishment. Committee On Sensible Transit (COST), Mothers against Drunk Driving (MADD), Save Our Surf (SOS), countless community organizations (CCO), and many others who dare challenge the status quo (MOWDCTSQ)—who are these people anyway?

Generally they are "real people" committed to a cause and ready to rattle society's cage. They are inventive and quick to learn how to communicate a point of view. They're usually better at advocating change than actually implementing anything specific. No single person or style dominates the arena. Skip Spaulding with a law book, Cliff Slater with a calculator, and Carol McNamee with traffic statistics have successfully protected the environment, stopped rapid transit, and curbed drunk driving. And when the battle was done, the gored oxen outnumbered the sacred cows.

Taken as a whole, the anti-establishment establishment is clearly a shaker and mover, vital to the yang and yin of Hawai'i's democracy. The Buster generation (18- to 30-year-olds) may not read newspapers, but they're not brain-dead either. Look for them to show us a whole new look and game plan. Pay attention. Governors, supreme court justices, union leaders, Bishop Estate trustees, and more than one journalist have passed through the gates of the anti-establishment establishment.

Missing in action. Surprisingly absent as forces in Hawai'i are the visitor industry and foreign investors. The industry is so important and yet lacks a unified voice or clear direction. Richard Kelley, scion of the Outrigger Hotels, has had some interesting ideas and hasn't hesitated to share them. But where's the rest of the industry?

Foreign investors own everything from bakeries to hotels. They are big-time employers here, but they have not emerged as political players or social movers. Is this discretion, ignorance, or simply a phase they're passing through? Probably the latter.

Over the past hundred years, people have used power to take control of Hawai'i from native Hawaiians; to build a military strong-hold in the Pacific; to develop blockbuster industries from sugar to travel; and to make Hawai'i the fiftieth American state. Especially since statehood, Hawai'i has looked for what Governor John Burns called "its rightful place in the Pacific sun." Whether you like it or not, key institutions will figure prominently in that search.

The Big Five may be an exclusive club. But hopes for Hawai'i belong to all of us. Remember . . . "power" is a neutral term. It's how people use power that makes it good or bad. Those who have it are worth watching. They may even be worth joining. And if they're not, they're certainly worth changing.

"THOSE WHO COMPLAIN THE MOST ABOUT GOVERNMENT ARE USUALLY THOSE WHO DON'T VOTE..."

CHAPTER 12

TOURIST DESTINATION

KEN TUCKER

Matson Distinguished Professor of Travel Industry Management
University of Hawai'i

"Is Hawai'i becoming less attractive as a tourist destination?"

A 1993 *New York Times*/CBS News poll asked people on the mainland where they would want to go for a dream vacation. Hawai'i was named more often than any other place—in the world! Add the fact that Hawai'i visitor counts rose steadily from 1984 through 1990 and it is natural to conclude that its attractiveness as a tourist destination has not diminished.

But there is a cloud overhead. Despite the poll's "dream results," the reality is that Hawai'i's visitor count is down—way down. Visitor spending reached a peak of $10.63 billion in 1991 and declined by 10.1 percent, to $9.56 billion, the following year. Is this drop merely a reflection of tough times in our two biggest markets, California and Japan, or is there more to it? Is it possible that the reality of Hawai'i today no longer lives up to the dream?

If Hawai'i's attractiveness is declining, then something had better be done about it. After all, tourism is the engine that drives our economy. If it starts to sputter, and can't be tuned up quickly, all of us are in trouble. As local newspaperman George Chaplin once said, "A sound economy doesn't assure a high quality of life, but a shaky or failing economy almost certainly precludes it."

Those of us who care about preserving paradise for future generations should not take tourism for granted. Hawai'i has a lot going for it, but not so much that tourists will continue flocking here regardless of our actions. There are lots of other destinations (more every day) vying for a limited number of tourists.

Comparative advantage. Hawai'i is a natural when it comes to tourism. It has attractions that will always appeal to a large segment of the traveling public. Economists call it "comparative advantage." In our case, it includes sun, sea, and sand, to be sure, but also cultural diversity and the aloha spirit. These last two items are increasingly important because of the growing number of "me too" destinations. Some of these look-alike alternatives—with lots of sun, sea, and sand— are attracting people who otherwise would have been expected to vacation here. Bali in Indonesia, Cairns in Australia, Phuket and Pattaya in Thailand, not to mention resorts in the Caribbean and Mexico, all have their special brand of dream-weaving magic.

A further dimension to the attractiveness of any given destination is what may be described as "differential advantage." How well do you present and deliver what you have? To achieve differential advantage, a location needs to build on its strengths with a goal of *exceeding* visitors' expectations. The basic idea is to provide more value or enhanced experiences with the quality and diversity of your facilities and activities. Not only can that set a naturally attractive destination apart from others, but it can also give a relatively unattractive location a chance to compete with the more photogenic ones. Singapore, for example, has limited natural beauty in a comparative sense, but it has been able to compete effectively by providing super-efficient service, interesting theme parks, superb infrastructure (such as a high-quality mass transportation system), and an exciting shopping experience.

By combining a destination's comparative and differential advantages, we obtain its "competitive advantage."

Problems in paradise. The most immediate threat to Hawai'i's competitive advantage is that its biggest fans, those *currently* dreaming of coming here, have lower income growth expectations or are concerned about their job prospects. The Hawai'i Visitors Bureau tells us that over 60 percent of all mainland visitors to the state are repeat visitors. Hawai'i may continue to be the place of their dreams, but that alone may not be enough. As they get older, they will probably tend to stay nearer home. And if their spending power declines, they may be priced out of Hawai'i and seek lower-cost destinations, in spite of our strong marketing and cut-price offers. A marketing program that targets aging travelers with these concerns would do little to boost long-term visitor numbers or expenditures.

Other visitors, such as recent college graduates, newly married couples, professional multiple-income families, or adventuresome singles (all of whom tend to be more variety-seeking in their behavior), may be enticed to visit other locations where they may experience a better range of attractions than are currently available in Hawai'i. They may strongly dislike something increasingly common in Hawai'i: mass tourism with its homogenous experiences.

There is also a danger that, without planning for longer-term community interests, "concrete jungles" and other ugliness may grow worse. Congested locations are not merely an eyesore; they compromise personal safety as well. Japanese visitors, in particular, place a high priority on security.

Capacity to cope. For a population of just over 1 million to be host to over 6 million guests each year—about 150,000 per day—requires a special effort if dreams are to be fulfilled. As our tourist count and expenditures decline, we have to wonder if Hawai'i is beginning to show signs of inability to cope with such a high volume of guests in one location. The Gold Coast of Australia has about the same population as Hawai'i but only about one-quarter the number of visitors. As a result, its coping capacity is in better shape and Australia is now taking market share away from Hawai'i. If the reality there is a better match for visitors' dreams, it suggests that they are not near the saturation point.

As the ratio of guests to hosts in Hawai'i increases, overload will show itself in a deterioration of physical appearance, damage to fragile environments, crowding in once-secluded areas, and increased crime. Traffic will be congested, and it will be increasingly difficult to be nice to so many strangers.

If local citizens feel that their taxes are already too high, they may resist further tourist-oriented government expenditures. What may appear to be isolated cases of unmanageable stress may be symptomatic of tourist overload.

The solutions probably lie in either spreading or sharing the impact. We can do this by creating controlled access to locations around the Islands and attracting carefully targeted tourists. For example, we might want to seek out tourists who are easy to manage, that is, those who wish to observe but not intrude and who can contribute more to the tax collections than they take to support.

Game plan. Of course, it's not simple to locate such "angels," but we're more likely to do it with a game plan than without one. Public interests and private gains must be reconciled or balanced. Industry and government strategies must be cooperative in their design and coordinated in their execution. At the present time, and without a plan, government, the hotel industry, and the community are focusing on potentially conflicting goals. It is difficult to be a good host if everyone pretty much goes his or her separate way.

What is needed is agreement on mission. Australia and New Zealand have strategic management plans for their tourist industries. Both are public documents with agreed upon objectives and measurable outcomes to the year 2000. Hawai'i needs such a strategic focus, one that is professionally objective and ruthlessly realistic about how much can be achieved.

One way to know how well we should be doing is to engage in benchmarking. This requires much more than simply asking people where they would travel to realize their dreams. It requires detailed analysis of where they actually are going and why. In addition, we cannot plan properly until we know what our competition is up to and whether or not it's working for them. It is essential that Hawai'i's performance be benchmarked by comparing tourist travel from newly industrializing countries—those with high-growth economies, econo-

mies with trade surpluses, and firm currencies. Monitoring the strategies and market share achieved by our competition is likely to have a better long-term payoff than promotion to repeat visitors.

It is estimated that over 80 million additional people between the ages of 20 and 40 will emerge as powerful consumers in the Pacific during the next decade. There are already a million millionaires in the People's Republic of China alone. A well-to-do travel-hungry class of business people are sure to emerge from what used to be the Soviet Union. The long-term health of Hawai'i's tourist industry *requires* that we tap into these markets. It simply won't happen by itself: those halcyon days are over.

Product development. There must be more emphasis on product development and less reliance on price-cutting or special promotions. Among the new product options are nature-based tours, health-related tourism, and educational opportunities that fit the interests and time constraints of our visitors. Already there are a few (too few) excellent examples of this: Waimea Falls has a new emphasis on teaching visitors about daily life in Hawai'i before contact with the West; whale-watching businesses on Maui have teamed up with the University of Hawai'i Sea Grant Program to create an experience that's both educational and exciting; Sea Life Park has replaced the silly prattle about "Fat Fred" with a presentation that shows sensitivity to its own interference with the animals' natural habitats; Kualoa Ranch has developed leadership training programs that provide physical as well as a psychological challenge to participants in a movie-maker's dream environment.

Less emphasis should be placed on growth in numbers and more effort devoted to growth in yield to the community and to the industry. This strategy will have implications for human resources policy. "High-yielding" tourists increasingly will come from different cultures. This might lead to less reliance on tipping as an incentive to staff and more attention to training and development. Investment in skills should be a higher priority than new buildings and other physical amenities. This applies particularly to small businesses.

Mindless focus. Finally, we must at all costs avoid the "if we build it, they will come" philosophy. A mindless focus on "supply" leads nowhere, fast. It's the "demand" side that needs attention. We've got to better understand why travelers want to come, where they will come from, what alternatives they have, and how many of them we can successfully host. Being someone's dream means nothing unless we can make it come true.

"I GOT IT! HOW ABOUT A STUDY TO FIND OUT WHY THEY DON'T COME HERE ..."

CHAPTER 13

GOVERNMENT SUPPORT

JAMES MAK
Professor of Economics
University of Hawai'i

WALTER MIKLIUS
Professor of Economics and Argicultural Economics
University of Hawai'i

"Why can't the tourist industry pay for travel promotion and a convention center?"

Many people believe that government should interfere as little as possible with the private sector. They argue that government tends to make markets work less, not more, efficiently. But that argument does not always apply. Sometimes government intervention and direct provision of public services actually increase efficiency in our economy. Tourism provides two such examples: destination travel promotion and convention center financing.

Tourism promotion. National governments around the world actively promote tourist travel to their countries. This is also true of state governments in the United States. All fifty states have government travel offices that promote local tourism. In fiscal year 1991/92, the budgets of these state travel offices totaled nearly $331 million. Most of that money came from taxes. Only Alaska (18 percent industry contribution), Hawai'i (11 percent membership fees and miscellaneous income), and Washington, D.C. (10 percent corporate sponsorship) received significant private contributions toward travel promotion.

Why can't the tourist industry promote itself? After all, industry-financed generic promotion—the promotion of a particular commodity rather than a brand name product—is a common practice in agriculture. For example, the Florida citrus growers got approval to tax themselves to finance their well-known television commercials. Here in Hawai'i, the papaya industry assesses fees on all its growers and uses the revenues to promote the sale of papayas.

These assessments on individual growers are based on either the volume sold or a percentage of the sales revenue, and therefore they are proportional to the potential benefits received from generic promotion. Growers are required by federal or state legislation to pay these assessments, although sometimes there are provisions to allow them to apply for refunds. There is no enforcement or compliance problem.

Free-riding. What would happen if there were no legislation to force papaya growers, for example, to pay for promotional expenditures? Even if each grower could see the need to promote papayas, he would know that he too would benefit from promotions paid for by others. This would be true even if he didn't contribute a dime to the promotion fund. Some growers (maybe all) would yield to the temptation to enjoy a free ride on the promotion spending of others. Of course, if many were to behave in this selfish way, there wouldn't be enough contributions to mount the size of promotion campaign the growers collectively want.

Legislation forcing all growers to contribute money toward product promotion also reduces the effort and cost (compared to private solicitation) of raising the desired level of money to promote their product. For these reasons, government intervention in the generic promotion of agricultural products increases economic efficiency.

The tourist industry also benefits from collective promotion, but free-riding is a chronic problem. When an airline, a hotel, or any other tourist attraction promotes Hawai'i travel on its own, other tourist businesses, which did not contribute to the promotion campaign, also benefit. But unlike the Papaya Administrative Committee, which promotes one specific product and has legal authority to compel compliance, the Hawai'i Visitors Bureau (HVB) is a voluntary trade association. It has no power to compel businesses that benefit from its activities to join or to pay their fair shares of the association's promotional expenditures. One study found that fewer than 7 percent of all businesses in Hawai'i belong to the HVB.

Reliance on government. Not surprisingly, the HVB never seems to have enough of its own funds to promote Hawai'i travel adequately. Consequently, it has had to rely increasingly on the state government to finance its budgets. In 1918, the territorial government's contribution to the HVB's predecessor (the Chamber of Commerce's Hawai'i Promotions Committee) represented 22 percent of the total budget. During the 1950s, the government's share of HVB budgets averaged around 50 percent. Through the 1960s and 1970s, state government contributions climbed to just over 70 percent of the budget. The government's share today exceeds 90 percent!

Since the tourist industry is unable to engage in collective destination promotion, the government has essentially taken over the function in Hawai'i. The HVB is a private entity only in the legal sense; every aspect of its operations is subject to review and approval by the state government.

How should the state government raise money to finance the HVB's tourism promotion? Ideally, we want tourism promotion taxes to fall on the parties who benefit from tourism promotion in proportion to the benefits each receives or is likely to receive. But, unlike the papaya industry, it is not easy to devise a simple and fair formula like so much per pound or per dollar-volume of sales. What makes tourism different from papayas is that it is difficult to pin down who benefits from tourism and its promotion.

Diverse industry. For one thing, tourism is a diverse industry representing businesses that sell a wide variety of goods and services. Moreover, businesses that sell to tourists also sell to local residents. Some rely more on tourists, others on residents. The percentages vary greatly, not only from company to company but from year to year. And that assumes each company has a practical way to determine who's a tourist and who isn't. That's not even close to being realistic in most cases. Plus, the economic benefits of tourism are widely dispersed. Most of us benefit at least indirectly from it, but a few may actually be worse off as a result of increased tourism. Where would we draw the line on who has to contribute to the HVB budget and how much?

Given this difficulty, governments use a variety of ways to finance travel promotion. Most states, including Hawai'i, allocate money from their general funds to finance their travel promotion. When the benefits of tourism are very large and diffused widely through the economy (as they are in Hawai'i), the use of general fund revenues for tourism promotion is appropriate.

Many states also use taxes that specifically target the tourist industry. The most popular industry-specific tax is the hotel room tax, used by nine states in 1991/92 to fund their state travel promotion. Four of those states use the hotel room tax exclusively to fund state travel promotion. Other industry-specific taxes used to fund state travel promotion in the United States include a tourist promotion tax (two states), car rental tax (two states), and gaming tax (one state). All these industry-specific taxes target a selected segment of the industry and bear no resemblance to the industry-wide "benefit" assessments employed in agriculture.

Several states use revenue sources that have no relation to tourism whatsoever. For example, West Virginia uses its lottery revenues to fund its state travel promotion, and in North Carolina 5 percent of the state travel promotion budget is derived from the sale of personalized auto license plates.

Earmarking. What about earmarking a specific tax—say, the hotel room tax—for tourism promotion? Earmarking is the practice of designating or dedicating specific revenues to finance specific public services. Indeed, when the legislature was debating the passage of the 5 percent hotel room (i.e., transient accommodation) tax in 1986, one argument in favor of its passage was that the new tax would enable the state to give more money to the HVB and also to fund the new convention center. However, the legislature chose not to earmark the revenues from the hotel room tax. Instead, it allocated the money into the state general fund. Earmarking would have assured the HVB a more predictable source of revenues. Currently, it has to beg for money from the state legislature every year.

On the other hand, earmarking would result in less fiscal accountability. The current arrangement requires the HVB to account annually for its intelligent use of the prior year's allocation. Plus, with earmarking, it's quite likely that the tax will generate either too much or too little for travel promotion. Hong Kong used to earmark its hotel room tax money for tourism promotion, but it stopped when it was determined that too much money was being spent on tourism promotion relative to funding levels for other worthy public services.

The case *for* earmarking is political rather than economic. The promise of earmarking increases the chances that the industry will support the passage or increase of the tax at the legislature.

Convention center. The same reason the tourist industry cannot successfully engage in collective travel promotion explains why the local tourist industry cannot be expected to raise the money to build and operate a convention center.

Convention center facilities usually operate at a loss, so no individual business wants to build and run them. The tourist industry cannot collectively finance the building and operation of a convention center because each tourist business in Hawai'i would benefit whether or not it contributed. As in destination promotion, the incentive would be to free-ride on the contributions of other businesses.

Voluntary solicitation would be inefficient and highly unlikely to generate enough money to build any kind of facility, much less the world-class convention center the industry wants (remember, fewer than 7 percent of all businesses in Hawai'i are dues-paying members of the HVB). As with the promotion of tourism generally, government intervention to provide a convention center increases rather than decreases economic efficiency. That's why large convention centers in the United States get built by state or local governments and not by private businesses.

In conclusion, government takeover of destination travel promotion and convention center development from the private sector does not necessarily imply state subsidy of the travel industry. It merely indicates a more efficient way to fund travel promotion and convention center facilities.

THE ONLY GAME IN TOWN...

CHAPTER 14

LEGALIZED GAMBLING

LEROY O. LANEY
Vice President and Chief Economist
First Hawaiian Bank

DAVID McCLAIN
Professor of Business Administration
University of Hawai'i

"Should Hawai'i roll the dice on gambling?"

It seems like a natural. The so-called experts, us included, have been emphasizing the need for the state to diversify its economy in areas related to its "core competence" of tourism. We've argued that this means, for example, building a convention center capable of attracting more business visitors.

What could be a more straightforward application of this principle than to bring gambling to the Islands, in order to attract even more tourists?

There are, of course, many kinds of gambling. Casinos, horse racing, dog tracks, lotteries—all provide someone who feels luckier, or smarter, than the next guy the opportunity to place a wager. In what follows, we'll focus on two of the most popular forms of gambling, casinos and lotteries. The sentiments we express, however, apply to other forms of gambling as well.

Casinos in paradise? Casinos and the games they offer—blackjack, baccarat, and the like—conjure up, at least to these middle-aged writers, scenes from James Bond thrillers with elegant and upscale players in such exotic destinations as Monte Carlo and Macao. These are the kind of tourists we want, aren't they?

Look at some of our competitor destinations: Las Vegas, located in the middle of an ocean of sand, built its reputation on gambling; Australia's Gold Coast seems to have gone to school rather well on the fruits of Bugsy Siegel's vision, the Flamingo, that started it all.

What's more, casino gambling might provide a revenue source for native Hawaiians if they are successful in their quest for sovereignty. Other native American groups have elected to permit gambling on the territories they control. And some of those Hawai'i residents who fly to Las Vegas for a fun weekend might spend their money at home instead.

To be sure, Donald Trump has had a bit of the rough time in Atlantic City, but isn't that just proof that nobody can make money when their primary market, in this case the Northeastern United States, is in an economic depression? Hawai'i's physical beauty, coupled with its proximity to the global growth dynamo of Asia, should ensure success in attracting the upscale traveler we want, starting from the get-go, right?

Wrong. Success, maybe and only maybe, in narrow financial terms. By almost any other measure, however, casino gambling would be disastrous for Hawai'i's image, and for its people. The principal reason: the Islands' success with tourists, and tourism's claim to a significant market niche, rests on the unique Hawaiian culture. Casino gambling would represent a distinct and perceptible conflict with that culture, blurring our image—carefully nurtured for well over half a century—in the increasingly competitive global tourist market.

Nor is there any assurance that Hawai'i would attract only the very upscale clients, such as those who frequent Monte Carlo. Monte Carlo's image has itself taken decades, if not centuries, to cultivate.

Organized crime. With the question of precisely who we attract comes the issue of organized crime, which seems to follow casino gambling wherever it goes. Just as Hawai'i's ecology is fragile, so is its social environment. We have our share of yakuza, mafia, whatever, already. Let's not attract more. By adopting casino gambling, we would be announcing to the world that Hawai'i is willing to put up with the acknowledged side effects of organized crime—not the kind of message non-gambling tourists would find appealing.

Finally, tourism experts in Australia observe that their Gold Coast casinos really bring very little new money into the economy. Much of the action comes from local Australians. The diversion of Hawai'i residents away from Las Vegas—and most would probably still head for the desert just to treat island fever—simply wouldn't do enough for the local economy to justify tampering with our image.

Oh, yes—where would we put the casino? O'ahu? By all accounts, Waikiki has crime concerns and is too commercial already. Maui, Kaua'i, the Big Island? It certainly would go against the pristine images these neighbor islands have sought to convey. Nor would we, personally, want to see Lana'i host to a casino. Could Moloka'i, starved for development, play Macao to Honolulu's Hong Kong? Only at the cost of an incredible affront to Hawaiian culture.

These concerns also mean that any attempt to build a casino in the Islands could well run into interminable delays—delays that would further cloud the financial picture for such a resort.

On cultural, criminal, social, and perhaps financial grounds, then, casino gambling is not for Hawai'i.

" I SWEAR THE YAKUZA HAS NOTHING TO DO WITH OUR HOTEL AND GOLF COURSE..."

Lotteries in paradise? There has been much talk about a state-run lottery. Surely this is a milder form of gambling, just a local indulgence, really, and the tourists would find it fun. Indeed, thirty-five states have already adopted some form of lottery. Here again, however, any benefits must be weighed against some rather sizable costs.

The purpose of such lotteries is always much more to provide state revenues than to offer another form of recreation. On average, existing state lotteries return only about 50 cents in prizes for each dollar wagered; about 38 cents reaches the state treasury, and the rest goes for expenses. The house take in Las Vegas is much less, and the prospects for winning much better. Gambling industry figures show that the average house takeout rate in a casino gambling game is 3 percent; on pari-mutuel horse racing it's 19 percent. Only illegal private gambling, such as the numbers game, has takeout ratios exceeding the 50 percent of state government lotteries.

Lotteries are managed by boards that focus on the bottom line of maximizing state revenues. Sometimes revenues are earmarked for specific state uses, such as education, but this does not necessarily mean those programs get more money. Legislators, aware of the earmarking, may be more sympathetic to other programs.

Deceptive advertising. Lotteries spend more on advertising per dollar of sales than the average private corporation. This advertising is sometimes misleading, distorting the odds of winning and often failing to mention that prizes may be paid in installments over the years, with a present value much less than the sum of the payments. (Not that many players realize that a $1 million prize paid in equal installments over a 20-year period has a present value, given a 6 percent discount rate, of only $573,000. They also may not realize that it's all subject to state and federal taxes, which can exceed 40 percent.)

Research indicates that, the higher one's educational level, the less one spends on lottery tickets—perhaps because the more educated person can better assess the odds. Even if average ticket purchases were the same across income classes, lower-income players pay a much higher proportion of their income for lottery tickets than do middle- or upper-income groups. Duke University economists Charles Clotfelter and Philip Cook argue that two-thirds of lottery wagers are made by only 20 percent of the players, with members of poorer ethnic groups

and those most dependent on public aid doing most of the gambling. Such repeat business, of course, could only come from the local population.

So the impact of this "tax"—even if it is voluntarily paid—is regressive in nature, falling disproportionately on the poor. Income taxes are usually progressive, falling disproportionately on higher incomes, while sales taxes—especially on things like alcohol, tobacco, and gasoline—are regressive. But a lottery "tax" is far more regressive than even these so-called sin taxes.

Discourage savings. Lotteries may also discourage saving over the long haul because of the belief, perhaps encouraged by advertising, that eventually a chronic player will strike it rich. Lower saving leads to lower investment and slower growth, which means lower state tax revenues. This lower growth can easily counter the intent of establishing a lottery in the first place, because actual lottery revenues are only a small portion of total state tax revenues.

In the eighteenth and nineteenth centuries, either lotteries were discontinued because of irregularities or they simply collapsed. Perhaps there's a lesson in that history.

There also is a reason why a small state like Hawai'i should be wary of a lottery. Lotteries generally have significant economies of scale; larger operations are able to provide services much more cheaply because they can spread high overhead expenses over more customers.

A state lottery would not damage our image as much as casino gambling. But if it's revenues we need, almost any other tax proposal would be better.

Gambling works best in states, or countries, which are either large enough to cope with the untoward side effects or so poor that they have no other economic alternatives. Hawai'i, too small to ignore these adverse consequences of gambling, is, however, not yet in such desperate economic straits that it has to wager its economic future on legalized rolls of the dice or spins of a drum full of marked ping-pong balls.

OPINIONS VARY ON LEGALIZED GAMBLING IN HAWAII.

Another View

As a result of updated air transportation, massive worldwide resort development and extensive marketing of other tropical sun/surf destinations around the world, Hawai'i has become just another leisure destination.

According to the Pacific Asia Travel Association, Hong Kong surpassed Hawai'i as the top Pacific/Asia visitor destination in 1992. Hawai'i, in second place, was followed by Singapore, Thailand, and Japan.

Aggressive marketing campaigns from countries such as Mexico, Puerto Rico, Guam, Saipan, and Australia have also made those markets highly competitive.

A recent survey by the Japan Travel Bureau indicated that for the months of July and August, Guam and Saipan are expected to show a 21 percent growth in Japanese visitors, bringing them to 206,000 Japanese tourists a month. That is approaching Hawai'i's level of 288,000 Japanese visitors a month. And Hawai'i is projected to show no growth in Japanese tourists. So what do we need to do to stay competitive in the marketplace? . . .

We need to take some risks! Let's stop analyzing and compromising, and start realizing and implementing!

Let's not re-create the wheel. Let's look at places that are successful in attracting visitors. For instance, look at Las Vegas. Once deemed "sin city," Las Vegas is now considered the master of visitor attractions.

Gaming is no longer a bad word. Las Vegas is the ultimate action leisure destination. It attracts the conventioneers, the gamblers, the show dazzlers, the shoppers. And now they have targeted family entertainment, creating theme parks and family entertainment casino centers. We should look at Las Vegas' success formula and translate it into a Hawaiian paradise success. . . .

Not only would we have action, but we would be able to offer quiet, secluded elegance along with our famed sun, surf, and beaches. What an unbeatable combination—something for everyone!

Dreams can be reality, so let's get our legislators, government officials, and visitor industry leaders to stop playing politics and get their fannies in gear to revitalize Hawai'i, 1990s style.

[Excerpted from a column in the *Honolulu Advertiser*, dated August 9, 1993, written by Ernest Watari, managing director of PKF Hawai'i, a CPA and consulting firm]

CHAPTER 15

TOURISM & JOBS

BRUCE S. PLASCH
President
Decision Analysts Hawaii, Inc.

"Does tourism provide mostly low-income jobs?"

A common complaint about tourism—voiced by many people, including influential government officials, community leaders, and University of Hawai'i researchers—is that most of the jobs it provides pay low wages. This is a serious allegation, since tourism is by far Hawai'i's largest industry, and misconceptions about its economic impacts can undermine public and government support.

Even though many jobs in the visitor industry do indeed pay low wages, the perception that tourism keeps Hawai'i incomes low is simply wrong. Quite the opposite is true. After adjusting for workers who hold two or more part-time jobs, nonwage incomes, and the many jobs generated by tourism which are outside the visitor industry, one finds that tourism generates respectably high incomes: nearly $30,000 per worker in 1991. Furthermore, the visitor industry supports far more jobs than is generally recognized. Counting all jobs directly and indirectly supported by tourism, the visitor industry is responsible for more than half of all jobs in Hawai'i.

Paradise "premium." Because of tourism, average per capita income in Hawai'i is 11 percent higher than that for the nation as a whole: $21,190 for Hawai'i in 1991 versus $19,092 for the nation. Although this "income premium" for living in Hawai'i is insufficient to fully compensate for Hawai'i's high cost of living, it is an amazing accomplishment, given our distance from major markets, lack of resources available to other states, limited area, and small population. If Hawai'i had not developed a visitor industry but instead remained heavily dependent upon agriculture, then incomes in Hawai'i would be much lower than they are today.

Furthermore, many people, some of them quite critical of tourism, are unaware that they themselves depend financially on the industry. Without tourism, many of these people would be unable to live here for lack of an income-producing job.

Low-wage tourism jobs. The basis for the misconception that tourism keeps incomes low is obvious: many jobs in the visitor industry *do* pay low wages. While in 1991 the statewide average annual wage was $23,176, hotels paid an average annual wage of $19,263, retail shops paid $17,112, and eating and drinking establishments paid $11,512. Although all three are lower than the average wage, three comments are in order.

First, low-wage jobs in the visitor industry are usually unskilled, entry-level positions filled by (1) those who lack language, education, and other skills and are therefore unable to obtain more advanced employment; (2) young people who are new to the labor force and who will gain work experience before they eventually move on to more advanced employment; and (3) young people from the mainland who work as part of an extended vacation before returning home. Many of these people would be unemployed if low-skill entry-level positions were not available. None of them, presumably, would be making more elsewhere in Hawai'i's economy, or they would go elsewhere. So, given their job qualifications and employment options, these workers benefit from having tourism jobs available to them.

Second, low wages do not necessarily mean low annual incomes. As explained further below, many jobs in the visitor industry provide substantial tip and other nonwage incomes.

Third, hotel, retail, and restaurant jobs account for only about 30 percent of all jobs generated by tourism. The remaining jobs are scattered throughout the economy (see Adjustment 6 below), and many of these jobs provide relatively high salaries.

Wage statistics can be misleading. To properly determine *real* income, we should consider six adjustments:

Adjustment 1: Part-time jobs. Many jobs in the visitor industry are part-time. For a person who holds two part-time jobs each paying $10,000 per year, the average annual salary *per job* is $10,000, but the average annual salary *per worker* is $20,000. If the average wage for hotel workers is adjusted to a 40-hour week, the average annual wage income is $23,069; a similar adjustment for retail workers results in an average annual wage of $22,080. (Data are not available to make the adjustment for restaurant employees.) These figures are significantly higher than the average annual wage for hotel and retail jobs on the preceding page.

Adjustment 2: Tips. Food servers, bartenders, busboys, bellhops, valets, maids, beach boys, taxi drivers, and other workers in the visitor industry earn substantial income from tips—income that does not get included in the wage statistics. Tips received by minimum-wage waiters and waitresses, for example, often triple their actual income. It's not unusual for bartenders to receive wage-plus-tip income that exceeds the incomes of many recent graduates with UH master's degrees.

Adjustment 3: Unreported cash income. Many visitors pay for goods and services with cash, and some people yield to the temptation to not report it as income. The economic incentive to do this is quite strong: for a person with a taxable income above $30,000, not reporting cash income can "save" federal and state taxes of more than $400 per $1,000 pocketed. It also results in statistics that make it look as though that job doesn't pay as well as it really does.

Adjustment 4: Income from profits. Owners of small businesses often derive income from profits rather than pay themselves a wage as an employee. This is often true of family-operated vendors such as those found in the International Market Place. Since income derived from such profits is not reported as wages, what may be substantial earnings simply do not show up in the wage statistics.

Adjustment 5: Benefits. Many small business owners/employees choose to take a portion of their compensation in the form of very generous health, retirement, and other benefits rather than as wages. Their incentive is to avoid a variety of employment and income taxes. This choice is perfectly legal, but it distorts wage statistics, making it look as though these workers earn less than they actually do.

Adjustment 6: Indirect jobs. The biggest adjustment is to account for all jobs that are directly or indirectly supported by the visitor

ADJUSTMENT # 2 : TIPS

industry—rather than just those jobs in hotels, retail shops, and restaurants.

Purchases of goods and services by visitors, by businesses that service visitors, and by employees supported by the visitor industry provide an enormous number of jobs dispersed throughout Hawai'i's economy. These include the many jobs provided by airlines and airports; companies that supply goods and services to airlines; car rental companies; bus companies; auto repair shops for rental cars and buses; oil companies that provide fuel for airplanes, ships, cars, buses, and trucks; the telephone, electric, and cable TV companies that service visitors and employees; construction companies that build, improve, or repair hotels, related off-site improvements, and homes of employees; building supply companies; furniture suppliers; shipping companies that import goods for visitors and employees; storage companies; trucking companies that deliver goods; landscaping and maintenance companies; banks and insurance companies that service businesses in the visitor industry as well as their employees; advertising companies; publishing companies; medical clinics and hospitals; schools to train employees. Many of these jobs pay high salaries.

Many farmers owe their jobs and their incomes to the visitor industry, since the farmers help feed the visitors and residents who are supported by the visitor industry. The two pineapple plantations on O'ahu, and farmers who grow fresh produce, flowers, and tropical plants for mainland markets, owe a major share of their income—if not their entire survival—to the excellent air transportation that has been established as a result of the visitor industry. They benefit from favorable backhaul rates and the frequent air flights to a large number of cities. Furthermore, tourism helps sell Hawaiian pineapple, macadamia nuts, papaya, and Kona coffee.

A great many government jobs are supported by the enormous tax revenues generated by the visitor industry. Revenues are generated by the 4 percent excise taxes on hotel construction, related improvements (roads, water systems, sewer), support businesses, and employee housing. Construction companies pay corporate income taxes and construction workers pay income and excise taxes. Visitors pay a 5 percent hotel room tax and taxes on fuel, liquor, tobacco, and other items. Hotels, resorts, and support businesses pay property taxes that are quite high because of the high value of their properties and the high tax rate (for O'ahu, the tax rate is more than twice that for residential property). Hotels, resorts, and support businesses also pay excise taxes and corporate income taxes. Employees who are directly or indirectly supported by the visitor industry pay personal income taxes, property taxes, excise taxes on their purchases, fuel taxes, motor vehicle taxes, liquor and tobacco taxes, and so on.

Income from tourism versus agriculture. Jobs generated by tourism generally pay higher wages than jobs in agriculture. In communities that have both resorts and plantations, the visitor industry generally bids workers away from agriculture, not vice versa. In addition, simple observation reveals that the residential neighborhoods that depend on tourism (e.g., West Maui, Kihei, Kona, Po'ipu) exhibit greater wealth than those that depend on agriculture (e.g., Ka'u, Honoka'a, Kekaha). Also, the few remaining communities that are far removed from tourism and still depend on plantation agriculture suffer from relatively high unemployment and low incomes.

Hawai'i compares favorably. As indicated earlier, the average per capita income in Hawai'i compares favorably to that for the nation as a whole, thanks largely to tourism. In 1990, with nearly the same average age in Hawai'i as in the nation (32.6 years for Hawai'i vs. 32.9 years for the nation) and nearly the same participation in the labor force (67.6 percent of adults vs. 66.8 percent for the nation), Hawai'i ranked tenth among the fifty states in per capita income.

Surprisingly, for the economy as a whole, Hawai'i had fewer multiple-job holders (5.2 percent vs. 6.2 percent for the nation), ranking fortieth among the states. Hawai'i also had fewer people below poverty level (11 percent for Hawai'i vs. 13.5 percent for the nation), ranking thirty-second.

In short, tourism may have its problems, but providing mostly low-income jobs is *not* one of them.

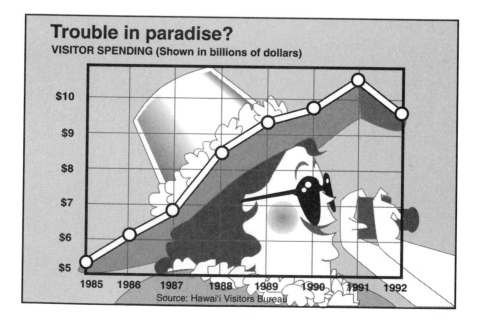

Trouble in paradise?
VISITOR SPENDING (Shown in billions of dollars)

Source: Hawai'i Visitors Bureau

" HAWAIIAN O'OS MIGRATING HERE BECAUSE OF RIDICULOUSLY HIGH COST OF LIVING IN THE ISLANDS..."

CHAPTER 16

PARADISE TAX

PETER S. ADLER
Executive Director
Hawaiʻi Bar Foundation

RANDALL W. ROTH
William S. Richardson School of Law
University of Hawaiʻi

JOANNE PUNU
Assistant Dean
William S. Richardson School of Law
University of Hawaiʻi

ERIC YAMAMOTO
Professor of Law
William S. Richardson School of Law
University of Hawaiʻi

"What is the paradise tax and what are its implications?"

Hawaiʻi's unusually high cost of living—nearly 40 percent higher in 1992 than the mainland average, according to Bank of Hawaii economist Paul Brewbaker—has sometimes been called a "paradise tax." We prefer to call this number a "cost factor" and treat it as one of two components of the paradise tax. The other component is the level of income a person can earn in Hawaiʻi compared to the amount that same person could earn elsewhere. By combining these two factors, one can better understand and compare the degree of financial sacrifice that has to be made in order to live in Hawaiʻi. One can also better understand the steady flow of relatives, friends, and neighbors—of all races, many in their twenties and thirties—moving to the mainland in search of more hospitable economic conditions.

Situations vary. A very small number of residents would see their incomes drop by more than 40 percent if they were to make such a move. Because these lucky people are enjoying an "income premium" that exceeds the 40 percent cost factor, they are not making a monetary sacrifice by living here.

Most people earn just a little more in Hawai'i than they could on the mainland. Their small income premiums help a bit but don't come close to offsetting the 40 percent cost factor. Consequently, they would be financially better off elsewhere.

Some folks, however, actually earn *less* income in Hawai'i than would be possible elsewhere. They, therefore, are incurring a double-whammy—an "income penalty" as well as the cost factor.

"Paradise Tax" = The cost factor minus the income premium (or plus the income penalty).
"Cost Factor" = The additional cost of living in Hawai'i, expressed as a percentage of the average cost of living on the mainland.
"Income Premium" = The additional income that is being earned in Hawai'i, expressed as a percentage of the mainland average.
"Income Penalty" = The additional income that could be earned on the mainland, expressed as a percentage of the mainland average.

Simple example. If Kim Kealoha pays 40 percent more to live in Hawai'i than she would in Las Vegas, but is earning 15 percent more here than she could there, her paradise tax is 25 percent. On the other hand, if Lisa Lee could be making 15 percent *more* working in Las Vegas than she's currently earning here, her paradise tax is 55 percent. Because Lisa's "tax" is higher than Kim's, her financial incentive to move is greater.

Unfortunately, data from the 1990 census are not yet complete, but retired state statistician Robert Schmitt, UH sociology professor Herb Barringer, and UH business professor Frank Abou-Sayf recently combined their considerable talents to provide a reasonable substitute set of data. What they found is quite interesting.

In 1989, Hawai'i residents who had completed fewer than twelve years of schooling enjoyed an average income premium of roughly 45 percent. The cost factor in 1989 was 31 percent (as compared to 1992's 40 percent), so this group enjoyed a paradise "bonus" of 14 percent that year. This bonus and the income premium which supports it may be linked to the fact that Hawai'i's economy is based largely on tourism and, to a much lesser extent, agriculture. These industries are known for generating jobs that require little in the way of formal education, yet workers in these industries in Hawai'i—perhaps because many of them are unionized—tend to earn high incomes compared to mainland counterparts.

Not all residents realize an income premium. Those with five or more years of college, for example, earned 5 percent *less* on average in 1989 than did their counterparts on the mainland that year. This slight income penalty, when added to the 31 percent cost factor, resulted in a paradise tax of 36 percent. Economist and UH business professor Jack Suyderhoud speculates that this figure may understate that group's actual paradise tax, because highly educated people tend to spend more educating their children and because of Hawai'i's comparatively progressive tax structure.

Different views. One view of the "bonus" for the lesser educated and the "tax" on the more highly educated is salutary: Hawai'i has less of an income gap between rich and poor than the mainland does. This might account in part for generally less volatile socioeconomic class conflicts in Hawai'i and generally more accommodating ethnic group relations.

Another view is that this bonus/tax phenomenon lessens incentives for residents to pursue further education, encourages more highly educated residents to move to the mainland, and discourages relocation here by outsiders with specialized training and education. In short, it may diminish the long-term chances of developing a vibrant, sophisticated economy.

New-starters pay more. The paradise tax also varies depending on when it was that a person settled in Hawai'i. Someone who bought a home ten, fifteen, or twenty years ago can more easily afford to live in Hawai'i than someone who is shopping for a starter home in today's market. People who have longer histories in Hawai'i also enjoy the cost savings associated with a *kokua* network of family and friends.

Conversely, for many *kanaka maoli* (Hawaiians), having been here longer than anyone else has not helped in terms of land and home ownership. Dispossessed of land and resources for over a century, many find themselves "new-starters" in their homeland, battling what some of them might term a "colony tax" rather than a paradise tax.

People who accept a particularly high paradise tax must really want to live here. Perhaps it's the pleasant climate and stunning beauty of the place. For many it's the intangibles like ethnic and cultural diversity and the aloha spirit.

People with deep roots here have those reasons, and more: it's always been home so there's probably an emotional, and maybe even a spiritual, connection. This makes it that much more special. Consider also the fact that a move from Hawai'i puts a wide ocean and expensive airline tickets between family and friends. A trip to see *tutu* or the kids becomes a very big deal. And yet, more than a few residents—*kanaka maoli, kama'aina,* as well as *malihini*—periodically think about moving to another place for economic reasons, and some actually do it. But most of us stay, despite the paradise tax.

Evidently, we can afford the price of paradise, at least for now. But we wonder about our loved ones. People with established roots in Hawai'i want their parents and grandparents nearby, and all of us want our children and their children to be able to call Hawai'i home. And yet the high cost of living can be increasingly difficult for retired people on fixed incomes whose paradise tax is now equal to the cost factor, and on young adults who are "new-starters" even if they were born and raised here.

No easy answers. Government could do things that would bring down the cost factor, especially to the extent that costs have been kept high through restrictive land use policies. But consider the implications. On the one hand, if the paradise tax gets too low, Hawai'i will be overwhelmed by people who want to live here. That, of course, would be the end of "paradise." Also, the home equity that many of us rely upon to educate our children or to retire comfortably might disappear, or at least drop significantly.

On the other hand, if government maintains a high paradise tax and does little more than attempt to reallocate its burdens, many of the sons and daughters of Hawai'i will continue to be pushed to leave the state.

So what's it going to be? Bring down the paradise tax and watch paradise and home equity deteriorate? Keep it high and watch our children and other loved ones settle on the mainland? Keep it high but try to give advantages to those we choose to favor in our community? Or something else?

Open discussion. No matter how difficult the choices seem, it's time for open and frank discussion. Even if we can't work out all the answers, clarity about the choices—and the implications that attend those choices—will serve us well. It is, in fact, one of the starting points for strengthening the quality of public life in our community, something that of necessity involves us all.

The hole in our wallets

Median family income in Hawai'i has consistently exceeded the comparable U.S. figure, but the cost of living in Hawai'i generally has exceeded costs on the mainland by a slightly higher percentage.

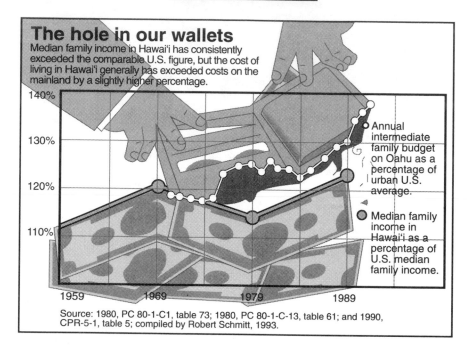

Annual intermediate family budget on Oahu as a percentage of urban U.S. average.

Median family income in Hawai'i as a percentage of U.S. median family income.

Source: 1980, PC 80-1-C1, table 73; 1980, PC 80-1-C-13, table 61; and 1990, CPR-5-1, table 5; compiled by Robert Schmitt, 1993.

Annual budget

The overall cost of living for a family of four was 38% higher in 1991 than for the U.S. as a whole.

1991 annual budget for four-person family in Hawai'i:

Source: State of Hawai'i, Department of Business, Economic Development and Tourism, Data Book 1992, table 418.

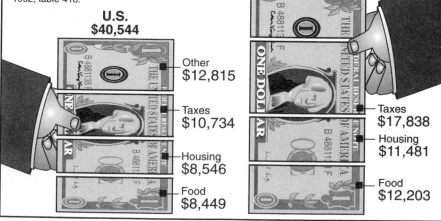

U.S.
$40,544

Other
$12,815

Taxes
$10,734

Housing
$8,546

Food
$8,449

Hawai'i
$55,833

Other
$14,311

Taxes
$17,838

Housing
$11,481

Food
$12,203

Opportunity costs vary

Highly educated residents of Hawai'i enjoy incomes that are higher than those of residents with less education. But when the income of each group's mainland counterpart is considered, it appears that Hawai'i's economy tends to attract people with less education and repel those with more.

1989 Median Earnings

Level of education	Hawai'i	Nation	Income Factor	
Less than 12 years	$13,195	$9,079	45%	(premium)
12 years	17,679	15,495	14%	(premium)
1 - 3 years college	21,454	20,073	7%	(premium)
4 years college	26,453	27,378	-3%	(penalty)
5+ years college	33,504	35,357	-5%	(penalty)

Source: C.P.R. P-60, No. 180 (August 1992); 1990 U.S. Census, public use microdata sample.

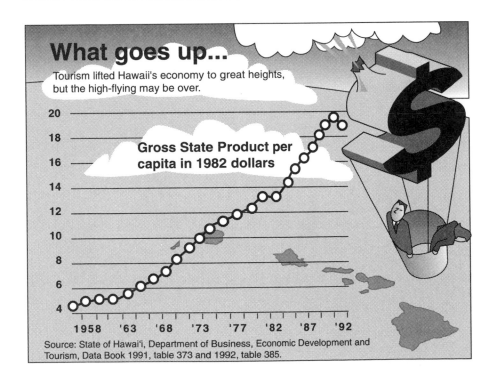

What goes up...

Tourism lifted Hawaii's economy to great heights, but the high-flying may be over.

Gross State Product per capita in 1982 dollars

Source: State of Hawai'i, Department of Business, Economic Development and Tourism, Data Book 1991, table 373 and 1992, table 385.

CHAPTER 17

GOVERNMENT & HOUSING

NICK ORDWAY

Director of the Hawai'i Real Estate
Research and Education Center
University of Hawai'i

"Is it the responsibility of the state and county government to make housing affordable?"

Didn't we already talk about this in the first volume of *The Price of Paradise*? Isn't this "déjà vu all over again," as Yogi Berra is often quoted? Actually, there are a few more things to be said—some of them might even be considered radical.

Whether you would *really* welcome a solution to the affordable housing problem depends on your point of view:

• If you are a parent, worried your children won't be able to buy a home in Hawai'i—say yes.

• If you are in business and find it difficult to recruit employees from the mainland because of high housing costs—say yes.

• If you are living like a gypsy, moving from one beach campground to another, because that is the only housing you can find—say YES!

• If you are an environmentalist concerned that Hawai'i's population is increasing too fast—say no.

• If you are a bureaucrat whose job depends on imposing red tape on private housing developers—say no.

• If you are a homeowner, afraid the value of your house will drop and your equity disappear—say NO!

Affordable housing in Hawai'i will solve problems for some people but create new problems for others. We'll get into how government could solve the housing problem, but first, a little background.

Reasons for unaffordability. Housing in Hawai'i has become less and less affordable for many reasons:

• A lot of people want to move to Hawai'i. This keeps the demand for housing up. High demand leads to high prices.

• Housing that could be used by regular residents sometimes is used for vacation rentals. This competition drives up prices.

• There is a scarcity of zoned urban land with suitable infrastructure (i.e., electricity, water, sewer, roads). Scarcity of land means higher prices.

• Labor and transportation costs for materials add to the production cost of housing. These costs are particularly high in Hawai'i.

• Hawai'i's unusually high excise and other business taxes are passed on to the consumer in the form of higher prices.

• It takes an incredibly long time and is ridiculously complicated to reclassify or rezone land for housing. This increases the carrying costs of land and adds the cost of otherwise unnecessary lawyers, accountants, and consultants.

• Government has not been paying its fair share for sewers and other infrastructure costs. It has imposed too much of these costs on home purchasers.

• Politicians frequently use legal blackmail to get developers to pay costs unrelated to their housing projects. These costs include tickets to political fund-raisers.

As this list makes clear, government and politicians currently are part of the *problem*. If we are to ever have affordable housing in Hawai'i, they must be part of the *solution*.

Possible actions. Government could revamp the system. Presently, landowners who are lucky enough to have undeveloped zoned land reap windfall profits. They are able to sell land to builders at artificially high prices. As indicated earlier, government then gouges home builders with excessive costs and expensive delays.

Some costs might drop if county governments had sufficient tax revenue to carry out their normal responsibilities. However, because our county governments don't have an adequate tax base, they shift more and more costs to private housing developers. State government,

"WE'VE FOUND THE SNAG..."

on the other hand, with too much tax revenue, has experimented with a wide variety of spending programs, many of which don't seem to be essential to the general welfare of our community. Any solution to the affordable housing problem must deal with the misallocation of tax revenue between the state and counties.

Government could zone land for housing development, reduce the time required to get building permits, provide more infrastructure, increase density, and reduce unnecessary building code provisions. It could also provide targeted subsidies, tax incentives to first-time buyers, and financing programs.

Another approach, seldom considered by policymakers, is to dampen demand. Demand for housing in Hawai'i comes from users (owner-occupants and renters) and nonusers (nonresident investors and speculators). Nonresident speculators create a burden on all resident taxpayers. They often buy houses that either remain empty or are used as illegal transient rental units. In both cases, these homes are no longer available to local residents. A solution is to raise property taxes and provide a tax credit to rebate the increase to people filing state income tax forms. We would benefit in three ways:

1. County tax revenues would increase, making it possible to fund new sewer treatment plants, mass transit, and other infrastructure. State tax revenues would decline, requiring the state to stop providing services that are the proper role of the counties.

2. Nonresidents who do not pay state income taxes (in some cases illegally) would pay more property taxes. This would deny them the free ride they have been enjoying and make them pay the real costs of the services their properties have been receiving.

3. The higher cost of operation to speculators not receiving tax credits would lower the value of their houses to them. This would cause many, if not most, to sell their houses to local users at reduced prices.

It might also be useful to tax people who speculate in zoned urban land—people who, as mentioned earlier, have been making windfall profits. A higher tax could be imposed on land that has not been developed within five years of being rezoned. In fact, consideration should be given to taxing the entire increase in value created by new zoning or by improvement of roads.

Another way to lower the cost of housing is to impose rent controls. But, unlike the first proposal, which shifts costs to nonresident speculators, rent controls would be likely to harm everybody except some renters in the short run and the bureaucrats employed to administer the rent control system. Rent controls can work in the short run as an emergency measure, but they create serious economic problems if left in place too long. Honolulu experimented with rent controls after World War II and dropped these controls in the early 1960s (much to the relief of nearly everyone).

Government could build or encourage more specialized housing. For example, the University of Hawai'i should be encouraged to build more student dorms and rental housing for faculty. The military should be encouraged to continue building more military housing. Government could build more housing for those of retirement age. Our *kupuna* should have the option of moving out of large single-family houses into smaller units designed to meet their special needs.

Hawaiian homelands should be distributed immediately and native Hawaiians given development grants to build their own homes. Much of the demand for housing could be satisfied simply by empowering native Hawaiians to control their own land.

Implications. When weighing the pros and cons of various solutions to the affordable housing crisis in Hawai'i, it is interesting to consider what would have happened if housing production and population size had continued to grow at the rates experienced in the 1970s. Toward the end of 1993, we would have had approximately 62,000 additional housing units and another 160,000 people driving 110,000 motor vehicles. These additional people would be adding to our traffic congestion and putting pressure on our water supply, sewers, schools, and other social services.

Who would be the newcomers to Hawai'i? Obviously, the state's low unemployment rate would attract those looking for jobs and raising families. There would also be three specific groups who'd find Hawai'i especially attractive:

1. Individuals of retirement age. Hawai'i's healthful climate and natural beauty make it attractive to retirees. Many of these individuals rely on pensions, which Hawai'i does not tax. They probably would be very nice people, but they would require extensive social services and place extra demands on the state's health care and social welfare system.

2. Transient workers of college age who would move to the state to surf and work in restaurants and hotels. Some of these people would work only as long as it took to qualify for unemployment benefits. Then they would arrange to be dismissed from their jobs. Fun in the sun would continue until their unemployment benefits ran out; then new jobs would be found to restart the cycle.

3. Young adults who would be returning home to Hawai'i after completing their college education on the mainland. It has been estimated that we lose up to 75 percent of these young adults. They leave for higher education, with a goal of returning, but they stay away because Hawai'i lacks affordable housing and high-paying job opportunities.

Mixed blessing. In other words, affordable housing would be a mixed blessing. The probable consequences would be a larger population, greater pressures on our physical infrastructure and social services, an increase in state and county taxes, and a decline in the quality of life for the middle and upper classes.

For those who currently are poor and homeless or under-housed, quality of life would improve. Our children would be more likely to settle in Hawai'i, and businesses would probably be able to attract and retain better-trained employees.

Should government get serious about solving the affordable housing problem? If you're middle or upper class, without children, and already own your own home, just say no. If you're just about anybody else, say YES! If your elected officials don't agree with you, just say NO! when they come up for reelection.

SPECIES DYING OFF AT THOUSANDS OF TIMES THE NATURAL RATE OF EXTINCTION:

HAWAIIAN BIRDS   HAWAIIAN TREES   HAWAIIAN FISHES   HAWAIIAN HOMEOWNERS

CORKY

BATTLE LINES ARE DRAWN AT SANDY'S...

CHAPTER 18

LAND REGULATION

KENT M. KEITH
President
Chaminade University

"Is Hawai'i being overdeveloped?"

Many battles have been fought over the development of land in Hawai'i, especially during the past thirty years. Political leaders have responded to public fears of overdeveloped land by enacting numerous planning laws and forming various commissions. Environmental and citizen groups have opposed specific projects, testifying at hearings, filing lawsuits, and launching initiative campaigns. Sometimes these efforts have been based on relatively selfless motives, other times not. The "not in my back yard" mentality has plagued developers as well as government officials who need to find places for public projects.

Battles over development will no doubt continue, but the entire community needs to understand a critical underlying truth: we are not overdeveloped, we are underpreserved. Once everyone understands that, we can shift our focus from regulation to preservation.

Lots of land. Over and over again, I have heard people in Hawai'i talk about our shortage of land. Actually, we have plenty of land, and most of it is open space.

The whole state consists of 4.1 million acres. Of that, 47.7 percent is in the Conservation District (mostly mountain tops and forests), and another 47.7 percent is in the Agricultural District (farming and grazing). A tiny amount is in the Rural District. That leaves 178,000 acres, or 4.3 percent, in the Urban District, the district that allows residential and commercial development. To put it the other way around, 95.7 percent of all our land in Hawai'i is in the Agricultural and Conservation districts, and most of the land in those districts is open space.

Then why the many battles over development? One reason is that most of us live and work on O'ahu, where the development is the most dense. The high densities are partly the result of a state planning strategy to build "up" instead of "out"—to build more densely in areas already zoned urban instead of spreading out into agricultural or other open space. A related reason is that complex multilayered government regulation has created an artificial shortage of land available for development. The rezoning and development of land for residential or commercial purposes takes years and years, and not all applications for rezoning are approved by government agencies.

In turning down applications, government agencies have been in tune with the large number of Hawai'i residents who fear unchecked urbanization. This fear is understandable—but misplaced. We can sustain significant growth in residential and commercial development, with only a small increase in the percentage of our land which is urbanized.

Housing. According to a housing study conducted by SMS Research and Locations, there was pent-up demand in early 1993 for an additional 25,608 housing units. Using construction at Mililani and Kapolei as a reference, one can build six to eight single-family homes, or fifteen to twenty multifamily units (in two- or three-story buildings), per acre. If three-quarters of the pent-up demand were met with six single-family homes per acre, and one-quarter were met with fifteen multifamily units per acre, it would take 3,628 acres to meet today's pent-up demand.

If pent-up demand were met, we would still need to continue building homes to meet population growth. The SMS/Locations study estimated that the number of households in Hawai'i will grow by 4,350 per year to the year 2010. Again, if three-quarters of this demand were met with single-family homes and one-quarter with multifamily homes, it would take 616 acres per year, or 10,472 acres to the year 2010. Adding the 3,628 acres to meet pent-up demand with the 10,472 acres for growth to the year 2010 totals 14,100 acres. That's only three-tenths of one percent of all the land in the state.

Let's take an even longer-term view. A century of growth requiring 616 acres per year would total 61,600 acres. That is only 1.5 percent of all the land in the state and would only increase the percentage of urban land in Hawai'i from 4.3 percent to 5.8 percent. That's not a big increase.

Agricultural lands. Urbanization is likely to encroach on lands in the Agricultural District, because they are often the easiest to convert to urban uses. The State Constitution protects important or prime agricultural land, but the Land Evaluation and Site Assessment Commission in the late 1980s concluded that 1,261,000 acres (64 percent of the 1.9 million acres in the Agricultural District) are *not* prime or important. And only 226,000 acres of the 700,000 acres of prime land are now planted in crops. That means that 1.7 million acres, or 88 percent of the land in the Agricultural District, is either not "important" or "important" but not planted.

We want to preserve agricultural lands, but there is significant acreage which has little agricultural value and can be considered for other uses. A century of housing, even if it were all built on agricultural lands, would use up only 61,600 acres, or 3.1 percent, of the 1,963,000 acres currently in the Agricultural District. That's not very much.

Hard questions. Though there clearly is enough land to meet our future development needs, hard questions remain: what should be done . . . and where? We have to use the right land for the right things, and not use some at all.

The problem is not simply development or urbanization. The problem is the potential misuse of land, private ownership of land needed for public purposes, and loss of environmentally important resources.

It is troubling, for example, when a beautiful beach needed for a public park is acquired by a developer and made into a private resort with limited public access. It is equally troubling to see an apartment building constructed on prime agricultural land when other land could have been made available. And it is not right to allow an ecologically important resource to deteriorate because of overuse. These preservation issues should concern us greatly.

Land Use Commission. It is in response to issues such as these that governments get involved in land use. The state government has regulated land use since the Land Use Commission (LUC) was established by statute in 1963. The LUC allocates all the land of the state into one of the four land use districts—Urban, Rural, Agricultural, or Conservation.

The basic concept of land use districts is that each parcel of land is better for some purposes than for others. Our community has many needs, and not all of them are fulfilled in the free market economy. For example, the concept of the "highest and best use" of land refers to its economic value. With no regulations prohibiting certain uses in certain districts, the economic "highest and best use" of a parcel of land would almost always turn out to be commercial or residential. Land use districts protect community values such as the preservation of agriculture, or aesthetic values such as the preservation of environmental resources, which would not be valued appropriately in the marketplace.

It made sense to establish the LUC in the early 1960s when the counties did not have fully staffed planning agencies and their general plans or development plans. They do now, however, and this has led to duplication in state and county zoning efforts. This duplication costs everybody time and money.

In 1984, the Department of Planning and Economic Development (DPED) did some informal research on LUC cases. Staff members found that in the LUC's first twenty years, from 1963 to 1983, 48 percent of all the cases that came before the LUC were for 15 acres or less. The DPED held workshops that included diverse members of the community and concluded that, except for Conservation lands, the state had little need to be involved in decisions regarding parcels of 15 acres or less. The DPED proposed, and the 1985 legislature adopted, a revision to the LUC statute so that parcels of 15 acres or less in Urban, Rural, and Agricultural districts would be handled by the counties.

The 1984 DPED research found something else. It revealed that in only 7 percent of the cases did the LUC's position on a land use issue really make a difference. In other words, the LUC's role during that period was not decisive in 93 percent of all the cases it heard. But its involvement slowed the process and increased project costs significantly.

The state government should remain very interested in land use, but it no longer needs the Land Use Commission. The regulatory work can be handed over to the counties, which are now fully qualified to do the planning and regulation.

State strategy. What the state needs now is a strategy for acquiring, developing, managing, and preserving public lands which will fulfill the values of the community. That is the essential contribution our government can offer future generations: the assurance that there will be enough land for public parks, recreation centers, community meeting centers, and public school and university sites. And it can make sure that ecologically important lands will be preserved. The focus should be on preservation, not regulation.

The state government, through its Department of Land and Natural Resources, should retain its management of the Conservation District and should continue to work with private organizations such as the Nature Conservancy in building the state's nature preserves. It should go further, however, to envision Hawai'i in fifty or a hundred years and set about acquiring the land our people will need to fulfill public purposes and community values in the long-term future. Rather than attempting questionable down-zoning and fighting bitter lawsuits, the state should just acquire the land the public will need for future generations. This can be done by purchase at a fair market price, or by land exchange, or by donation.

There is enough land in Hawai'i for development. We need to take action now so that, regardless of the rate of urbanization, land is set aside to guarantee that Hawai'i will still be Hawai'i in the centuries to come.

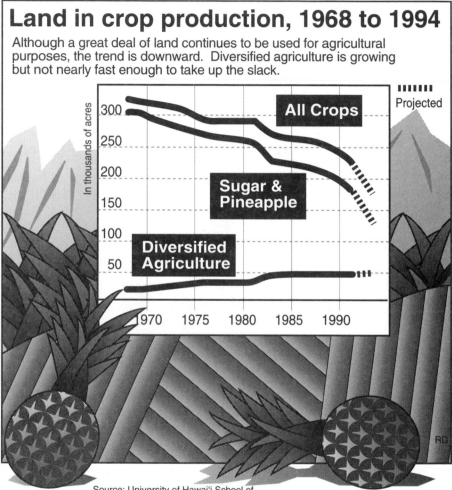

Land in crop production, 1968 to 1994

Although a great deal of land continues to be used for agricultural purposes, the trend is downward. Diversified agriculture is growing but not nearly fast enough to take up the slack.

Projected

In thousands of acres

300
250
200
150
100
50

All Crops

Sugar & Pineapple

Diversified Agriculture

1970   1975   1980   1985   1990

Source: University of Hawaiʻi School of Agricultural and Resource Economics.

CHAPTER 19

AGRICULTURAL LANDS

PETER GARROD
Professor of Agricultural and Resource Economics
University of Hawai'i

BRUCE S. PLASCH
President
Decision Analysts Hawaii, Inc.

"What's to come of all the land released from sugar and pineapple?"

About 177,000 acres have already been or will soon be released from sugar and pineapple cultivation in Hawai'i, including land undergoing final harvest on three sugar plantations. This is an enormous amount of land—more than half the total amount used for crop production just twenty-five years ago. 177,000 acres is equivalent to a strip of land 609 feet wide (slightly more than the combined length of two football fields) stretching from Honolulu to San Francisco!

Unless there are some drastic changes soon—an increase in the federal support price for sugar, a major and favorable change in the world sugar market, or a technological breakthrough that increases yields, lowers costs, or utilizes by-products—more land will be released from plantation agriculture as unprofitable sugar plantations are forced to close.

The future of pineapple isn't quite so bleak. When it comes to canned pineapple, Hawai'i can't begin to compete with Thailand or the Philippines because our production costs are much higher. For example, the *hourly* wage rate for farm workers in Hawai'i is higher than the *daily* wage rate in some other countries. Pineapple production for the canned market has already been shut down completely on Kaua'i, Moloka'i, Lana'i, and O'ahu, leaving only one plantation on Maui growing pineapple for this market. In most years, however, our fresh pineapple sales remain profitable. This is the result of a superior product, a shift in consumer preferences from canned to fresh fruit, and the availability of cheap backhaul rates to the mainland. The two plantations on O'ahu grow pineapples for the fresh market.

The land already taken out of sugar and pineapple production may provide a clue as to the fate of any additional acreage that becomes available. Perhaps you're wondering how much of it is being used to grow other agricultural products.

Diversified crops. Just about any agricultural use other than sugar and pineapple is referred to as "diversified agriculture." Roughly 20,000 acres have been replanted in diversified crops (macadamia nut production being the largest new use). That's a lot of land but amounts to only 11 percent of the 177,000 acres in question.

Why hasn't more land been used for diversified agriculture? Two reasons: Hawai'i's high production costs and small markets for profitable crops. Our production costs are substantially higher than those in the competing regions, particularly the cost of labor, water, and imported inputs such as fuel, equipment, and agricultural chemicals (not to mention the cost of owning land). In fact, production costs in Hawai'i are among the highest in the world, even if we ignore the cost of land!

In addition, fruit fly infestations have burdened producers with both added restrictions and costs; particularly hard hit in recent years has been the papaya industry. On the mainland, in contrast, the winter freezes conveniently kill many pests.

There are two markets for Hawai'i's diversified agriculture: the local market and overseas markets. The local market is small, only 1.25 million residents and visitors. There is no local outlet for excess or off-grade production. Small, specific product markets are easily saturated: for many crops, there is sufficient demand for a single producer to make a living, but if two producers are unfortunate enough to produce the same crop at the same time, they can both go broke.

A significant portion of the produce consumed in Hawai'i is already produced locally. Of the 290 million pounds of fresh fruit and vegetables entering the Honolulu market in 1991, nearly 30 percent was produced in-state. This is a very significant amount when one considers the importance of nontropical produce in our diets (e.g., potatoes, apples, head lettuce, onions, and tomatoes) and the seasonal nature of most crops. For those crops that have proved to be viable in Hawai'i, only about 2,000 acres are needed to expand production to meet local demand.

If effective agricultural use is to be made of the lands released from sugar and pineapple, crops destined for out-of-state markets must be produced. This is not new information; the agriculture industry has always been aware of it. In fact, it is fair to describe the history of agriculture in Hawai'i as the continuous search for, and the development of, viable export commodities. The major agriculture activities historically have been sugar and pineapple, which are export crops. Recently, macadamias, papayas, coffee, flowers, and ornamentals have become increasingly important.

With land being released from sugar and pineapple production, why has the export market for other crops increased so slowly? The reason has nothing to do with Hawai'i's ability to produce a desirable commodity but has everything to do with Hawai'i's ability to produce and market commodities at competitive prices. The closest major markets for tropical agricultural products are the east and west coasts of North America, thousands of miles away. The major regions producing competing products (California, Mexico, the Caribbean, and Florida) are much closer to the large mainland markets. As a result, their shipping and spoilage costs generally are much lower than costs for products shipped from Hawai'i.

Notable success. Given the constraints, Hawai'i producers are to be commended for doing as well as they have in overseas markets. Notable successes include flower and horticultural products, macadamia nuts, ginger, and fresh pineapple. Hawai'i has captured a share of these markets by producing a superior product, taking advantage of the Hawai'i mystique, and utilizing the frequent airfreight and shipping services to many markets at relatively low rates (thanks to the high volume of flights generated by tourism).

Clearly, it is not a scarcity of land that has limited increases in the production of agricultural products for either local or overseas markets, but rather the costs of production and marketing, combined with strong competition from both U.S. mainland and foreign producers. Thus, it isn't very likely that the availability of more land will have a major impact on expanding Hawai'i's production.

Other uses. So, if only 11 percent of the 177,000 acres has been used for diversified agriculture, what has happened to the rest? About 10,000 acres have been used for housing and other urban uses (that's another 6 percent), and 3,000 acres (that's less than 2 percent) are now golf courses. So what has or will happen to the other 81 percent? The answer is simple, and it has major implications for the future of Hawai'i. All that land—over 140,000 acres of it—either is or will soon be used to graze cattle, or is lying or will soon lie fallow. A brief trip to a former plantation—North Kohala, Puna, and soon North Hilo and Hamakua on the Big Island, Moloka'i, Lana'i, Kahuku on O'ahu, and Kilauea on Kaua'i—will underscore this observation.

It's not as though Hawai'i's beef industry is enjoying good economic times: every major feedlot in the state has been shut down over the past five years, and two out of three large slaughterhouses have also closed.

Why, then, is land being used to graze cattle? There are primarily two reasons for this: (1) when there is no demand by more intensive agriculture uses, grazing is the only agricultural use that has the potential of producing a positive (although small) return on the land; and (2) as long as the land is being put to agricultural use, it is assessed at a very low value for property tax purposes. If the land is not used for agriculture but instead is allowed to lie fallow, property taxes can increase by ten to fifteen times—from about $9 to $125 per acre per year. Saving on taxes provides a strong incentive to find some agricultural use for the land (such as grazing), even if profits are very low or small losses are suffered.

Future use. If history is a guide to the future, most freed-up land will go into livestock grazing, while some land will be used for diversified agriculture, some will lie fallow, some will be urbanized, and some will be turned into golf courses.

These last categories—urban use and golf courses—offer the only real hope for significant return to the landowners. But the market for these two uses is limited, and each requires many government approvals— which are difficult to obtain.

As mentioned, some of the lands released from plantation agriculture will go into other crops; in fact, the greater the success of replacement crops, the more rapidly will land be released from plantation agriculture. The amount of land that remains in pro-

"NEW LANDMARKS FOR OLD..."

duction will depend on market factors, the entrepreneurial ingenuity of farmers, and the willingness of government to modify its official and informal policies on land use.

Despite an abundant and growing supply of land available for profitable diversified agriculture crops, farmers frequently have difficulty obtaining use of this land, for two reasons. First, agricultural lands can be subdivided into smaller parcels, for sale or for lease, only if the landowner agrees to install infrastructure such as hard-surfaced roads and buried water supplies. Never mind that agriculture does not require and cannot afford such luxuries. Second, there has been a history in the state of existing agricultural tenants successfully protesting land use conversion, thereby obtaining a long-term right to farm the land. Such past successes make current landowners very hesitant to lease their land to farmers for fear they'll never be able to get it back.

Suggestions. If the state is serious about diversified agriculture, it should examine its restrictive land use policies closely. Government policies should be modified to increase the access that farmers, both large and small, have to land. Also, far more land can be made available for housing or recreational use without adversely affecting the growth of diversified agriculture.

© 1993 JOHN S. PRITCHETT

CHAPTER 20

LAND PLANNING

FRANCIS ODA
Chairman and Chief Executive Officer
Group 70

"What might Hawai'i look and feel like years from now?"

Within the next two decades, about one million acres of land in Hawai'i may lose market viability. Close your eyes and visualize how the lands of Hamakua, Waialua, Ka'anapali mauka, and virtually every other large agricultural parcel might look without sugar, pineapple, or cattle production. Do you see anything? No?

Well, you are not alone, for few alternatives to our current large-scale agricultural uses of land have proved to be viable. Attempts at developing crops such as coffee, macadamia nuts, and guava for two decades have yielded only 42,400 acres of land cultivated by 1991, or 2.5 percent of Hawai'i's agricultural lands. All that seem to thrive on ex-agricultural lands are subdivisions.

Close your eyes again and imagine the Hawai'i of future generations. Do you see the lands of Waialua and Hale'iwa covered by a patchwork quilt of asphalt-shingled rooftops stretching to the sea? This apparition may prove to be true, but there is an alternative. Its ingredients are housing (and other urban uses), agriculture, and tourism. Taken separately, these ingredients are competing, and they don't add up to a preferred future. The key is to combine them in a special way.

Land use in Hawai'i today. Agriculture, as we know it, is an endangered industry. As of mid-1993, most of Hawai'i's cattle are sent to Canadian feedlots and slaughterhouses at prices that seem to foreshadow the demise of that industry, except, perhaps, as a property tax shelter. Sugar and pineapple are having difficulty competing with growers elsewhere. Small-scale, diversified agriculture is struggling with high land costs (often in competition with urban land uses for the most convenient parcels) and the high cost of infrastructure, such as roadways and water source development and distribution. In addition, diversified agriculture is hard-pressed to find large-scale markets or subsidies to ensure sustainability.

Housing is in short supply, and new housing is largely provided in faceless subdivisions and dense high-rise complexes. With high prices a major determinant, simply owning a home is the issue—a "Hawaiian" lifestyle is not. Only a generation ago, housing in Hawai'i existed in the context of defined communities and neighborhoods. These—and with them our Hawaiian sense of place—have largely given way to impersonal sprawl, especially around Honolulu.

Hawai'i's tourism and its infrastructure are based on group travelers isolated in resort destinations and zones. Waikiki, Ka'anapali, Po'ipu, and West Hawai'i have become places where tourists experience the fantasy world of other tourists. Little of the real Hawai'i seeps through. This situation does more than offend our sense of how things ought to be; it also flies in the face of a worldwide ecocultural tourism trend. If not addressed, this approach will eventually leave Hawai'i at a severe disadvantage in the competitive tourist market.

Working together. We can base a new vision on the premise that housing, agriculture, and tourism are essential to each other's viability in a preferred Hawai'i.

Close your eyes again and picture this: modern housing clustered like the old plantation villages and surrounded by tree farms of bioengineered native hardwoods, macadamia orchards, dryland taro gardens with state-of-the-art drip irrigation, flower nurseries, grazing lands, seed corn plots, botanical gardens, community gardens, individual garden plots, and banana patches. Imagine these villages focused around little centers with a convenience store, churches, postal service, day care center, and even a McDonald's. Several would have schools, some a library. The communities would be small enough to know neighbors, yet large enough to support common services. Critically, these communities would not expand beyond specified limits.

Agricultural lands surrounding these villages would be "perpetual

open spaces" via easements in favor of the residents of the villages. The value of these outlying lands would be maintained at sustainable agricultural levels by agreement of the village property owners, the original developers, and government. This would be feasible because of the increased values attributed to the residential component. In addition, infrastructure costs often unaffordable to farmers would be borne by residential development. This approach would reverse the current competition between small-scale agriculture and housing, where an either/or choice seems necessary. Housing would support, and be supported by, agriculture..

Envision agricultural tourism as another critical ingredient to this mix, for low land costs alone will not ensure the viability of agriculture. Locals and visitors may take tours of agricultural operations, such as the native hardwood tree farms within which other native flora and fauna are nurtured and featured; buy taro products such as cakes, cookies, chips, and slices at a farm where *kupuna* explain the importance of taro in the Hawaiian culture; and overnight at a bed-and-breakfast farmhouse on a tropical flower farm that features tours, cut flower sales, wood products, and lots of aloha. Imagine guest ranches with working cattle and horse operations which allow one to experience Hawai'i's *paniolo* lifestyle. Such places would meld host communities and visitor accommodations in a manner that would satisfy the growing desire, even among group tourists, to experience the unique cultures of their destinations. The true ecocultural tourists would be able to reside in small numbers throughout the community.

Finally, envision these villages as transit nodes interlocked in a system that gives easy access to each village as well as to urban centers. With well-planned mass transit, computer modems, telephones, and fax machines, one would not have to have an agricultural job to live in these villages.

What it will take. For this vision to be realized, current concepts in housing, urbanization, agricultural activity, and tourism must change. Existing land use laws that mandate "contiguity"—urbanizing only land that is next to existing urban land—ensure urban sprawl and therefore must be rethought. Land use priorities that pit agriculture against housing and tourism must be changed to achieve an enforceable balance. The concept of contained group-tourism facilities (resort "ghettos") must give way to allow the thin spreading of tourist lodgings and activities throughout the community to accommodate the emerging ecocultural-agricultural tourism market.

Other communities offer models for this approach. The Swiss have firm boundaries for their settlements and have maintained a balance between urban development and agriculture for generations. A recent study of agricultural lands along the historic Connecticut River valley argues for the creative physical and economic balance of historic agricultural uses and new development. More and more notables are championing a worldwide movement toward "livable towns," with old-fashioned principles of community design, as the consequences of not doing so become clear.

Do we have a choice? The time has come, indeed, been forced on us, to create a new way of linking sustainable agriculture, housing, and tourism in Hawai'i. Close your eyes for a last time and reenvision the lands of Waialua sprawling to the sea in a quiltwork of forest patches and agricultural fields with a variety of crops. Villages that look like groves of trees dot the landscape, and they're all linked by transit. Within the villages, our families, friends, and relatives live a Hawaiian lifestyle similar to that of our parents and grandparents. Guests from the mainland or abroad stay at nearby bed-and-breakfasts and experience the real Hawai'i.

Is this dream too far-fetched? Not if we choose to set aside conventional wisdom and determine to hold on to our cherished visions of Hawai'i.

"YOU GOTTA ADMIT THIS ALTERNATIVE PLAN GOT RID OF ALL THOSE CARS CLOGGING OUR ROADS..."

CHAPTER 21

TRAFFIC CONGESTION

LOUIS A. ROSE
Professor of Economics
University of Hawai'i

"Is there a long-term solution to traffic congestion?"

How much would you pay to get an extra half hour for yourself each day? You might use it to play with your kids or take a stroll with your spouse or read a book or do volunteer work or exercise or take a nap or enjoy a hobby—the possibilities are endless. Sounds pretty good, doesn't it?

If you're like most people, you waste at least an extra half hour on most days (15 minutes each way) contending with traffic congestion. There are over 600,000 vehicles on O'ahu, and it probably seems as though most of them are on the road exactly when you have to drive to and from work. Buses are available, but for most people that option is even more time-consuming.

Most people would be willing to pay a reasonable fee to get from here to there faster. But before explaining how this fact of life supports what I call a "market approach" to traffic management, I will provide a bit of background.

Traffic management. Road use generally is regulated by government planners and engineers. In Hawai'i, these well-intentioned experts have tried to relieve congestion primarily by better managing traffic on existing roads through use of devices such as contraflow lanes, coordinated signals, and HOV lanes; widening and extending existing roads and providing new ones; and providing and improving public transit services. I would hate to think of how bad traffic would be without these band-aid, short-run solutions. But, while most of these efforts have been socially beneficial, none of them permanently solves the problem.

Ironically, Hawai'i's efforts to relieve congestion are part of the problem because they encourage more driving at each improved location. Drivers who formerly traveled at other times or on alternative routes soon converge on an improved road. In the long run, developers create new subdivisions along the road, feeding additional drivers into its lanes.

The same is true of new or improved mass transit facilities (such as better bus service or a fixed-rail system). Whatever relief they provide tends to be short-lived as newly uncongested roads become magnets for yet more cars.

In short, government planning and engineering are absolutely necessary, but they only forestall the inevitable. A permanent solution requires a market approach.

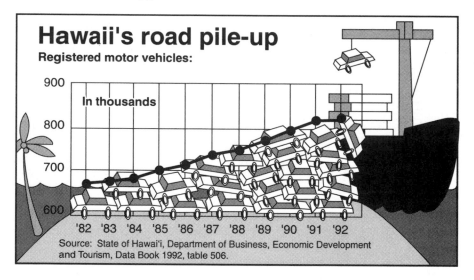

Hawaii's road pile-up

Registered motor vehicles:

In thousands

900
800
700
600

'82 '83 '84 '85 '86 '87 '88 '89 '90 '91 '92

Source: State of Hawai'i, Department of Business, Economic Development and Tourism, Data Book 1992, table 506.

The market approach. The provider of roads should charge for their use, just as the providers of electricity and long-distance telephone calls charge for what they provide.

Roads are like power plants or telephone systems. Most of the time they have a lot of excess capacity. It is only during the peak demand periods that their capacity is overloaded and cannot satisfy everyone.

The power and telephone companies wisely charge higher rates at such times, thereby encouraging some of us to use electricity and make calls at other times of the day. Thus demand is spread out over slack periods.

The road charges would not be applicable at most places or at most times of the day—only at locations and times when there would otherwise be traffic congestion. The amount charged would be whatever is necessary to get the traffic flowing at a reasonable speed. Perhaps a typical commuter vehicle on H-1 would incur a charge of one dollar for a 7:00–7:30 A.M. trip and another dollar for a 5:00–5:30 P.M. return home. A half hour later, the charge might be only fifty cents, and an hour later there might be no charge at all. If these charges failed to reduce congestion to the desired level, they would be raised. It wouldn't take long to determine the proper charges.

These charges would not affect the commuting behavior of most drivers, but they would affect enough to bring about a permanent reduction in the number of vehicles on otherwise-congested roads. Some people would carpool to share the charges, or drive at an off-peak time to avoid them completely. Others would drive on alternative (uncongested) routes, and still others would take the bus or use available paratransit services. In the long run, some would even rearrange work hours, work at home, or move closer to their jobs to avoid paying the charges. Without a doubt, this method would *permanently* solve the congestion problem.

The technology for electronic collection (rather than inefficient toll booths) is currently in use on toll roads and bridges in mainland states; and several European nations are on the verge of installing similar systems for congestion control. The newest systems are easily administered and enforced without invasion of privacy by government, and the cost of installation and operation is typically only 5–10 percent of the revenues collected.

Other possible solutions. There are a couple of other tactics that would permanently provide congestion relief. Both of them are based on market incentives rather than government decree. The first is simply to raise the gasoline tax. This instrument is sufficiently powerful, but too blunt for curing the congestion problem. That's because it discourages driving at all times and locations, not just at the times and places of congestion. Thus it is wasteful in the sense that it discourages

Electronic collection is easy

1 Sensors in road detect on-coming cars.

2 Electronic reader above highway continuously sends out radio signals.

5 Sensors trigger camera to take picture of each car.

3 Credit-card size tag on windshield receives signal, reflects an account code back to reader.

4 Lane controller sends code to main computer which charges pre-paid account.

6 If no tag or account balance, owner is mailed a violation notice. Other pictures are destroyed.

Source: USA Today, June 30, 1993, p. 1.

otherwise worthwhile trips. (This may be a desirable effect for purposes of reducing pollution, but that is the subject for another discussion.)

Another approach is to deter rush-hour driving by discouraging parking at the end of the commute. Many public and private sector employers currently subsidize parking for their employees, thereby encouraging them to drive their own cars to work. Government should stop this practice and encourage employers to offer cash instead of subsidized parking. It could also levy surcharges on morning parking. These tactics would immediately reduce the number of vehicles on the road during the two rush hours of the day.

Government should also rescind its requirement that developers provide a specified amount of parking spaces with each new office building. This would have a similar effect in the long run.

Fairness. One way to define what's fair is to say that those people who cause others inconvenience should compensate them for it. Those who would be persuaded by the charges to stay off of the road could be compensated for their inconvenience by those who enjoy uncongested rush-hour driving. The compensation could be in the form of lower gasoline taxes financed by collected road charges. A reduction in gas taxes equal to the net amount of road collections would appeal not only to those who endorse this concept of fairness but also to those who oppose new taxes.

Another way to define what's fair is to say that the group of people who are charged should receive corresponding benefits. This rule is satisfied for those who pay and commute during the rush hours, since they enjoy time savings. It is further satisfied if the annual collections along any given route are expended on socially beneficial transportation improvements for the users of that route. Improvement proposals currently in need of funds include encouragement of commuter-van pools, car pools at designated pickup points, shared-ride taxis, small-van jitneys, demand-responsive services, subscription vans, and BusPlus. Although these improvements cannot approach the cost effectiveness and fairness of road charges, they do promise to be socially beneficial, and they could be subsidized by net road charges.

"AT LEAST IT'S FAIR...**NOBODY** GETS ANYWHERE..."

Still another notion of fairness is that user charges should be at least proportional to income. Regressive charges (ones that require lower-income people to pay a percentage of their income that is higher than that required of higher-income people) are unfair. Though existing studies indicate that road charges satisfy this rule of fairness, additional research needs to be done to clearly establish this conclusion. The gasoline tax, however, is highly regressive, so using road charges to reduce the cost of gasoline would be consistent with this notion of fairness.

No pain, no gain. Nobody likes to pay for something they have been getting for free. But, in the long run, you have to hit motorists in the pocketbook to get the traffic flowing.

Surely you would be willing to pay *something* for that extra half hour mentioned at the beginning of this chapter. And make no mistake, the amount of time you waste in traffic will slowly but surely increase (as will taxes needed for additional band-aid solutions) unless we take a market approach. Can you even imagine what traffic (and taxes) will be like for our kids and their kids if we don't make a commitment to a long-term solution?

For whom the road tolls

Tolls will soon be collected electronically all over the country.

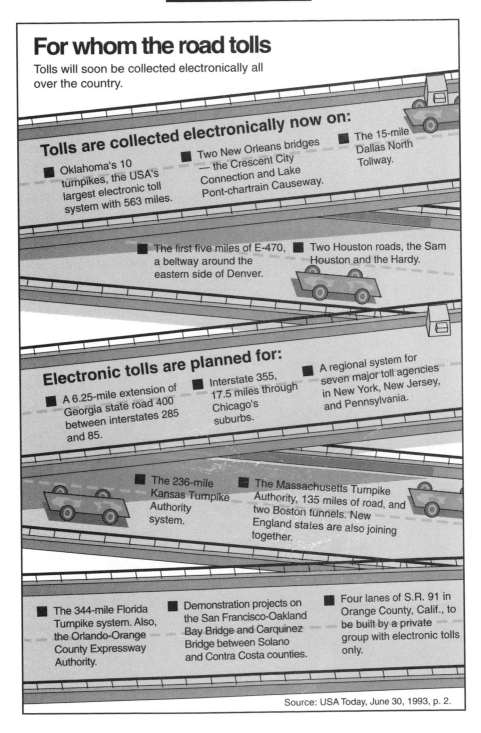

Tolls are collected electronically now on:

- Oklahoma's 10 turnpikes, the USA's largest electronic toll system with 563 miles.

- Two New Orleans bridges — the Crescent City Connection and Lake Pont-chartrain Causeway.

- The 15-mile Dallas North Tollway.

- The first five miles of E-470, a beltway around the eastern side of Denver.

- Two Houston roads, the Sam Houston and the Hardy.

Electronic tolls are planned for:

- A 6.25-mile extension of Georgia state road 400 between interstates 285 and 85.

- Interstate 355, 17.5 miles through Chicago's suburbs.

- A regional system for seven major toll agencies in New York, New Jersey, and Pennsylvania.

- The 236-mile Kansas Turnpike Authority system.

- The Massachusetts Turnpike Authority, 135 miles of road, and two Boston tunnels. New England states are also joining together.

- The 344-mile Florida Turnpike system. Also, the Orlando-Orange County Expressway Authority.

- Demonstration projects on the San Francisco-Oakland Bay Bridge and Carquinez Bridge between Solano and Contra Costa counties.

- Four lanes of S.R. 91 in Orange County, Calif., to be built by a private group with electronic tolls only.

Source: USA Today, June 30, 1993, p. 2.

CHAPTER 22

DYSFUNCTIONAL LEGISLATURE

ROBERT M. REES
Producer and Host of KFVE's "Island Issues"
Lecturer of Business and American Studies
University of Hawai'i

"What's wrong with our state legislature?"

This question strikes most of those in the state legislature as the wrong question. Speaker of the House Joseph Souki says that a better approach is to ask what's right. Vice Speaker of the House Jackie Young thinks the question is polarizing, negative, and cynical. Still, it's comically and painfully clear that *something* is wrong. There has been one slip on a banana peel after another.

In 1992, for example, the Senate realized too late that it had forgotten to vote on a key bill it had already publicized as one of its major accomplishments.

In 1993, the legislature set as its primary objective the selection of a convention center site. It failed to do so not for any of the right reasons but for all the wrong reasons. Relying primarily on vested interests for intelligence—which is like asking the foxes for honest input on how to keep the chickens safe—the Senate and the House pushed different site schemes for two different developers. Then, attempting to reach a last-minute Cinderella compromise that would have let both interests stuff their feet into a single glass slipper, a Senate-House committee worked out a quick deal with the governor and the developers. Finally, in its haste to beat the midnight deadline, the committee actually signed the wrong papers. All was for nought, except that this slapstick debacle offers a near perfect microcosm of how the legislature operates. That reality has its roots in six factors:

1. One-party control. The single most important characteristic of our state legislature, and its only unique trait, is lack of control over its own destiny. Hawai'i's state legislature is little more than a bureaucratic extension of Hawai'i's power elite.

The essence of political power is access to the decision-making process, and most of Hawai'i's legislators are simply not in that loop. The legislative procedures have been designed over time so that power is concentrated in the hands of only a few well-disciplined party loyalists. The others have learned that in order to get along they have to go along.

For example, the Hawai'i Supreme Court ruled in 1988 that without remedial legislation citizens have no right to vote directly on land use issues. At that point it seemed appropriate for the legislature at least to debate the issue. But in each of the next three years, proposals for land use initiatives were killed without discussion.

There has been some reform, and both the House and Senate are working on ways to make the legislature more accountable to the people. It is easier now than it used to be to pull bills out of committee and force a vote. But most of the reform measures are at best inadequate. A recent highly touted reform package calls for things most voters assumed already existed: cost-effective, most direct travel; limits on free postage; a requirement of a quorum for committee decision-making. These changes don't come close to altering the stark reality of a closed system dominated by the power elite.

2. Part-time legislators. Speaker of the House Souki, when asked what one thing in our legislative process needs fixing the most, says we ought to "lengthen the session. We need more time so that there are fewer compromises due to the clock."

The Republican minority leader in the House, Representative Cynthia Thielen, disagrees and argues that it's not time but incompetence that gets in the way. To others, asking for longer legislative sessions may seem like the restaurant customer who first complains that the food is inedible and then that the portions are too small.

But the Speaker makes a good point. The 60-working-day constitutional limitation on our legislature makes it almost impossible for a complicated and controversial bill to pass through in deliberative fashion. Anything important will necessarily be subjected to last-minute compromises.

The Speaker of the House points out another and perhaps more serious problem with a part-time legislature: conflicts of interest. Many legislators arrive and leave with other things on their minds, including the best ways to supplement a base salary income of $37,000. Most discover that being a legislator offers advantages when it comes to making money. Conflict of interest is nearly inevitable even if sometimes unintended. This constant appearance of self-seeking erodes voter confidence.

3. Greed and self-interest. Greed is not unique to our legislature. The big difference is that in Hawai'i the closed legislative system has made the blatant pursuit of self-interest all the easier.

"THERE'S JUST NO MONEY FOR ANYTHING..,
IN FACT WE WERE LUCKY TO FIND ENOUGH
TO FUND OUR PAY RAISES..,"

In the 1993 legislature, the very first order of business for the House was to accept a salary increase of $5,000 while refusing to give up a $5,000 expense allowance that was supposed to be in effect only until the pay increase had been approved. One member of the House, Representative David Hagino, did argue that the allowance ought to be rescinded, but he was shouted down by his colleagues and accused of showing off for the voters.

This relentless pursuit of self-interest was equally apparent when in 1992 the travel habits of our legislators were revealed. It turned out that some of them had been treating themselves to first-class travel along with generous per diem allowances for days spent out of state on supposed legislative business. One senator went to Russia to pursue his own business interests at taxpayer expense and justified the trip on the theory that what's good for his business is good for Hawai'i.

Lieutenant Governor Ben Cayetano notes that some legislators have become disconnected from the public and lack fundamental principles. "What we have," says Cayetano when asked what's wrong with the legislature, "are too many legislators living a life of content-ment."

4. Power politics. A fourth factor that determines how our legislature operates is its inordinate fear of, and respect for, three kinds of power—votes, money, and favors.

It's not so much the voters our legislators fear and respect as it is blocs of votes. Any bill or issue that appears to have unified support or opposition will be treated with special caution. The former minority leader and fourteen-year veteran of the House, Whitney Anderson, says that what's wrong with the legislature is that most legislators "have no guts and never take a stand." They follow the dictates of either the power elite or the outspoken and visible voting blocs.

Most bills, of course, don't draw the attention of voting blocs and thus are affected more by the other two kinds of power, money and favors.

Politicians who accept money from others but claim not to be influenced by it are not to be trusted. Money talks. Contributions by political action committees, businesses, and wealthy individuals pay off. That's the reason the contributions keep flowing.

Our legislature's historical reluctance up until 1993 to pass laws aimed at tobacco, the only product that kills when used as directed, is connected to Philip Morris's being the third-largest contributor to our legislators (trailing only the University of Hawai'i's teachers lobby and the Hawai'i State Teachers Association).

The third kind of power—the ability to grant favors—is the primary reason the Senate president and Speaker of the House were reluctant in 1992 to change first-class travel policies. In just one year, one member of the Republican *opposition* racked up $16,000 worth of first-class travel in addition to per diem expenses for thirty-seven days out of town. All this had to be okayed by the Democrats. It would be naive to think this busy traveler didn't feel a tad bit indebted to Senator Wong for his okay.

It becomes difficult for legislators, living in the fairytale land of favors, to understand what's bothering the rest of us. Some legislators come to expect to be treated differently than ordinary people. Freebies like memberships in the Aloha Airlines Executive Club and in country clubs are accepted without qualm. According to sources at Punahou and University of Hawai'i professional schools, state legislators are notorious for attempting to influence admissions decisions.

5. Secrecy and anonymity. Former heavyweight boxing champion Joe Louis once said of a speedy opponent, "He can run but he can't hide." For our legislators it's different: they can run and they can hide and then they can run again. One of the things that helps incumbents preserve their good reputations is that so little of what they do is known.

The 1992 legislature named Senate president Wong's aide and friend to the Office of Ombudsman, where, in theory, he would investigate complaints from citizens. But one of his first decisions was to continue the policy of *not* publicizing the office; he was concerned that it might generate too many inquiries.

Anonymity is helped by the budget process. The general appropriations bill is not voted on until the last day of the legislative session, and even the Legislative Reference Bureau, the department with the most expertise in finding out what's going on, acknowledges that the bill is impossible to access in meaningful ways.

No outsider can know who is voting for what because the legislators themselves aren't sure. Toward the end of the 1993 session, not even Senator Dennis Nakasato's office could determine whether one of his projects, continued sponsorship of a hot rod dragster as an advertising medium for tourism, had been included in the general appropriations bill.

6. Reelection process. Two Democratic senators and fifteen Democratic representatives (30 percent of the House) ran unopposed in the 1992 general election.

As long as an incumbent "goes along to get along" and doesn't make a fatal mistake, chances of reelection are good. State employees, who get a paycheck from the government and are apt to fear change, now account for a huge bloc of votes. Money will come from those who have been given favors. Support will come from the party machine. Publicity and coverage will come from uncritical newspaper and television reporters. Votes will come from blocs which have been satisfied and from complacent voters for whom name recognition is everything. Reelection is almost certain.

What it means. The problem is ours. As long as we continue to tolerate our legislative follies, then for that long we'll continue to get what we deserve. It's as simple as that.

One-party government

1990 Hawaii campaign expenditures

Election	Democrats	Republicans
Primary	$7,181,777	$1,378,294
General	$2,188,532	$1,420,964
Supplemental	$1,437,965	$164,373
Total	$10,808,274	$2,963,631

Selected Offices		
Governor	$3,806,074	
Lt. Governor	$373,375	$685,065
State Senator	$698,652	$18,899
State Representative	$2,356,231	$105,743
		$783,768

Source: Hawaii State
Campaign Spending
Commission, Oct. 14, 1991

State legislature party membership

Number of members

70
60   Democrats
50
40
30   Republicans
20
10
0

1963 '65 '67 '69 '71 '73 '75 '77 '79 '81 '83 '85 '87 '89 '91 '93
Year

Source: State of Hawai'i, Department of Business, Economic
Development and Tourism, Data Book 1992, table 268.

CHAPTER 23

CHECKS & BALANCES

NORMAN H. OKAMURA
Associate Specialist
Social Science Research Institute
University of Hawai'i

RANDALL W. ROTH
Professor of Law
William S. Richardson School of Law
University of Hawai'i

"What in the world is High-3?"

Have you ever wondered why some legislators avoid criticizing the administration—no matter what it does or does not do? Have you ever wondered why legislators, whose part-time salary is less than the full-time pay of many school teachers, receive a retirement income that sometimes is three or even four times as big? Have you ever wondered why so many legislators get appointed to other government positions?

"High-3" is a popular name for a way to increase the pension benefits of former legislators dramatically. Its importance is best appreciated by first taking a look at what it has helped to create and then working through a simplified example of how it works.

Cozy relationship. Some people are suspicious of the cozy relationship that seems to have developed between the legislative and executive branches of government. We believe this coziness reflects a "political spirit of aloha." Roughly translated, that means "To get along . . . you gotta go along!"

The "get-along, go-along" spirit may not always be in the best interest of the public. The separation of the legislative and executive branches of government is an integral part of a "checks and balances" design that promotes accountability and helps to keep the public informed of what government is or isn't doing.

Checks and balances work best when the legislative and executive branches of government are truly independent. Both sides are forced to articulate and defend specific policies and priorities. They keep each other honest as they vie for public support.

One reason for the "go-along" mentality is the administration's power to reward political supporters. For example, non-bid contracts can be given to firms that contribute to the political campaigns of go-along legislators; pet projects can be expedited; and a High-3 appointment can be made when the time comes.

Pension calculations. To understand the High-3 phenomenon, and why it's so attractive to state legislators, you have to know how pension benefits for state government employees are calculated. A simplified formula is summarized as follows:

Annual			Average of
Retirement =	Accrual*	x Years of x	Highest
Income	Rate	Service	3 years of income

* Accrual rate depends on job classification. For example, teachers have a rate of 1.25% unless they were hired before July 1, 1984 and have chosen to make regular contributions to the pension plan. The accrual rate for teachers in such a "contributory" plan is 2%. Legislators have a rate of 3.5% and their plan is always contributory. But unlike the teachers, who get a higher accrual rate for contributing to the plan, legislators get an annuity based on the amounts they contribute. This annuity is in addition to their retirement benefits under the usual formula. In comparing the benefits of a retired teacher to those of a retired legislator, we use accrual rates of 1.25% and 3.5% respectively, and ignore the extra annuity income paid to the legislator. To preserve this "apples to apples" comparison, we use an accrual rate of 1.25% for the legislator after appointment to another job. Readers should keep in mind that this is simplistic and is done solely to illustrate the effect of a legislator's appointment to a high-paying job.

Simple example. Assume that we have two state employees: a legislator and a teacher, both with 17 years of service. Assume further that the legislator's average salary over the highest three years is $35,000 and the teacher's is $45,000.

(A) ERS member	(B) Years of service	(C) Accrual rate	(BxC=D) Retirement benefit rate	(E) Ave. of highest 3 years of income	(DxE=F) Annual retirement income not counting sup. annuity
Legislator	17	3.5%	59.5%	$35,000	$20,825
Teacher	17	1.25%	21.25%	$45,000	$9,563

Despite having been a part-time employee and having earned a lower salary, the legislator can expect to receive annual retirement income that is more than double that of the teacher. This is simply a reflection of the legislator's higher accrual rate. It does not yet illustrate the so-called High-3, but is helpful in explaining how it works.

Now assume that the same two people work three more years at their current jobs and (for simplicity sake) at their same salaries.

(A) ERS member	(B) Years of service	(C) Accrual rate	(BxC=D) Retirement benefit rate	(E) Ave. of highest 3 years of income	(DxE=F) Annual retirement income not counting sup. annuity
Legislator	20	3.5%	70%	$35,000	$24,500
Teacher	20	1.25%	25%	$45,000	$11,250

Three additional years increased the legislator's advantage over the teacher. Again, that's pretty straightforward. It too is just helpful background.

But now assume that the legislator, rather than stay in the legislature for those last three years, receives from the administration an appointment as, say, the manager of Aloha Stadium or a public utilities commissioner at $80,000 per year, and serves in that capacity for three years.

(A) ERS member	(B) Years of service	(C) Accrual rate	(BxC=D) Retirement benefit rate	(E) Ave. of highest 3 years of income	(DxE=F) Annual retirement income not counting sup. annuity
Legislator/ Political Appointee	17/ 3	3.50% 1.25%	63.25%	$80,000	$50,600
Teacher	20	1.25%	25.0%	$45,000	$11,250

Believe it or not, the legislator/political appointee's expected retirement more than doubles, jumping from $24,500 to $50,600 per year as a result of the appointment. This dramatic increase is called a High-3. Incidentally, it pushed the legislator/political appointee's annual retirement income to almost four and a half times that of the teacher.

What it means. The possibility of a High-3 can be used as a powerful tool in the hands of the executive branch. There is no good policy rationale for this method of calculating benefits, and it adversely affects our system of checks and balances. It's money coming out of taxpayers' pockets that hasn't been earned except in a strict legal sense.

If government in Hawai'i wants to begin the process of restoring public confidence, it should do away with the High-3. It might also consider reducing the spread between the accrual rates of legislators and teachers (and other public employees). Currently, legislators enjoy an accrual rate that is "second-to-none." Now where have we heard that expression?

CHAPTER 24

GOVERNMENT SPENDING

LOWELL KALAPA
President
Tax Foundation of Hawai'i

"What ever happened to the state's fat surplus?"

The sackcloth and ashes routine around the State Capitol during the 1993 legislative session was a far cry from just a few years earlier when the unappropriated general fund balance contained nearly $650 million and questionable special funds hid another $150 million. The most recent estimate calls for the former to dip below $100 million by the end of the 1993–1995 biennium. The latter has been "found" and mostly spent.

The legislature likes to blame the dramatic decline in these balances on the slowdown in Hawai'i's economy. The *real* story is a bit complicated but highly instructive. It tells us much about how government works (or doesn't work) in Hawai'i.

How it all began. Our tax system is such that government's slice of the economic pie grows faster than the pie itself. For example, when Hawai'i's economy grows by 10 percent, state tax revenues increase 12 percent.

Tax revenues were pouring in so fast during the economic boom of the late 1980s, they simply could not be spent intelligently, at least not right away. State administrators and lawmakers, worried that taxpayers would demand a rebate or a tax cut, or both, did their best to spend or hide these funds as fast as they were collected.

One way to hide them was through the use of "smoke and mirrors" (see Chapter 11 of *The Price of Paradise*, Volume I). This approach channeled what should have been general fund receipts into newly created special funds. So, even if all available funds weren't spent during any particular year, the remaining balance would not lapse back into the general fund. These special funds never showed up as part of the surplus. Presto chango . . . and the surplus vanishes before your very eyes.

"Parking" excess funds. Another tactic was to earmark general funds for programs or projects that were expected to be canceled eventually or financed differently. For example, the 1991 session of the legislature appropriated $28 million in general funds for a controversial housing project that was unlikely to be built any time soon (if at all). People who understood the true purpose of this appropriation—to "park" excess funds out of taxpayer view—were not surprised when the means of financing was changed by the 1993 legislature.

Another example was the state's disingenuous offer to use its extra cash to pay for several county projects. Given the historically contentious relationship between the state and counties, it was highly unlikely that this would become a reality. Sure enough, the 1993 legislature "reclaimed" the cash it had authorized for certain county projects, like the Honolulu police telecommunications system and a foreign trade zone warehouse for Hilo.

Yet another way. Parking as a way of hiding surplus funds worked for a while, but when the amounts that needed to be hidden got bigger, the focus shifted again, this time to paying "cash" for major projects.

Capital projects (such as roads, sewers, and public buildings) are usually considered one-time expenditures that ought to be financed through bond sales. The basic idea is that facilities expected to last a long time should be paid for with taxes collected from the people who are actually benefiting from those facilities. But our lawmakers, wanting to tie up as much of the excess general fund cash as possible, appropriated staggering amounts from the general fund (nearly $500 million dollars) for capital improvement projects.

This approach, virtually unheard of outside Hawai'i, flies in the face of a basic public finance principle: the burden of long-term capital projects should be borne by the people who will directly or indirectly benefit.

The scheme worked in that it relieved the pressure to rebate the surplus or lower taxes, but it was also a major reason the constitutional spending ceiling was exceeded in each of the past four fiscal years. That's another story (oh, what a tangled web we weave).

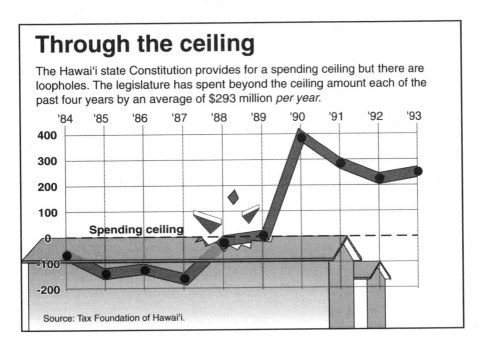

Through the ceiling

The Hawai'i state Constitution provides for a spending ceiling but there are loopholes. The legislature has spent beyond the ceiling amount each of the past four years by an average of $293 million *per year.*

Source: Tax Foundation of Hawai'i.

Money is "found." This charade became obvious when state revenues dropped and, in a frantic search for cash, officials allowed many cash-financed capital improvement projects to lapse or changed the means of financing from cash to bond sales (which is how they should have been financed in the first place).

Government spending during these "hide and seek" years was illusory in the way it was accomplished but real in that an awful lot of money was eventually spent. For example, the size of state government, as measured by the number of employees, increased dramatically. This is clear, even if one accepts the state's version of the numbers, which does not reflect the many temporary and appointed positions. These hidden positions tend to be held largely by political appointees who generally serve as special assistants to special assistants. They are the people who can be found on street corners during political campaigns smiling broadly and waving signs.

A more accurate indication of just how much government grew during this period is the ratio of operating expenditures to state personal income (i.e., government's slice of the economic pie). State operating expenditures between 1986 and 1991 grew by more than 70 percent while total personal income was growing by less than 50 percent. In other words, government's forced share of the economic pie grew considerably faster than did the pie itself.

This might not have been cause for concern if the quality and quantity of government services had been increasing. But much of the growth was unproductive fat rather than hard-working muscle. An obese government that perhaps would be tolerated if times were still good is being roundly criticized now that the economy is hurting.

For example, voters might not have been up in arms a few years ago if they had been told the public tush would be sitting on $1,700 koa benches or that the governor would be affixing his "John Hancock" to the latest revenue-raising measure on a $10,000 koa desk. These amounts are pocket change to a multibillion dollar operation like the Hawai'i state government. How they were spent, however, says a lot about what happens when a giant surplus falls into the hands of a spendthrift government.

Broken promises. Perhaps you're wondering about all those wonderful promises to upgrade schools, repair roads, and improve government services. Those projects may be a long way off as a result of lower revenues, the switch to bond financing, and prolific spending in earlier years.

In fact, during the 1993 session of the legislature, when the reality of the economic slowdown finally hit them, lawmakers switched more than $82 million of infrastructure financing from general funds to bonds and lapsed another $20 million in projects. This freed up more than $100 million for operating expenses but resulted in the delay or cancellation of promised projects.

If general fund revenues continue to limp along, administrators will be faced with a self-created bottleneck in the state's capital improvement program. The amount the state can borrow is based on the percentage of general fund revenues available to make payments on its debt. Ironically, the trick of siphoning general revenues into special funds has caused the state to bump up against the constitutional debt

"COULD YOU HOLD ON? I THINK THAT PAPER'S ON THE MAKAI SIDE OF THE DESK…"

limit. This will slow the effort to upgrade public infrastructure. In short, if you're waiting for your kid's elementary school to be repaired, don't hold your breath.

State misled the public. If you still don't recognize "smoke and mirrors" bookkeeping and "hide and seek" banking for what they are, consider this: despite all the hype about cuts that would have to be made to the budget, the 1993 state legislature actually increased its spending. Overall operations funded through the state budget grew by 11.6 percent from fiscal year 1993 to 1994. This percentage is a bit misleading because of certain changes in accounting, but even after adjusting for them the state operating budget grew by 6 percent.

If that's not enough to convince you that the state was not as bad off as officials wanted you to believe, consider this: no cuts were made in public employment. The total number of jobs funded by the 1993 legislature actually *grew*. By the time the budget had been massaged by the 1993 legislature, there was a net increase of 1,077 positions for fiscal year 1994 and 344 positions on top of that for fiscal year 1995. Tough times indeed.

Why it's bad. A few officials have suggested that taxpayers should be thankful that our clever leaders hid, er . . . "banked," all that money during the boom years so we wouldn't be caught short when times weren't so good. They contend that because state officials resisted the temptation to refund the surplus or lower taxes, we had enough money in 1993 to keep things going.

Granted, we kept government fed. But what if the economy is slow to recover? We are now saddled with a bloated government that has outgrown the economy. We satisfied its appetite in 1993 with money that had been hidden in prior years. But what will feed the dragon next year? Another round of tax increases?

You may not have noticed, but the 1993 legislature quietly increased taxes to supplement its hidden reserves. There were no broad-based tax increases that might upset the general public. The legislature just picked on this or that constituency group too small to complain. Actions included a doubling of the conveyance tax, a new tax on hospitals and nursing homes, and something called "fees" which are a lot like tax increases. Over $60 million in new taxes and fees were raised. That was another big bite out of a pie that hasn't been getting any bigger.

Conclusion and prediction. So, where did all that surplus money go? Well, first it was hidden behind the smoke and mirrors of special funds, and then when the tax review commission and state auditor demanded a more honest approach, state officials started financing capital improvements with excess cash rather than through bond sales.

As the economy weakened and tax collections flattened, state officials managed to get by on the previously hidden money and quietly enacted new taxes. But the secret stash soon will be exhausted, leaving a big government with a big appetite. Don't be shocked by talk of more tax increases if the economy doesn't improve. At this time, a self-imposed diet is not even being considered.

In short, if you think things are bad now, wait till the state government's creative bookkeeping and love of band-aid solutions catch up with us. The individuals who created the mess won't be around; they'll be pulling the rip cord on their golden parachutes. We're the ones who someday will have to explain to our kids and to their kids how it was that we let this happen.

"EVERYBODY ELSE WILL HAVE TO GO ON DIET..."

"THIS IS THE STATE BILL FOR THE $5 MILLION GEAR...
WE ONLY BROKE IT DOWN TO PURCHASE ORDERS OF
UNDER $7,000 FOR ...UH, MORE ORDERLY ACCOUNTING."

CHAPTER 25

PROCUREMENT REFORM

"How sound are the state's buying practices?"

RANDALL W. ROTH

Professor of Law
William S. Richardson School of Law
University of Hawai'i

Legislators gathered in early September of 1993, determined to reform the state procurement code. Everyone, it seemed, wanted to junk the current law: bureaucrats complained that it made their jobs unnecessarily difficult; Governor Waihee called it "complex beyond workability"; and outside experts labeled it a "disaster." Immediate action was obviously so imperative and imminent one tended to forget that the law in question had been around since 1909. So why the sudden outbreak of reform fever?

Background. State government spends over $800 million each year just on supplies, printing, advertising, and consultants. That's a lot of money, and yet as of mid-1993 Hawai'i was the *only* state that didn't have centralized purchasing.

Consequently and incredibly, no one could keep track of how money was being spent. A 1993 state auditor's report pointed this out and went on to call Hawai'i's procurement law "old, fragmented and vague . . . inefficient and costly . . . out of date, incomplete."

Serious abuses. It's not just that the law was flawed—there had been allegations of serious abuse of it as well. By the late 1980s, contracts were being routinely awarded to politically connected people who did not have to compete. Often these and other contracts were later amended upward, again without public scrutiny. Even when bidding was required, well-positioned vendors had been permitted to write the specifications before bidding, thus abling them to favor themselves over their competitors. In fiscal year 1990/91, one division alone—"Airports" in the State Department of Transportation—issued more than half its contracts without competitive bidding. These non-bid contracts represented well over $40 million of taxpayer money.

Ian Lind, then with *Hawaii Monitor*, reported an uncanny correlation between contributions made, and non-bid contracts received. Public cynicism was growing, but procurement reform seemed a distant possibility, at best.

All of this greatly troubled the state's Director of Purchasing and Supply Division, Earl Dedell. Now retired, Dedell likes to stress that no law is people proof: "Our procurement law has never been a disaster. If everyone did what the law calls for, there wouldn't be a problem. The problem is with people, not with the law." Nevertheless, Dedell urged in the late 1980s that the law be studied, hoping this would lead to meaningful reform of the entire "system." He formed a study group of high-level bureaucrats who worked closely with a mainland consulting firm, Lallatin and Associates. To no one's surprise, they found that there had been minimal competition in the awarding of work during the late 1980s. Lallatin's 1990 report recommended major changes and this led some observers to believe that reform would be forthcoming.

The first clue that certain interests would do what they could to prevent procurement reform was not long in coming. The most important recommendation of the Lallatin report—to remove the buying function from each government agency and place it in a centrally controlled and responsible division—was mysteriously changed in the report's final version to allow each agency to continue to be autonomous. No one would explain publicly just how this major reversal of position came to be. Dedell later revealed that the change was made at the insistence of other agency officials.

The second clue was the administration's reaction to the progress of Dedell's study group. When that seven-person body indicated it was close to coming up with specific recommendations for change, the administration quickly added another ten people to the group. The reconstituted group unsurprisingly was unable to come up with any recommendations.

Jurassic Park

Vetoed bill. A 1992 legislative effort to reform the law produced a bill that passed both the House and the Senate but was vetoed by the governor because of a provision that would have held state employees criminally liable for knowingly violating the law. The governor considered this reason enough to scuttle the entire bill, despite the fact that such a provision is commonly found in other jurisdictions. Evidently, the governor didn't think it fit our unique political culture.

"OH, SURE—WILL YOU PUT IN YOUR BID WITH THESE OTHERS AND WE'LL CALL YOU..."

The state legislative auditor was then directed to retain a qualified consultant to conduct yet another study. The National Association of State Purchasing Officials (NASPO), whose membership includes the nation's leading experts on governmental buying practices, was chosen to do the work. NASPO examined Hawai'i's procurement law and practices and then issued a report that was specific and complete. Boiling their conclusions down to one word (their word), our procurement system was a "disaster."

This and an equally critical report, written by the state legislative auditor and issued a few days before the opening of the 1993 legislative session, again raised hopes for procurement reform.

Another try. The NASPO bill, which was later passed by the State Senate and came to be known as the "Senate bill," called for a central purchasing authority responsible for policymaking and oversight of public contracting. It also provided for a chief purchasing officer with stringent requirements for appropriate professional (as opposed to political) experience. The bill went on to carefully define the accountability, responsibility, and authority of central purchasing but authorized the delegation of power where that made sense. The stated goals of the bill were to (1) serve the best interests of the taxpayers by encouraging competition and focusing on value; (2) provide the entire business community with fair and open access to government business; and, (3) meet the needs of state agencies in securing goods and services in a timely and cost-efficient manner. This Senate bill caused great consternation among many, including the Waihee administration.

A different procurement bill—written by the administration—was intentionally made to look very much like the Model Procurement Code which had been recommended by the state legislative auditor in her 1993 report. But as the experts from NASPO quickly pointed out, what the administration really was offering was the same old wolf in sheep's clothing—the status quo reincarnated. This one came to be called the "House bill."

Failed reform, again. The lobbying effort mounted to prevent real reform was awesome. Everyone who benefited from the current disastrous law did everything possible to fight the Senate bill. Their strategy was part Pinocchio, part Keystone Cops—and it worked. Believe it or not, supporters of the administration-backed House bill worked out an oral agreement that was acceptable to supporters of the Senate bill; then, when the compromise bill was put into writing, it mysteriously lacked key provisions that had been agreed upon orally. Outraged supporters of the Senate bill refused to vote for the version that had been handed to them, and there was no time to correct the "error." The ultimate irony is that they then were accused by the administration of having killed procurement reform.

Many observers concluded that this "mix-up" had been carefully planned by forces who wanted to sound like reformers without actually changing anything.

A few months after the session ended, Governor Waihee ordered the legislature into special session and listed procurement reform as a high priority item. Cynics suggested this was "damage control," necessitated by a Senate committee's investigation. More than a few bureaucrats and cronies had just been caught doing things they shouldn't have done, and the governor blamed it all on the procurement system: "And I believe what you'll find in most instances, at worst, are people who short-cut an impossible system in order to do their jobs more effectively." The governor's comments seemed to suggest that all these people had put their hands into the procurement "cookie jar" out of confusion and for the noblest of reasons.

The 1993 special session resulted in what initially appears to be a greatly improved procurement code. That's good news but not reason to forget about the circumstances of its enactment.

Skepticism warranted. We can only wonder why it has taken years of bumbling (or conniving) and a Senate investigation to get a system of procurement that is based on competition, impartiality, professionalism, and openness. And given the events of the past few years, the public is well-advised to be skeptical. Even a well-written procurement code can be abused if powerful people are so inclined.

"TOO MANY OF OUR MEN ARE GETTING CAUGHT BREAKING THE LAW SO WE THINK IT'S TIME WE JUNK IT..."

E.R.S. MEMBERS

SPECIAL INTERESTS

© 1991 JOHN S. PRITCHETT

CHAPTER 26

EMPLOYEES' RETIREMENT SYSTEM

BILL WOOD

Freelance Journalist

"Is the State Employees' Retirement System being abused?"

I'll tell you a few things about the Hawai'i State Employees' Retirement System (ERS) and let you draw your own conclusions.

Background. Nearly all state and local governments have retirement plans for their employees, some worth billions of dollars, such as the California government's $60 billion program. Each typically is governed by a board of trustees, whose primary job is to make sure there is enough money in the kitty to cover their workers' retirement benefits.

What we now call the ERS was set up for Hawai'i government employees by the territorial legislature in 1925. Since then its membership has grown from a few hundred to about 55,000 active state and county workers and some 24,000 retirees and their families.

From 1986 to 1992, the number of working participants in the system increased 20 percent; the number of retirees rose 47 percent; and the value of ERS assets climbed 83 percent, thanks mainly to a soaring stock market. The surge in assets was a godsend because of the fund's climbing commitments. The ERS now has total assets of about $5 billion, with two-thirds invested in U.S. stocks and bonds and the remaining third divided among five other categories of investments, the biggest of which is real estate.

Direct investment in real estate offers the possibility of a comparatively high return, but at a relatively high risk. As a percentage of the overall fund, the real estate segment of investments is relatively small but has grown the fastest in recent years.

The fund had not directly invested in real estate prior to 1989. Governor John Waihee says he suggested the move then as a means of broadening the fund's investment base. His administration paved the way by convincing the legislature to double the statutory ceiling on real estate investments to 10 percent.

Run by trustees. The ERS is administered by seven unpaid trustees and a paid staff. Three of the trustees are elected by the members of the system, three are appointed by the governor, and one, an ex-officio but voting trustee, is a member of the governor's cabinet, the director of the state's Department of Budget and Finance. So the governor appoints four of the seven trustees.

The trustees have a great deal of discretion in day-to-day operations, notably in managing the system's $5 billion in assets. They do, however, get lots of help with their investment decisions. Currently, about thirty investment advisory firms—some local, some not—monitor and make buy-sell recommendations. And there is other help. ERS's data processing, legal and actuarial work, and financial audits are done by outside firms.

Okamoto, Himeno & Lum. In 1989, when the trustees made their first direct real estate investment, the purchase for $68 million of the newly built City Financial Tower in downtown Honolulu, they decided the legal advice they had been getting in-house—mostly through the state attorney general's office—was inadequate. They needed specialists. So they hired an outside law firm, known then as Okamoto, Himeno & Lum. The firm's partners were Kenneth Okamoto (whose wife, Sandra, was an assistant to then-State Attorney General Warren Price), Sharon Himeno (Sandra's sister and by November of that year Warren Price's wife), and Bettina Lum (the law firm's real estate expert).

Bettina Lum assisted the ERS in its purchase of City Financial Tower. She also helped the trustees evaluate the many mortgage loan applications that were coming in to the ERS as a result of a decision to step up that activity. Much of the $628,000 in fees earned by the law firm from the ERS account between 1989 and 1992 came from evaluating these applications.

Not all the fees came directly from the ERS. Some loan applicants paid Okamoto, Himeno & Lum directly for help in preparing and evaluating their applications. One of these applicants was Waikele Commercial Associates, a partnership seeking a $154 million loan from the ERS to develop a shopping complex on land purchased from Amfac/JMB in central O'ahu. Governor Waihee now says he had urged the ERS trustees to increase their loans to Hawai'i businesses such as Amfac/JMB and Waikele Commercial Associates "because it makes good economic sense."

Political tool. Some people complain that the governor has openly used the ERS as a political tool and improperly interfered in its decision-making. They contend that this amounts to abuse. The governor and his political allies have responded by denying any improprieties. The ERS trustees are proud of their investment record and say that's what really matters.

Though none of the advisors employed by the ERS is required to bid for their contract, nobody associated with the fund or the administration thinks that's a problem. They say the trustees selected Okamoto, Himeno & Lum, for example, for the real estate expertise of Bettina Lum, not for the political connections of her partners.

The ERS trustees used more than Lum's services in buying the City Financial Tower. They also hired the local real estate firm Marcus & Associates. That firm had been recommended by trustee and budget director Yukio Takemoto, who was a golfing buddy of its chairman, Marcus Nishikawa. Marcus & Associates was named exclusive leasing agent for the 24-story City Financial Tower and given the contract to review the leasing program for the building.

Marcus & Associates also participated in other real estate purchases. Later in 1989, it was a player in the ERS's $26 million purchase of the CentrePointe office-warehouse complex in Carson, California, and in the 1991 purchase, for $17.5 million, of Huntington Plaza, another commercial center in Southern California. In each case the real estate firm was paid a six-figure commission, not by the ERS, but by the sellers.

A quick $3 million. The CentrePointe purchase came back to haunt some of its participants. That deal began when Honolulu businessman Stanley Himeno (father of Sharon Himeno) approached the ERS trustees wanting to borrow money to buy the California property. Marcus & Associates got involved and soon it was decided the ERS would itself buy the property. CPAs Ernst & Young, who had started to work for Himeno, appraised the property for the ERS trustees at $26.2 million, and the ERS then offered Himeno's company $26 million. The offer was quickly accepted and the sale closed. The trustees later said they had no idea Himeno had bought the property for only $23 million and arranged back-to-back closings, thus making an apparent $3 million gain in a matter of minutes.

Okamoto, Himeno & Lum declined to participate in that particular purchase because of the obvious conflict of interest. Besides the family relations, Sharon Himeno and Sandra Okamoto were officers and directors of the Himeno company that bought and sold the CentrePointe property. Another law firm was hired to help out: Hoe, Yap and Sugimoto, Governor Waihee's former law firm.

Himeno's firm continued to review loan applications. One was for an $11 million loan that would have gone to Nansay Hawai'i, a Japanese-owned development company. The money was to be used not by Nansay but to shore up a failing Kona aquaculture company called Ocean Farms Hawai'i, which the administration wanted as a showcase operation and which Nansay had already been coaxed into supporting. But when the development tradeoffs of the loan became unclear, Nansay balked. The loan wasn't made and Ocean Farms folded quietly. The governor's supporters see this as a noble attempt to help a local business survive. Others call it a blatant example of government interference and misuse of the ERS's funds.

Jurist resigns. Late in 1991, the trustees voted to pay $31 million for Wood Ranch, a California golf course. That deal had been brought to them by Honolulu developer Rodney Inaba, a friend of ERS trustee Gordon Uyeda. But retired Hawai'i Supreme Court justice Edward Nakamura, who had been appointed an ERS trustee only months before, strenuously opposed the purchase. He also had grown upset over the pending $154 million loan to Waikele Center Associates. Saying he couldn't stomach such treatment of public funds, the respected jurist resigned his trusteeship when the Wood Ranch acquisition was approved by a majority of the board.

The governor then told "Yuki" Takemoto to kill the deal and the trustees reversed their decision. Another trustee later said Takemoto told the board the governor "didn't want the hassle."

By mid-1993 the ERS had made one other real estate investment, a 400-unit apartment complex in Arlington, Virginia, that cost $38 million, and it was considering two others. Both of the latter involved conversion of existing mortgage loans into equity interests. One was the $154 million loan to Waikele Center on O'ahu and the other a $31 million loan to Ka'ahumanu Shopping Center on Maui. The conversions seemed certain of approval. ERS administrator Stanley Siu considers them prime examples of what the governor meant by "investing in Hawai'i."

But in the summer of 1993 the ERS faced a State Senate special committee probe into its investment decisions and contract practices. Governor Waihee labeled the investigation "McCarthyism." The ERS met the challenge by hiring another consultant: Hill and Knowlton, a high-powered international public relations firm that specializes in crisis management. The first thing the big PR firm did was launch a newsletter for ERS members called "Safe & Sound." The first issue contained blanket denials of any wrongdoing.

"NOTHING TO BE CONCERNED ABOUT... JUST FAMILY SPATS..."

CHAPTER 27

GOVERNMENT CORRUPTION

NORMAN H. OKAMURA
Associate Specialist
Social Science Research Institute

"Is government in Hawai'i corrupt?"

Will Rogers once said, "All I know is what I read in the newspapers." Perhaps there's more to government procurement in Hawai'i than we read about, but that alone is enough to concern many people. Here's a summary of a few newspaper articles from recent years. Most of these were written by James Dooley of the *Honolulu Advertiser*.

• Aloha Stadium manager Ken Kiyabu resigns with full retirement benefits after being caught intentionally circumventing the procurement law by parceling $50,000 of purchases to friends. Governor Waihee calls Kiyabu an outstanding employee who "made a mistake." Waihee's appointed attorney general, Robert Marks, decides not to prosecute Kiyabu, saying he has suffered enough.

• Public Utilities Commission and other state officials attend expensive golf tournaments sponsored by GTE Hawaiian Tel and other companies that have received large state contracts from, or are regulated by, these same officials. Some receive gifts such as golf clubs worth about $1,000.

• Data House, a computer consulting company that provided services and leased computer equipment to the political campaign of John Waihee, receives $10 million in non-bid contracts after Governor Waihee assumes office in 1987. The president of Data House, Dan Arita, is a close friend of State Director of Budget and Finance Yukio Takemoto and golfs with him about forty times a year. But Takemoto says he did not realize that Data House had helped in the governor's campaign.

• An engineering firm known as M&E is awarded a $150,000 consulting contract during an early phase of the state's $2.5 billion airport improvement project. That contract is then amended numerous times over the years, without competitive bidding or outside review. As of early 1993, amounts paid out under the amended contract exceed $52 million. A principal of the company, James Kumagai, is the former head of the Democratic party. M&E has many retired state officials on its payroll and is a large contributor to the Democratic party.

• Employee Retirement System (ERS) administrator Stanley Siu says he was instructed by his bosses not to answer questions about activities of the $5 billion ERS fund. Taking these marching orders literally, he ignores inquiries from not only investigative reporter James Dooley but also Lieutenant Governor Benjamin Cayetano. The chairman of the ERS board publicly denies issuing the gag order. State Director of Budget and Finance Takemoto writes a letter apologizing for the "misunderstanding" but doesn't admit giving the gag order or reveal who did.

• A company called SS/168 sells an office complex (CentrePoint) to the ERS, minutes after having bought it for $3 million less than the sales price. A part owner of SS/168, Stanley Himeno, is the father-in-law of Attorney General Warren Price. Himeno's daughter is a principal in a law firm that billed more than $600,000 to the ERS over a three-year period for non-bid work on other matters. Governor Waihee later nominates Sharon Himeno to the Hawai'i Supreme Court.

• State director of environmental quality Marvin Miura pleads guilty to federal charges of fraud, bribery, and tax evasion relating to kickbacks received in the awarding of large non-bid consulting contracts.

An insider's perspective. Even Will Rogers's opinion of government in Hawai'i would be colored by these and similar stories. I'm a little jaded, too, not just from reading the newspapers, but from what I saw as a high-level bureaucrat in state government. Until recently, I was administrator of the Information and Communication and Services Division of the Department of Budget and Finance(ICS Division). In this position, I had a ringside seat for watching how government in Hawai'i operates.

Before going any further, I want to emphasize that the vast majority of government workers in Hawai'i are honest, hardworking, and committed. Many of them have been at least as frustrated and angered as is the public by the actions of a few high-level people in government. Some have taken courageous actions: Peter Crosby, a Budget and Finance employee who was yanked off his assigned project when he questioned a particular non-bid contract, went public by filing a "whistle-blower" lawsuit; Hideto Kono, Richard Barber, and two others resigned from the nine-person board of the Hawai'i Information Network in reaction to political appointments that they perceived as being based on connections rather than competence; former Supreme Court Justice Edward Nakamura quit as a director of the ERS rather than be a part of something he couldn't stomach. The list could be much longer. The point is that people inside government have taken stands against what they perceived to be abuses of the public trust.

I personally saw and struggled with many of the cases reported in the papers. It was not easy. I was often torn by my conscience and the demands of others, continually trying to find compromises that did not exist. I made formal and informal appeals of troubling decisions, but the situation just got worse. Eventually, I quit my job in frustration. I simply grew tired of beating my head against a brick wall.

Leaving the Budget and Finance Department was one of the most difficult decisions I've ever had to make. The people working with me had worked very hard, and we had accomplished some really good things. The work itself was interesting and challenging, and there was a lot more that needed to be accomplished.

Ironically, I did not intend to voice my concerns publicly at that time. It didn't seem likely to be productive, and I quickly had gotten involved in a time-consuming new job.

Economic buttons. But then a key person in state government somehow got the impression that I was partly responsible for newspaper and legislative investigations that started in early 1992. He called me in and told me to "back off." I can still hear his words: "Hey Norman . . . when the economic buttons get pressed, you're going to get hurt. Your family is going to get hurt. And, the company you're working for is going to get hurt." It was like something out of the *Godfather* movies.

At first I was shocked. Then I was resigned to whatever was going to happen. Finally, after going home and playing with my children, I became angry—so much so that I decided to do something about the practices that caused me to leave my job with the state. My first step was to resume the academic life I had left ten years earlier to work in government. As an associate specialist in research at the University of Hawai'i, I would be able to look into social concerns, such as abusive procurement practices, without too much fear of retribution. Several additional steps, including this chapter, followed. I can't say I've had an impact just yet, but I feel good about trying, especially since so many others are working equally hard, if not harder, for change.

Matsuura's committee. There is an excellent chance for government reform thanks to the work of a special committee of the State Senate. How it came about is itself an interesting story.

Senator Richard Matsuura, a Democrat from Hilo, together with Senator Mamoru Yamasaki, a Democrat from Maui, began raising questions publicly in 1992 about the general purchasing practices of the Waihee administration. They were concerned about costly sole-source and exempt procurements, the practice of amending contracts without

Senator
Richard Matsuura

review, a specific contract with GTE Hawaiian Tel for the state's telephone system, the length of time the administration took to switch from costly interisland long-distance calls to the state's own microwave system, and the investment practices of ERS. These are some of the very things that had caused me to quit my job.

The administration's initial reaction to the Senate probe appeared to be based on a threefold strategy: not respond to inquiries; pressure the senators to halt the investigations (including the threat that this would "hurt the Democratic party"); and criticize existing procurement law while voicing support for reform.

Tactics fail. When these tactics failed to contain the inquiry, the administration tried to gain control of the Senate through the reorganization that followed the retirements of Senate president Richard Wong and Senator Yamasaki. But Senator James Aki ended up president of the Senate, and he supported the investigation. By December 1992, the Senate had formed a special investigative committee and assigned it the task of investigating procurement and the ERS. The governor lobbied against giving subpoena power to the committee but was unable to sway the Aki-organized Senate.

Toward the end of the 1993 session, and shortly after the polls revealed a substantial drop in his support, Governor Waihee again went on the offensive. First, he called for an end to political contributions from companies doing sole-source and exempt work. Then, he accused the Senate of killing a procurement bill for political reasons and for being more interested in conducting an investigation than in working for meaningful reform. Finally, he instructed all agency personnel to respond to questions from the committee only in writing and to send a copy of their responses to the offices of their particular director and the governor.

Charges of McCarthyism. Just before a committee hearing involving a Data House contract to provide services to his own office, the governor went so far as to charge that the investigation was reminiscent of McCarthyism. The governor's offensive posture, it seems, was designed to create the impression that the investigation was somehow politically motivated and to portray Senator Matsuura as being on a witchhunt. However, the press didn't buy it and neither did the public, who were beginning to wonder what was making the governor so nervous.

It was at about that same time that the administration hired Peter Wolff, a criminal defense lawyer. Wolff quickly sent a letter to the committee, challenging its right to operate between legislative sessions and saying he had advised state officials not to show up for the hearings. And he pledged to fight the committee's authority to issue subpoenas all the way to the Hawai'i Supreme Court.

Although the governor's public relations ploy did not succeed in stifling the Senate investigation, the decision to test the committee's subpoena powers at least slowed it down.

Crisis of confidence. There is a growing crisis of confidence that will not end soon. The Waihee administration's strategy appears to be to delay any resolution, leaving the mess for the next administration. That doesn't instill faith in government.

Regardless of how it plays out, there are lessons to be learned and reforms to be made. At a minimum, we need a new procurement code. That's obvious. But we also need an independent watchdog agency to keep things honest. Normally, a second political party would do most of this, but Hawai'i's Republican party has itself been fairly inept and one of its standard bearers has had to deal with allegations of wrongdoing himself (remember Kukui Plaza?). The absence of a viable second party has left the work of political reform to the newspapers and independent-minded Democrats in the Senate.

We also need an independent attorney general, someone who defines the client as the public rather than the governor.

Finally, we need political leaders who concern themselves with the spirit as well as the letter of any law and who run for office to serve the people rather than themselves and their friends. The vast majority of people who work for the State of Hawai'i are honest and hardworking. Yet they get tainted by the practices of a few. Whether those few are corrupt or just unethical doesn't matter all that much. The mere appearance of corruption is reason enough for the public to demand reform.

A DEATH IN THE FAMILY

CHAPTER 28

GOVERNMENT BAILOUTS

SEIJI NAYA
Professor of Economics
University of Hawai'i

BRUCE VOSS
Freelance Writer

"Should the state bail out failing private companies?"

Hamakua Sugar Company worker Isaac Fiesta phrased the question a bit differently. "How come the governor's doing nothing to save our jobs?" Fiesta angrily asked at a meeting two weeks before the planned shutdown of the 110-year-old plantation. "Waihee's a Honoka'a boy; how come he no show face?"

Obviously stung, Governor (and Honoka'a native) John Waihee came lumbering to the rescue on a proverbial white elephant. Waihee proposed an $8 million state loan guarantee—quickly rubber-stamped by the state legislature—to finish the final harvest of the bankrupt sugar company and avoid the "economic and social fallout" of an immediate shutdown. State attorneys told the bankruptcy court there was at least a reasonable chance the harvest could be completed and the loan repaid. What a deal! Hamakua's main creditor, already $115 million in the hole but needing cooperation from the state to sell off the plantation lands, found it difficult to say no.

Traditional pattern. State officials, mindful that times were tough elsewhere around the state, emphasized that this was merely a loan guarantee, not an outright giveaway. Still, the Hamakua deal followed

203

the traditional pattern, where politics and personalities rather than long-term planning and policy considerations trigger state aid to dying companies. Ultimately, taxpayers' money will only forestall the inevitable.

When the state gave Hamakua Sugar its initial $10 million rescue loan in 1988, owner Francis Morgan declared that he needed only temporary help to get over some weather-related and cash-flow problems. The state agricultural director proclaimed, "The loan is fully collateralized. . . . the state will get its money back no matter what happens."

Such sweet talk is cheap; sugar production is not. Although Hamakua stayed alive for another five years, nothing was done to diversify the district's economic base or prepare for the inevitable shutdown. In the end, Hamakua was charged with violating federal environmental laws; it had run up millions of dollars more in debt to creditors (including local businesses); and it had let its workers compensation insurance fund lapse so that the state had to shell out at least $6 million to cover employees' claims. That's on top of what it will have to pay for unemployment insurance and any default on the final harvest loan guarantee. And no matter how the harvest goes, all jobs will be history by late 1994.

By comparison, the $8.5 million state loan to Hilo Coast Processing Company in 1989 has been a success. That loan is current, and the company appears well managed. Moreover, because the money was used to buy and continue operating the plantation's 18-megawatt electricity generating plant, the Big Island had fewer rolling blackouts than surely would have followed a shutdown.

Nonetheless, when Governor Waihee signed the bill for the Hilo Coast loan, he announced that it would "help save 700 jobs." Not for long. In 1994 that plantation will also close, leaving just thirty employees to run the power plant.

Beyond the bottom line—and in spite of the imminent death of King Sugar—there might be legitimate social arguments for state aid to sugar companies, given the sheltered, self-contained nature of plantation communities and their historic role in Hawai'i's development. Unfortunately, none of those arguments fit the state's $12.6 million loan guarantee on behalf of Hawaiian Airlines.

Recent bailout. By early 1993, Hawaiian Air had the look of a fiscal dodo bird. Its operating losses over the prior four years had totaled $350 million (about $240,000 a day); it was in default on its aircraft leases; and its outside auditors had expressed "substantial doubt about its ability to continue as a going concern." Only Boris Yeltsin had a worse credit rating. Still, the state government made and then defended the Hawaiian loan guarantee as a "good, conservative business deal."

No one disputes that interisland air travel is critical to Hawai'i's economic health. To justify the deal, government business analysts projected that shutdown of Hawaiian Air would result in a loss of 3,500 jobs and $94 million in annual household income statewide. Those doomsday guesstimates, however, rested on the highly questionable assumption that no new competitor would enter the Hawai'i market with comparable service.

Besides being just plain wrong, that assumption was more than a trifle self-serving on Hawaiian Air's part, given its past efforts to kill one competitor (Discovery Airways) and keep out another (United Airlines). Business practice and common sense should have dictated that

"TURNED DOWN OUR LOAN AGAIN 'CAUSE THEY WANT SOMEONE TO GUARANTEE THE STATE LEGISLATURE'S GUARANTEE..."

there would be new entrants in the interisland air market (perhaps Mahalo Airlines) and that they would hire mostly local people.

State legislators' response to Hawaiian Air's plea was classic Marx (Karl, not Groucho). Along with the loan guarantee, lawmakers voted to reregulate the interisland air business via a state commission with the power to set fares and restrict new competition. In an amazing display of double-talk, Governor Waihee claimed regulation would "foster competition by keeping the industry economically viable."

Our elected officials were convinced not by numbers but by bodies: the hundreds of Hawaiian Air employees who descended on the Capitol to plead for help to save their jobs. Honest, tearful testimony can be devastatingly effective, and in this case it was.

More to come? Such bailout plans consume an extraordinary amount of time and attention that might be better spent on more productive state business. History shows that bailouts provide a false sense of long-term security for employees. And with the floodgates now open, more "worthy but troubled" companies surely will stagger up to the trough. How can their pleas be denied?

Rather than ricocheting from crisis to crisis, the state has to determine what's crucial to its long-term economic prosperity—and then stick to it. A dying duck cannot be transformed into a phoenix. Belated government intervention, whether with loans or price controls, will only make an inefficient business less efficient.

It is ironic that Hawai'i, a state with close ties to Asia, has not yet learned this economic lesson. From Thailand to South Korea, countries are deregulating, privatizing, and encouraging private companies to work out their own problems. In Singapore, even government-backed enterprises are allowed to go bankrupt. Meanwhile, starting and operating a business in Hawai'i is an increasingly byzantine paper chase.

Government role. This is not to say that Hawai'i government should be a disinterested observer. Some regulation of business is important to protect the health and welfare of consumers. But it is just as critical to distinguish between those regulations that promote the free market and those that interfere with it. One cannot see the difference while sitting behind a desk; government officials must get out and talk to the thousands of business people who are forced to live by the rules.

Hawai'i's state government, especially its business development department, must set clearer goals and provide some direction for future growth. The 1978 Hawai'i State Plan never got much respect, was generally ignored, and is now just an expensive relic. Nagging new questions need answers: Which tourism markets will we target over the long term? Do we want more foreign investment? Do we even really know how foreign investment affects Hawai'i?

Only when those bigger issues are settled can government effectively provide incentives to encourage desirable new industries, instead of bailing out businesses that should be laid to rest. It is interesting to see that the state's 11-year-old Innovation Development Program, intended to promote the development of new products, had made only three loans by the end of 1992.

State officials have always defended the relatively high delinquency rates on other state loan programs by noting that the state is a "lender of last resort." That is, businesses who borrow from the state must show they can't get the money from anybody else. Such spin-control reflects a jumbled mind-set. Rather than a lender of last resort, the state government must be a facilitator of first ideas.

Broader vision. Economic development officials have recently said that they're focusing on making Hawai'i a sports and film-making center. Those may be worthy goals, but a strategic plan must have a broader vision. For example, the state might decide to target "knowledge-related" industries, high-tech niches that don't require large land areas or mass production. With a wonderful climate to attract both doctors and patients, Hawai'i might become a center for medical research and treatment—a sort of Mayo Clinic of the Pacific.

And in spite of the recent furor over foreign investment, the state must foster closer ties with Asia. Billions of dollars of goods and services now fly over Hawai'i every day between Asia and the U.S. mainland. We must be outward-looking and ready to compete if we are to become a part of that action. Bailouts are inward-looking activities that make Hawai'i a place serious business people like to fly over.

Consider this: Despite the lack of a convincing policy rationale, there was meager opposition to the Hawaiian Air loan guarantee. Evidently legislators worried more about a small but vocal bloc of votes than a large number of silent votes. Surprised?

CHAPTER 29

DEMOCRATIC MACHINE

THOMAS P. GILL
Attorney at Law
Gill and Zukeran

"Hawai'i's political malaise: Does anyone care?"

Hawai'i's government is falling apart politically, if not ethically. Some people complain, some profit, others worry; but who is doing anything about it?

I suggest we look back to get a sense of how we got to this point and, more important, where we are headed.

Those of us "mature" enough to have grown up in the 1930s knew about depressions, overt discrimination, and a territorial government that took care of the economic and political "in-crowd" of the time. However, thanks to the federal New Deal and its programs in Hawai'i, we had a sense that government could *do* something if people got together and made it happen.

Pearl Harbor. December 7, 1941, was a shock to Hawai'i, in more ways than were obvious at the time. A multiracial society in which all groups were minorities, and most with a fair degree of internal cohesion, was literally kicked where it hurts.

The attack on Pearl Harbor was conducted—in the language of the time—by the "Japs." It might have been easy, as it was on the mainland, to transfer the public anger into a form of "ethnic cleansing," but that didn't happen. We had military government but little internment or relocation in Hawai'i. Too many people of Japanese ancestry were woven into the blue collar base of our economy, and they were too large a portion of the population. Hawai'i had to continue to function because it was essential to the Pacific War.

The university ROTC was mobilized on December 7, immediately after the attack. All the Japanese Americans who showed up, including the group which later became known as the "AJAs," were given rifles and assigned to sentry duty at pumping stations and other public facilities.

A few weeks later, the military government decided it was unwise to have young men of Japanese ancestry with loaded rifles doing guard duty in Hawai'i. So it stripped them of their guns and uniforms. The personal trauma was tremendous on a group of young people who considered themselves Americans but who also were subject to all the emotional tugs of a close-knit ethnic group with parents or grandparents whose native land was now the enemy.

Heroic service. This humiliating expulsion led to the gutsy decision by many young men to prove themselves. The Varsity Victory Volunteers was formed to perform needed work and service for the military and the community. From this group (along with others, including those who had been serving in the National Guard) came the now-famous 442nd and 100th units. It was their triumphant return from heroic service in Europe that gave a potent and ethnically oriented surge to a political wave. The ethnic cohesiveness of the Japanese community before the war was reinforced by their wartime experience. They had proved themselves as Americans, and now, fifty years later, the drum beats on.

Of course, many other people in Hawai'i, of all ethnic groups, young and old, served in the military during World War II, in all branches of the service; but they returned home as individuals, not as members of a clearly identified ethnic unit. The political wave that began to form in the late 1940s and early 1950s included veterans and their families of all ethnic backgrounds, but the organized core was the AJAs. The vestiges remain today. It is interesting to wonder what form postwar politics would have taken if the military government had not moved as it did in 1942.

The political wave of the early 1950s included optimism and altruism throughout the different ethnic and social groups involved. It also had an undercurrent of self-interest, perhaps more accurately phrased "now it's my turn."

Road to power. Politics became the road to power. Government could change things where the Republican Big Five would not. You had to win elections, which meant different people had to vote. This meant you had to register them and get them to the polls. The old method of holding musical rallies with free food wasn't enough. Many who would vote Democratic didn't want to be identified as such—just yet. So you had to go door to door, talk to them, and sign them up. Once registered, they usually voted, and voted for the new Democrats.

There was another key element. Some people sensed that a new wave was coming, but they needed assurance that it stood for something different. Much of the definition came from "university types" and other "intellectuals," who provided just what the candidates and power seekers needed, ideas like "taxation according to ability to pay," "stronger unions," and "land reform." After all, it could be embarrassing to just stand up and say, "Vote for me because I'm like you." The new voters wanted more.

For a while they got it. Most of our basic social reform legislation relating to land, taxes, monopolies, wages, and working conditions was passed by our state legislature in the late 1950s and early 1960s. Then the more durable part of the surge took over—self-interest.

Complacency sets in. Inevitably, if you were in office for a few terms, your most important goal shifted from furthering a party platform to getting reelected. The old local axiom "no make da wave" resurfaced, politically. Once your voting constituency felt it was no longer excluded from political power and was now part of the in-crowd, it was not smart for you to push for big changes. This could make people nervous, and they might vote against you.

In the 1960s money began to talk as the cost of campaigning through the media climbed higher and higher. To get money you had to please special interests. Lobbyists multiplied like rabbits and easily hopped over party barriers. The former Big Five began to hire the new politicians—as they had the old—along with their political operatives. In the last session of the territorial legislature, in 1959, some labor groups led by the International Longshoremen's and Warehousemen's Union cut deals with minority Republicans and neighbor island Democrats to maintain their political clout. The Democratic platform, after its brief moment in the sun, effectively disappeared.

Government, initially seen as an agent of change, became viewed as a source of employment. And once the governorship was finally captured by the Democrats in 1962, a vast new job haven opened. First it was political appointments, then the civil service. The new power brokers could now reward their supporters and, more important, ensure their continued support. The ethnic composition of the civil service shifted markedly over the next several decades while its numbers increased dramatically. Eventually, the government-worker voting bloc merged with the Democratic AJA's and became the most important and reliable in the political arena. The Land Use Commission, originally designed to bring some statewide sense of planning to then chaotic individual county systems, opened a state door to ambitious developers with big money. At the same time, it opened doors to big landowners, such as the Big Five, who became less interested in agriculture and more in using their vast land holdings to grow "bucks." Today they continue.

Eventually, after appointing a majority of the Hawai'i Supreme Court, the new in-crowd could put their people into the most powerful private land trust of all, Bishop Estate. When you stir together the control of land use with the biggest private landowners, and then add a dash of monetary seasoning (including developers and the state retirement system), you have a potent pot of stew. It is now beginning to bubble, and some claim they don't like the smell!

Wave broke, now receding. So the Democratic political wave that began in 1954 has broken and is now receding, leaving some disturbing flotsam. Now what?

The label "D" is still important—note the "R" candidates who become "Ds" when it suits their purpose—but this is largely because the Republican party is little more than a source of media comment. The "D" voting bloc has shrunk in size but not in importance, since it—and particularly its AJA core—still shows up to vote in a shrinking and disinterested electorate.

The pundits have yet to predict a new sea change that will move us again. But all is not lost. New tides are astir. Our local population is changing. Marriages between ethnic groups are much more common than they used to be. Many young people are questioning the "gimme" values of the 1970s and 1980s. The older functionaries of the political

Voter turnout

system are retiring to the golf courses or dying off. There are new sets of "outs" who are more than mildly disgusted with what they see in the government and private sectors. In addition, many politically motivated people who became active during the barren 1970s and 1980s, but who concentrated on single issues, may have begun to sense the need to pull it all together again. Most important of all are the multitude of potential but unregistered voters.

If some group, or collection of groups, can put together a real political program that catches the attention of the bored and disillusioned, things could move. But they will have to register new voters in sufficient numbers to break the old patterns. It will take new ideas and lots of work.

New "outs" want in. We should not expect a sea-change event like World War II to force political adjustments. It is more likely to be a change in the sea itself, as new minorities are pushing for a place on the beach. They come from such places as Malaysia, the Philippines, and the South Pacific. And some are "new haoles," locals as well as those from the mainland, who have also been excluded. Interestingly, one of the most excluded groups is the most local of all—Hawaiians. If they can continue to gain pride in their culture, and in themselves, without setting up privileges and barriers that alienate the rest of Hawai'i, they can once again become a potent force in our society. Just repeating the mantra of "sovereignty" won't do it; many non-Hawaiians are curious as to what the word is supposed to mean. Given the land potentially involved, this could turn into Hawai'i's biggest cookie jar.

All these, and others, are the new "outs" who would like to be "in." Or, at the very least, they would like to feel comfortable with a government that is lean, efficient, and run in the interest of most of the people—not just those groups who contribute heavily to campaigns and hire political cronies.

History is out there, waiting to be made. Does anyone care?

"THEN THEY WONDER WHY PEOPLE DON'T VOTE..."

A Voice That Is No More

The *Hawaii Observer* was Tuck Newport's five-year attempt to provide what he called a "reflective" brand of journalism. Rather than compete for breaking news, he wanted to carefully investigate and thoughtfully cover the most important issues, institutions, and people in the community. He encouraged his staff to be less concerned with daily ephemera and more alert to the underlying forces that shape society in the Islands.

Tuck had some particularly interesting things to say in a *Star Bulletin* guest editorial on March 4, 1978:

> Industrial civilization is approaching a day of reckoning for which we are ill prepared.... government in Hawai'i is in the throes of disintegration. The creative energy, spirit of reform and capable leadership of the Democratic Party from World War II through the early years of Statehood have dissipated. Meanwhile the local economy has ridden the waves of war and tourism. No major, productive industry has evolved in these Islands since Jim Dole started the Hawaiian Pineapple Company at the turn of the century.
>
> Hawai'i has been coasting economically and politically for decades. It's been a nice ride—in many respects one of the most comfortable on the planet during the middle portion of this century—but it won't last long.... every increase in tourism leaves us more vulnerable to dislocations over which we have no control.... In truth, we don't know what kind of community we want; in fact the majority of us have abdicated responsibility for trying to decide.

CHAPTER 30

POLITICAL POWER

JOHN C. McLAREN
Attorney at Law
Law office of Dennis W. S. Chang

"Have we left the plantation era?"

For many years, powerful business and political interests, typified by the Big Five, used laborers from Asia and the Pacific Islands as their principal vehicle for success. Today, while plantations have declined significantly in size and influence, and the Big Five are gone or greatly reduced in importance, most Hawai'i residents continue to feel the powerlessness and exploitation of plantation life. And they wonder why.

One-party state. Hawai'i's Democratic party came into power in the early 1950s in reaction to the exclusionary philosophy of wealthy, mostly Caucasian Republicans. The Democrats' rise took Hawai'i on a path of unprecedented social and economic growth that led many to believe the exploitive aspects of plantation life would never return. Unfortunately, in the 1970s many of Hawai'i's young Democrats began to advocate an exclusionary political philosophy called "Palaka Power," named after the blue and white plaid clothing worn by thousands of Hawai'i's plantation laborers. These Democrats espoused a then-radical social and political agenda and were unique in their goal of promoting "local" talent to the exclusion of others. They also sought control of Hawai'i's economy and news media.

Nearly twenty years later, Hawai'i's current Democratic leaders, many of whom were proponents of Palaka Power, find themselves trying to explain flagrant abuses in political fund-raising and government procurement. An outraged public knows something is wrong but is confused about the details. Meanwhile, calls for higher ethical standards for government officials go unheeded.

Leaders of the Democratic party have become a "machine" without any apparent redeeming, progressive cause to advance on behalf of the people they were elected to serve. They seem to have lost themselves in their hunger to maintain dominance. They have become the "lunas" the nisei Democrats sought to eliminate in 1954.

Loss of ideology. A growing number of politicians in Hawai'i have lost nearly all their ideology in favor of simply seeking election to public office. This has been done in the name of expediency and is best illustrated by the members of both political parties who have switched their affiliation—sometimes more than once—rather than work toward consensus or constructive change within their original party.

Rewarding friends and punishing enemies has become commonplace in Hawai'i politics as a direct result of this focus on achieving political control. Perhaps Mayor Frank Fasi described this pragmatic approach most clearly in a speech some years ago: "Simply stated, *all else being equal*, you help your friends, you don't help your enemies." Many observers would not be terribly upset by this if they thought the "all else

being equal" part was always kept in mind. Others, including myself, are disgusted by it in any event.

Political fund-raising. Most political experts agree that money is the life blood of a successful campaign. The ability to collect large amounts of monetary and in-kind contributions is the principal reason incumbents consistently beat "no-name" opposition.

One of the hallmarks of a democracy is the right of any citizen to support any candidate for public office. But as documented by *Star-Bulletin* reporter Ian Lind, there are disturbing signs of abusive and unethical fund-raising activities in Hawai'i politics. High on the list is the large amount of money donated (directly and indirectly) to incumbents and to the Democratic party by regular recipients of large government contracts. The strong connection between who gives and who gets to feed at the government trough is shocking.

Some have described this practice as nothing more than a bastardized version of religious tithing applied to the political world. At least a few contributors have acknowledged privately that their political contributions are "required" as a part of doing business with the state and local governments. I view it as the reciprocity element embodied in the Japanese concept of *on*: a custom involving the conferring of a benefit and the begetting of a suitable obligation in exchange. It's a principle that has social merit, but it should not be a part of government practices.

It is not uncommon for wealthy political supporters to arrange for the purchase of costly fund-raiser tickets by their family members, friends, and employees. This practice is a patently unlawful device for getting around the limit on the amount any one individual can give, but it's difficult to enforce. And it's masked by the throngs of "ordinary" people one sees at a typical fund-raiser. Generally, many of these latter folks were given tickets or enticed to attend by the offering of valuable prizes.

Practice versus theory. In theory and under Hawai'i's current campaign spending law, no candidate for state or county office should receive more than $2,000 per election from any one individual, business, or political action committee. In practice, many candidates receive much more than this amount by exploiting various loopholes in the law and relying on lax enforcement by the Campaign Spending

Commission. For example, as documented by Lind, since 1988 candidates seeking election to a four-year term have been allowed to accept more than $2,000 for a single election by holding fund-raisers in nonelection years, effectively doubling the maximum contribution limit to $4,000 per election.

Even Governor Waihee has used this loophole to receive significant contributions, despite the fact that he is prevented from running for a third term as governor and federal campaign spending law prohibits use of such funds in any campaign for federal office. The Campaign Spending Commission finally decided in 1993 to draft rules to control this nonelection year fund-raising practice.

In the past few years, at least a few clever individuals have formed multiple political action committees involving the same people, apparently to act as conduits to fund their favorite candidates. This practice clearly circumvents the spirit of the law and almost as clearly is unlawful. But because it has not yet been *expressly* prohibited by the legislature or tested in the courts, some people call it a loophole and do it anyway.

Some candidates take out enormous loans from themselves and from wealthy family members with no apparent intent to actually repay the loans. I believe this sort of thing is done primarily (if not solely) to get around a state law that prohibits candidates from using more than a total of $50,000 of their own money and gifts from family members to seek office.

A similar federal law has been held unconstitutional, and Hawai'i's version probably would be, too, if it were tested. But politicians who don't like it ought to challenge it directly rather than utilize cute deceptions that encourage others to "wink" at all fund-raising rules. There ought to be more concern about the spirit of such laws and the need for those who would serve in government to hold themselves to the highest standards of conduct.

"Customary and appropriate." Office of Hawaiian Affairs Chairman Clayton Hee, when asked about the propriety of sending a fund-raising letter to companies several days after inviting them to compete for the right to manage $136 million in OHA funds, called the practice "customary and appropriate." Unfortunately, Hee was right about it being "customary." State lawmakers, for example, typically hold their

fund-raisers during decision-making time at the legislature.

An executive at one of the companies solicited by Hee refused to comment on it publicly, saying, "We're in the middle of the selection process. . . . I don't think I should say anything." With a lot riding on a pending decision, who can blame someone for not commenting? Do you think this executive refused Hee's invitation to make a contribution?

Retired businessman Herb Cornuelle has suggested that any one company can't really afford to say no when asked to make political contributions, and things will change only when the entire business community "takes the pledge." Cornuelle added that a group decision to just say no probably won't happen, in part because of clouds over Hawai'i's economic future.

The wave has broken. No one disputes the unparalleled economic prosperity enjoyed by many of our citizens over the past forty years. It is also true, however, that many—particularly native Hawaiians and recent immigrants of all races—have not shared in this economic largesse. The wave of economic prosperity never arrived for them. As for Hawai'i's more fortunate residents, the wave has long since broken and is headed back out to sea.

Instead of simply waiting for the next wave of prosperity to hit our shores, we must now concentrate on preparing to become a stronger, more diverse, self-reliant, and fundamentally citizen-oriented community that is less dependent on the vagaries of tourism for its survival. We must also recognize that the social norms of conservative behavior, obedience to authority, conformity, and honoring obligations virtually at any expense—all highly valued in Asian and Pacific Island cultures for centuries—have been taken advantage of by political opportunists. As a result, power and dominance, the worst parts of Hawai'i's plantation system, have survived intact and continue to flourish within Hawai'i's government and its two major political parties.

This is an especially bitter irony for those residents, including myself, whose parents or grandparents toiled in Hawai'i's sugar cane and pineapple fields in an effort to leave the plantation and its physical and economic hardships behind.

Time for change. No single candidate for office ever has served or ever can serve as more than a messenger of change. Instead, grassroots members of all parties must take an active role in shaping the upcoming debates on what Hawai'i's cultural, economic, and political directions should be as we prepare to enter the twenty-first century. In particular, we must demand not only that elected officials obey the law, but that they behave within the highest ethical standards of conduct. We must also demand that our elected officials advance first and foremost the interests of all citizens of this state. Over the past few years, we have witnessed far too many signs of just the opposite.

The emperor has no clothes, and it is high time we told him.

CHAPTER 31

ETHNICITY

FRANKLIN ODO
Director of Ethnic Studies
University of Hawai'i

SUSAN YIM
Freelance Journalist

"Are race relations in Hawai'i getting better or worse?"

We aren't getting along as well as we used to, largely because we tend to ignore certain ethnic pressure points.

Brief history. We started out as a thriving society of native Hawaiians; then came contact with the West, colonialism, the arrival of immigrants from Asia, Europe, and North America, and eventually statehood. It was the critical addition of immigrant workers for the sugar industry, beginning in the mid-1800s, that created modern Hawai'i's multiethnic complexion. By the late 1800s, their numbers had changed the demographics of the Islands forever. During most of the 1900s, there was a Caucasian power elite symbolized by the Big Five and Republican rule, but everyone was part of a demographic minority.

World War II and the postwar changes in Hawai'i shifted some of the power. Japanese and other Asian Americans banded together to propel the Democratic party into power. Coupled with the dramatic rise of organized labor, especially the International Longshoremen's and Warehousemen's Union (ILWU), this new element radically changed electoral politics.

"Made in America." In this multicultural setting, isolated from Asia and the U.S. mainland by the Pacific Ocean, Hawai'i has evolved into a unique society. Yet, as different as we may be, Hawai'i is still "made in America." Our educational system and the media are two powerful factors in our socialization. What we are taught and how we are taught (our teachers' methods, our textbooks) and what we see on TV (the cartoons, the news, the sitcoms) are very much like those in California or Iowa or New York. With this socialization come negative values, including racism. So you find many of the same stereotypes and prejudices here—toward Caucasians, Asian immigrants, African Americans, and native Americans.

Yet, perhaps because we're an island society and have lived together in a confined space, or because our plantation past taught us to coexist in multiethnic communities, we've learned how to live together better than people in other places. Then again, maybe it's just the natural consequence of a uniquely welcoming host society.

Visionary leadership. We also had the good fortune of visionary leadership from individuals who understood the critical value of creative public policies that were mutually respectful of Hawai'i's ethnic groups. During the years just before, during, and immediately after World War II, the Islands benefited from the joint efforts of military, private sector, and public sector leaders who took a look at Hawai'i's society as a whole, studied the pressure points among the ethnic groups that could fractionalize the community, and with great care and thought anticipated and addressed problems.

Out of this effort, three individuals—Shigeo Yoshida, Hung Wai Ching, and Charles Loomis—emerged as remarkable leaders who were able to talk to different ethnic groups, as well as to leaders in the military, government, and private sector, and thereby influence public policy in ways that addressed the concerns of the diverse community. They were part of the military's "morale section" that was formed to maintain the morale of the civilian population during the war. Their basic approach was to talk about ethnic issues openly and in constructive terms. The long-term result was that a fairly harmonious Hawai'i emerged from the war better prepared for the changes that were to follow.

Island stew. Today people from different ethnic groups are thrown together all the time: a mix of family and friends gather for a graduation party—or, more likely a wedding. The largest and fastest growing ethnic group in Hawai'i, according to veteran state statistician Bob Schmitt, is the mixed-race group. Schmitt calculates that approximately 60 percent of the children born in 1992 were the offspring of interracial unions. Membership in this "hapa" group will continue to grow, not only in size, but as a percentage of the entire population.

There is a general notion that having large numbers of interracial people eliminates prejudice, stereotypes, and racism. Hawai'i is proof that this is not necessarily the case. Indeed, it is not uncommon to find individuals who hold negative images of ethnic groups that are part of their own backgrounds.

The truth of the matter is that ethnic tension in Hawai'i is growing and a tradition of tolerance tends to mask this.

Pressure point 1. We have difficulty, as a society, with newcomers to the Islands, whether they're highly trained, predominantly white professionals who come here to enter the private sector, new immigrants from Asia who are highly educated but speak English with an accent, or the working-class groups from various islands in the Pacific.

The Caucasian newcomer often resents the "haole" label and is also unprepared for the degree of Asian or "local" influence and the extent to which nonwhites wield power. Too many anticipate a move to Honolulu as being no different than a move to any other U.S. metropolitan area and refuse to learn or accommodate. And Hawai'i residents tend to view this group with suspicion and mistrust. But this is a large, powerful, and growing population; our ability to interact in a positive fashion will help determine how they fit and participate in the community.

African Americans, like others, are a diverse group, ranging from student athletes to retired military personnel to business professionals and laborers. There are stories of successful accommodation—John Penebacker came to Hawai'i with the military, subsequently attended the University of Hawai'i where he was a basketball star, eventually became a school board member, and is now a state administrator—but Hawai'i can be brutally racist in its treatment of this particular minority.

Many of the new Asian immigrants come to Hawai'i from different backgrounds than those who came as contract laborers for the plantations. They're urban, educated professionals in the countries of their birth. They resent being treated like second-class citizens just because of their accents and refuse to accept our attitude that they should "wait their turn" to rise on the economic, social, and political ladder.

Pressure point 2. We are facing social problems created by an economy that employs a large number of less-educated immigrants and newcomers in the tourist industry, who often work more than one job for wages on the low end of the pay scale. This economic situation leaves a younger generation often unsupervised while parents and older siblings work long hours to make ends meet. This is related to the troubling presence of youth gangs.

In the days when Hawai'i was not as urbanized, when parents were working long hours on the plantations, there were institutions such as language schools, the YWCA and YMCA, and churches to serve as caretakers for the children of laborers. Today these organizations need far more assistance.

Pressure point 3. A new and still developing tension is fueled by the changing image of the Japanese American in Hawai'i. Since World War II, most have enjoyed a comfortable middle-class lifestyle, defended the status quo, and expected education and upward mobility to be as much a reality for their children as sun and surf. As a result, they suffer from the "model minority syndrome": people expect them to be perfect, cooperative, productive citizens. Japanese Americans expect the same of themselves. But, like any other group, they have crime, failure, and dysfunction. This doesn't fit their image.

Just as entrenched is the image that they run this place: that an enormous Japanese American elite and bureaucracy control the inner workings of government. Japanese Americans, as a result, become the logical target as a group that has overstayed its welcome, taken more than its fair share of power and glory—and the historical explanation of how they got there doesn't much matter.

Every ethnic group has its own perspectives and concerns, but the case of the Japanese American is especially critical because they have dictated, in so many ways, the status quo. If they feel threatened, they will respond by circling the wagons. Like most groups under siege, they will become defensive, protect their steadily diminishing areas of influence, and succumb to the temptation to use more nepotism rather than to become more egalitarian and inclusive. Because of their sizable population and political influence, this could further fractionalize the community in considerable ways.

Pressure point 4. The movement for Hawaiian sovereignty is kindling a range of emotions. It has the potential to put people into "us versus them" camps since the issue can be perceived as threatening to other ethnic groups, large or small.

Although this is a pressure point, the native Hawaiian community is the one group that has seen things change for the better recently. This momentum may have gotten its kick start with the Hawaiian renaissance of the 1970s and the surge of pride in native culture and arts. Since then, native Hawaiian groups have organized and mobilized politically as well as culturally. They've seen that education and community participation can make a difference, and that they can be active players in determining their future.

Need for policy. There is much more to this complex story, of course, and some of the statements here are overgeneralized and simplified. The crucial point is to recognize the existence of some positive ethnic and racial patterns; the persistence of some long-standing negative ones; the threats imposed by new developments; and, most important, the need for policy considerations to protect and enhance our ability to tolerate and respect different heritages and aspirations. Perhaps it's time to establish a modern-day morale corps to address these pressure points. For sure, every large institution in the Islands (military, universities, hospitals, etc.) should provide "orientation" for newcomers. It might be as simple as a reading list or perhaps a video that constructively addresses the unique qualities of Hawai'i, including an honest airing of ethnic pressure points.

Race relations aren't as good as they used to be, and for them to improve we and our elected officials need to recognize this area as crucial to the future of Hawai'i.

"NEVER MIND THE...UH, KISS, FELLA..."

CHAPTER 32

GENDER EQUALITY

CORI LAU
Executive Director
Hawai'i Institute for Continuing Legal Education

"Should same-sex couples be allowed to marry?"

This issue can be difficult to discuss. People who answer the question in the negative are sometimes called homophobic or just plain intolerant of others. The yes crowd often are accused of promoting homosexual activity or labeled "politically correct" (the 1990s version of "bleeding heart liberal"). Rather than answer this question directly, I'll try to list all the arguments against same-sex marriages, and possible responses to each one. I hope this will help you think through the issues and form an opinion that makes sense or feels right to you.

Background. It's not illegal in Hawai'i to be homosexual or to engage in homosexual activity. Perhaps this is a reflection of Hawai'i's liberal political tradition, or maybe it has something to do with our cultural backgrounds. For example, UH professor Lilikala Kame'eleihiwa tells us that bisexuality has been accepted for centuries throughout eastern Polynesia, and UH professor and director of ethnic studies Franklin Odo has pointed out that the Japanese historically have been tolerant of homosexuality among samurai, Buddhist monks, and kabuki actors.

Prior to a 1993 Hawai'i Supreme Court decision (the "Baehr case"), the law in Hawai'i was that members of the same sex could not marry. The Baehr case at least clouded things and probably turned them upside down. The legal analysis is fascinating to lawyers but confusing to others. Basically, it goes something like this: because the law lets persons of the opposite sex marry, it is discrimination to not allow marriage simply because the persons to be married are of the same sex. Importantly, the Hawai'i Constitution generally forbids discrimination based solely on sex, just as it does when race is the basis.

In a way, the rationale is logical and simple. But there's no getting around the fact that same-sex marriage is revolutionary. No other state has yet to do what Hawai'i has done with the Baehr case, regardless of how logical it might be.

The Hawai'i Supreme Court's decision in Baehr was not the final word. The state *can* discriminate if it can show a compelling reason to do so. Whether it has a compelling reason to prevent same-sex marriage must now be argued in a lower court, but most lawyers are predicting that the state will lose and that same-sex marriages will be allowed.

There is also talk that the administration will support a "domestic partnership" law which would, with limited exceptions, provide the rights and responsibilities of marriage—it just wouldn't be called marriage. And unlike marriage, it wouldn't be recognized outside Hawai'i.

Arguments and responses. Here are the primary arguments being made in the community against same-sex marriages, with a possible response to each one:

"Same-sex marriages are wrong because homosexuality is wrong." Whether or not it's "wrong," homosexuality is legal. Consequently, homosexuality is not a proper legal basis for restricting any of the benefits currently being provided to others.

"The state should not sanction a union in which procreation is impossible." It must be remembered that marriage is possible for senior citizens well past childbearing age, sterile individuals, and heterosexual couples who have no intention of ever having children. The intention to procreate is not a requirement for marriage.

"Marriage will be abused by homosexuals seeking only tax breaks, health care coverage, Social Security benefits, and other such possible advantages." Hawai'i law does not currently prevent heterosexual individuals from marrying even if done to get these same benefits. Moreover, some of

these rights and benefits carry concomitant obligations. Although tax structures may benefit married couples in a traditional household where only one spouse is the breadwinner, two individuals who both work (the more likely scenario for a same-sex couple) typically pay *more* in taxes as a married couple. Also, spouses generally have a legal obligation to support one another. This, for example, can prevent one from qualifying for welfare or medicaid.

Same-sex couples are more likely than the average married couple to both be in the working force; consequently, they are more likely to be earning many benefits (e.g., Social Security, health insurance) on their own and less likely to be dependent on a spouse for such benefits.

"The state has a right to uphold religious values." Religious groups and denominations do not universally agree on the issues of homosexuality and same-sex marriages. Those opposed to same-sex marriage, however, would not be required to perform, sanction, or even recognize such marriages. They could even condemn them if they so chose. Perhaps this is a bit like divorce, which is not recognized by some religions yet *is* recognized and sanctioned under the law of every state.

"The state should respect deeply held community values." This argument might be more convincing if its proponents could demonstrate how they would be adversely affected by same-sex marriages. Perhaps an analogy can be made to miscegenation laws, which for decades prevented interracial couples from marrying in some states. After all, interracial marriage did offend the sensibilities of many people in the states that had such laws. Yet most Americans today realize that miscegenation laws deprived individuals of a basic civil right. Here in Hawai'i, nearly half our marriages involve individuals of different races!

The lower court decision in the Baehr case recognized that Hawai'i has a "history of tolerance for all people and their cultures." Along these lines, Hawai'i already has statutory protection against discrimination in the workplace on the basis of sexual orientation. If our duly elected officials have made it wrong to discriminate in this way in the workplace, perhaps such discrimination should be just as wrong at the altar.

"Same-sex marriage will make Hawai'i a haven for homosexuals." Homosexuals may indeed flock to Hawai'i to marry. However, because the U.S. Constitution requires that each state respect the laws of all other states, the home states of same-sex couples who marry here are supposed to accept the marriage as legal. Domestic partnership laws, however, are recognized only in states that have adopted such legislation. Consequently, gay couples would be more likely to settle here permanently should domestic partnerships be legalized as an alternative to allowing same-sex marriages. It also could be argued that gays and lesbians—including those who don't care to "tie the knot"—will be attracted to Hawai'i, perceiving the people here as more tolerant of their lifestyle.

Migratory behavior is notoriously difficult to predict, but let's assume for a moment that gays will be attracted to Hawai'i in relatively large numbers. From a purely economic standpoint, that may be very good news for Hawai'i. It is well documented that the homosexual population's household and per capita income are well in excess of national averages. According to the July 18, 1991, issue of the *Wall Street Journal*, the average annual income of homosexuals at that time was $55,430, compared to a national average of $32,144. The April 1992 issue of *Honolulu Magazine* reported that the average household income for the homosexual population in Hawai'i was $56,218. The *Journal* article also noted that 49 percent of homosexuals held professional and managerial positions, as compared to 15.9 percent of the national population.

If we assume that the gay and lesbian population of Hawai'i will grow, several other questions come to mind. Will professional and skilled jobs become harder to find if gays and lesbians are statistically more likely to be professionals? Will well-heeled homosexuals drive up housing prices? Will increased gay tourism or a reputation as the "San Francisco of the Mid-Pacific" discourage tourism by individuals who dislike being around gays and lesbians? We simply don't know the answers to these questions.

"Allowing gay marriage encourages homosexuality and the spread of HIV." It is a widely held perception that homosexual men are more likely to contract HIV than heterosexuals. However, homosexual men who currently have AIDS are dying of the disease at a higher rate than heterosexuals because of high-risk behavior that occurred many years ago. In fact, HIV infection today cuts across all lines: sexual orientation, sex, social status, religion, and ethnicity. The World Health Organization estimates that five out of eleven new infections occur in women and that, by the year 2000, 75 percent of those with HIV infection or full-blown AIDS will be heterosexual.

Whether public perception of AIDS is correct or incorrect, homosexual men are not going to change their sexual activities or become heterosexual if denied the opportunity to marry. Some people argue that community encouragement of long-term monogamous relationships among the homosexual population (i.e., allowing them to marry) would serve to reduce the spread of HIV.

But migratory uncertainties are a particular concern in this context. What happens if a large number of homosexual men are attracted to Hawai'i and a certain percentage of them are already HIV infected? That could place a tremendous financial burden on the state.

"Homosexuals are antisocial troublemakers." The perception that there is a disproportionate incidence of antisocial behavior among gays and lesbians is fueled by the outrageous antics of groups such as Act Up

and Queer Nation, whose "in your face" activities are expressly designed to shock and dismay the average "straight" person. Perhaps their radical behavior can be likened to the extreme actions of Black Panthers or other highly visible extremist groups from an era when equality for them was just a dream. As civil rights legislation became more and more a reality, most radical groups disbanded.

Gender equality. In case you've been thinking the Baehr case doesn't directly impact heterosexuals, think again. By deciding this case the way it did, the Hawai'i Supreme Court has made it much easier for victims of sex discrimination—who usually, but not always, are women—to sue and win! Before the Baehr decision, sex discrimination was permissible as long as the government had an important objective in mind and the discrimination was substantially related to achievement of that objective. Now, a "compelling" reason to discriminate must be shown—and that's much harder to do. So, while the headlines may speak only of same-sex marriage, future generations (especially of women) might look back on this case as a landmark decision for them.

CHAPTER 33

BISHOP ESTATE

DESMOND BYRNE
Owner
Honolulu Information Service

"Are we adequately compensating the Bishop Estate trustees?"

I hope you're kidding.

First of all, it's not the most important question to be asked about the Bishop Estate. Second, it's not even the second most important question. Finally, it's obvious to everyone except perhaps the trustees themselves that their compensation is way out of line. I'll explain why this is so and then talk about more important matters.

Adequate compensation? The trustees think of themselves as undercompensated because they give back some of the fees to which they're entitled by law. They can't seem to understand why people aren't more impressed by their generosity.

The truth is, the law does not set their fees; they do. All the law establishes is a maximum. The governing statute says commissions "shall be *limited* to . . . ."

The trustees point to that figure and say, "That's what we're entitled to." Baloney. It's a legal maximum and nothing else. Corporations can *legally* pay their executive and directors billions in salary. Does that mean they should? Of course not. The fact that an amount can legally be paid doesn't begin to address the issue of reasonableness.

The trustees paid themselves a salary of $860,652 for the year ended June 30, 1992. That's $860,652 *each*. Most major foundations, universities, hospitals, museums, and other nonprofit organizations pay their trustees *nothing*. That's right, most are unpaid volunteers. (Some nonprofit organizations use terms other than "trustee," but the responsibility and liability are those of a trustee so I'll use that term for the sake of consistency.)

In a 1990 foundation report—which did not include information on the Bishop Estate, since it is not technically a foundation but rather a charitable estate—the Council on Foundations noted that the highest fee paid to a foundation trustee in the nation, to their knowledge, was $74,000. A 1989 article on trustee compensations at the country's ten wealthiest foundations indicated that the highest 1988 trustee fee was $56,200. By contrast, each Bishop Estate trustee made $659,558 that year.

Most Fortune 500 companies pay their directors—de facto trustees responsible for setting policy—annual fees in the range of $20,000 to $50,000. Once in a while one hears of fees as high as $80,000—an amount that is less than 10 percent of the fees received in 1992 by each Bishop Estate trustee.

Five CEOs. Bishop Estate trustees consider such comparisons invalid since directors and other trustees aren't as active as they are in actually running things. Unfortunately, they're right. It's unfortunate because the Bishop trustees, as a group, don't seem to have the strongest possible credentials to run the Kamehameha Schools or manage upwards of $10 billion in assets. And yet, perhaps in an attempt to justify their astronomical salaries, the Bishop Estate trustees don't confine themselves to setting policy and overseeing the work of skilled managers the way a board of directors, for example, might do. Instead, they function as five separate chief executive officers (CEOs). If they were volunteering their time, I'm sure they would delegate more to a professional staff that would actually run things.

How much does it take to attract top-notch staff? The two highest-paid Bishop Estate employees—other than the trustees—are paid less than $200,000 per year, despite having outstanding credentials. One has to wonder: are they underpaid . . . or are the trustees overpaid?

A 1992 issue of the *Chronicle of Philanthropy* reported that salaries of CEOs at major charities and foundations ranged from $200,000 to a high of $509,000 (which went to the CEO of the J. Paul Getty

Foundation). Not only does the Bishop Estate pay far more than that highest amount, it pays it to each of five trustees.

It would be interesting to see what kind of job each of the estate's trustees could get outside Hawai'i. Oswald Stender was the only one earning a "big league" salary prior to his appointment.

Any way you cut it, the Bishop Estate trustees are grossly overcompensated. They should be ashamed. *Someone* should be outraged.

More important issues. Much more important than the adequacy of compensation is the issue of to whom the trustees are accountable. Who is that someone who should be outraged?

The five justices of the Hawai'i Supreme Court select the trustees, but they make no effort to oversee their performance. The selection process itself has been rather unstructured. Up until the last two appointments, the justices did not even interview the candidates. There have been no written selection criteria (at least none were advertised) despite the fact that each trustee sits atop wealth measured in *billions*, with a responsibility to a group of people (native Hawaiians) who collectively are at the bottom of every have-not list in the state of Hawai'i (see Chapter 30 of *The Price of Paradise*, Volume I).

The probate court makes sure the trustees do not violate the law, but it doesn't seem to concern itself with the quality of the job being done. Do the Kamehameha Schools produce superior graduates? Is everything possible being done to resolve the educational problems of *all* native Hawaiian children? These are just a few of the many important questions that need to be asked. Unfortunately, the probate court doesn't ask them.

No "standing." The probate court does appoint a master to review the Bishop Estate's annual report in accordance with certain guidelines. The master's report is then reviewed by the state attorney general on behalf of the Kamehameha Schools. Interested individuals can attend certain hearings but can't intervene since they lack what lawyers call "standing." That means they don't have the legal right to represent the estate's beneficiary, the Kamehameha Schools. Other than to write letters (to the trustees, the governor, the master, the probate court, the attorney general, the supreme court), citizens—including native Hawaiians—are powerless.

Much of the public discussion about the Bishop Estate is ill informed, mostly because the estate makes little effort to provide information about the quality of its work. I'm talking *information*, not the slick propaganda one sees in the newspapers.

Political plum. The governor appoints the people who select Bishop Estate trustees. He also appoints the attorney general, who represents the public interest in the proper administration of charitable trusts. It's all a bit cozy—too cozy. Nobody is really watching out for the people Bernice Pauahi Bishop had in mind when she established this trust more than a century ago. Rather than ask who can do the most for Hawaiians, the question on some people's minds seems to be "who's next in line for this political plum?"

Are you surprised to hear that the legislature never finds enough time to debate the issue of compensation of trustees? This was particularly maddening in 1992, when a resolution calling for a study of the trustees' compensation died somewhere between two Senate committees—nobody would admit to killing it—and then a few months later Senate president Richard "Dickie" Wong was appointed a trustee.

Representative Henry Peters (also a trustee) and Senator Milton Holt (a Bishop Estate employee) have been accused by some observers of being overly active in defending the interests of the estate whenever they arise in the legislature, which is often. And yet, the Bishop Estate did not report any amount spent on lobbying when it filed its most recent tax return. It maintained that it had not attempted to influence legislation or to influence public opinion on a legislative matter.

Hawaiians. The native Hawaiian community has not been particularly critical of the Bishop Estate trustees. Many Hawaiians say it's difficult to attack something that's uniquely theirs, especially if it would have to be done in full view of non-Hawaiians. Many Hawaiians value the institution not just from a practical viewpoint but as a symbol of what little is left of their heritage and their land. Besides, they don't have "standing" to really do anything.

Aimoku McClellan, a 1966 Kamehameha Schools alumnus, was outraged upon returning from many years on the mainland and finding the appalling conditions of Hawaiian children on the Wai'anae coast. According to him, "the real accountability is to the children of Hawaiian ancestry who are often at the bottom of the educational and social scale, and if that is the criterion then the trustees are not doing their job. The only way to get out of the mire today is education, and the focus should also be on the public schools which are not doing an adequate job." McClellan has suggested criteria for the selection of Bishop Estate trustees. He and many others feel that the selection of well-qualified trustees is the most significant improvement that can be made to the estate.

Office of Hawaiian Affairs (OHA) trustee Rowena Akana has also voiced concerns: "Compared with OHA the estate has a smaller mandate but bigger bucks, and I am tremendously disappointed that more Hawaiian children are not better educated, especially with the resources of the estate."

Oswald Stender is the only trustee who is universally considered to be up to the job. He was quoted in the spring 1990 issue of *He Aha Ka Meahou Me Kamehameha* as saying, "I want people to love Kamehameha Schools/Bishop Estate. It has a great story behind it and a mission, yet it has the worst image of any large business in Hawai'i. Bishop Estate has a major influence in the community and we're not meeting this challenge." Amen.

"TO THINK JUST YESTERDAY WE WERE THE HEALTHIEST STATE IN THE NATION..."

CHAPTER 34

LEASEHOLD CONVERSION

NEAL MILNER
Professor of Political Science
University of Hawai'i

"How should the leasehold controversy be resolved?"

The controversy over leasehold land has heated up again, this time with respect to condominiums. County councils and the state legislature are working on solutions, but every piece of legislation will no doubt be tested in court. That's unfortunate, because litigation takes time. For example, over twenty years elapsed between the passage of the Land Reform Act of 1967 (the legislation setting in motion lease-to-fee conversions for single-family homes) and the U.S. Supreme Court decision that upheld its constitutionality. Four more years passed before mass conversions began. The slow pace of litigation would keep many anxious and frightened land and condo owners in limbo for a long time.

Litigation never produces a happy ending for everyone. In fact, it is quite possible to end up with a definitive, well-reasoned court opinion that satisfies no one. For example, a court might force landowners who do not want to sell to anyone to offer land for sale at prices that many condo owners cannot afford to pay. Plus, certain unappreciated facts about the leasehold controversy are likely to get lost completely in litigation. These features are terribly important and, once understood, may suggest other ways of dealing with the conflict.

1. The Bishop Estate and other landowners are more different than alike. It is politically useful for Bishop Estate to ride the coattails of the small landowner (like the Hanohano family mentioned in many estate-funded commercials), but the differences between the estate and all other landowners are vast. The Bishop Estate owns much more land than any of the others. It is a large, powerful organization with a clear mission. Other landowners are mostly families and small groups that are neither politically powerful nor as explicit in their goals.

None of these differences alone is very important. What makes them more significant is:

2. Unlike the Bishop Estate, small landowners do not want to sell their land. Time and again in their testimony before legislative bodies, small landowners have emphasized that their land is their legacy, not something they ever want to sell. As one put it, "My wise mother-in-law instilled in us 'buy land in fee simple. It cannot be lost, stolen, or taken away. This ownership of land is security for your children and for your children's children.'"

While the Bishop Estate's words do not distinguish it from the small landowners, its deeds certainly do. Its strategy over the past ten years has been to invest the bulk of its wealth outside Hawai'i. Selling out to lessees (i.e., condo owners) would allow the estate to continue that plan.

3. Condo leasehold raises moral, as well as legal and economic, issues. Home ownership occupies a special status in America. Owning a home signifies that you have paid your dues by scrimping, saving, struggling, and sacrificing in order to become someone who has "permanently" settled into the community. Financial security is part of this success, but so is the feeling that by owning a home you have done things right.

This theme has come up again and again in testimony about leasehold conversion. Condo owners talk of the sweat and sacrifice they have put into their homes. They have done everything expected of a homeowner and now they might lose it all. The landowners talk about the sacrifice, toil, and postponed gratification that went into the purchase and development of their land. People on both sides are especially angry and afraid because they see basic, cherished American values threatened.

4. Landowners differ from condo owners on racial and ethnic lines. Almost 90 percent of those testifying at O'ahu council hearings on behalf of the condo owners had Western (haole) surnames, while nearly two-thirds of the landowners had Asian, Hawaiian, or other

Pacific Island names. At leaseholder meetings I have attended, approximately 90 percent of the attendees and about the same number of active participants appeared to be Caucasian. The results of a 1987 survey support my casual observations and further note that the condo owners group included very few Hawaiians and Filipinos at that time. Presumably, that has not changed.

These sensitive and imprecise observations become more important when combined with:

5. Landowners typically brand condo owners as outsiders. Time and again the landowners distinguish themselves from the condo owners whom they think of as, and sometimes call, outsiders. Specifically, they have argued that condo owners do not have a sufficient stake

Condo ownership in Hawai‘i

• Approximately 22% of Hawai‘i's resident population live in condos as of April 1993.

• The percentage of Hawai‘i residents living in condos is expected to increase.

• The total value of all condos in Hawai‘i as of 1992 was nearly $22 billion.

• As of 1993, 39.3% of condos in Hawai‘i were on leased land.

RD

Source: Locations, Inc., research department.

in the community and are mainly interested in the profits they can make from real estate speculation. Landowners often introduce themselves with phrases like "I am one-eighth Hawaiian," "I am a third-generation American of Japanese ancestry," or "I am keiki o ka 'āina." The condo owners never describe themselves in ethnic or racial terms.

6. There are important similarities between the small landowners and condo owners. The small landowners and the condo owners share a sense of victimhood. Both sides see themselves as victims of larger forces. Landowners feel exploited by increases in housing prices, far in excess of their expectations at the time they agreed to offer low lease rents. As a result, they feel victimized by condo owners who have made gigantic profits on condo sales. Condo owners who haven't sold out also feel victimized by the unanticipated run up in prices because it threatens their home ownership. Each feels vulnerable because things that used to be taken for granted—"my land will stay in my family" and, "if I work hard and save, I will be able to pay off my mortgage and live comfortably by the time I retire"—are now slipping away. Both have done everything they were supposed to do but see their dreams slipping away.

Again, the Bishop Estate is in a different situation. Given its size, mission, and political connections, it is much less vulnerable to outside forces and in fact has benefited tremendously from these unanticipated

Lease to fee conversion

Bishop Estate's condominium lease-to-fee conversions

	No. of units offered fee	Average cost per unit
1991	2,588	$46,926
1992	942	$56,810
1993	1,222*	$93,199

*Includes a greater mix of townhouses, which have more land area per unit. Data as of March 1993.

Estimated dollar value of Hawaii lease-to-fee conversions.

■ All single-family residential, 1970-1990 (24,000 homes at average $50,000)	$1.2 billion
■ Private condo conversion, 1982-1991 (9,258 units at average $21,158)	$195.8 million
■ Campbell Estate condo conversions, 1991 (496 Makakilo units at average $23,092)	11.5 million
■ Bishop Estate condo conversions 1991-1993 (4,752 units at average $60,784)	288.8 million
■ Projected Bishop Estate condo conversions for 8,120 remaining units	756.7 million
■ Total estimated cost: (assumes all condo units are purchased.)	$2.4 billion

Source: Honolulu Board of Realtors Research Department.

changes. It is anything but a victim.

What it means. Facts 4 and 5 indicate that this conflict could broaden and become a nasty battle between "insiders" and "outsiders" precisely when, because of the likelihood of Hawaiian sovereignty, those of us living here can least afford that kind of conflict. The leasehold controversy has the potential to ignite a broader conflict over who belongs here. For all people in Hawai'i, sovereignty requires a sophisticated recognition that, on the one hand, some important benefits will be allocated on ethnic lines while, on the other, accommodating ourselves to one another will become an even more necessary goal than ever before. Certainly Ka Lāhui, the largest sovereignty organization, has been very clear in its emphasis on both exclusion and inclusion.

In the heat of battle it becomes tempting to avoid such subtlety. Condo owners who hear themselves labeled outsiders may see this labeling as part of a general sentiment to exclude them from Hawai'i.

One Bishop Estate trustee in particular, Henry Peters, has been more than willing publicly to consider opponents of the estate's policies as culturally insensitive outsiders who should leave if they do not like his sense of what Hawai'i is all about.

Facts 1, 2, and 6 indicate the need for a range of ways of dealing with leasehold issues. If small landowners do not wish to sell their land, and lessees do not wish to pay high lease rent, then these parties should be encouraged to work out some sort of profit-sharing arrangement. Perhaps in exchange for an acceptable lease rent the condo owner would share profits with the landowner when the condo was sold. Leases could be written to discourage speculation and to reward those who live in their condos for a long time. Such arrangements could be worked out through private negotiation, mediation, or arbitration. If the state legislature wants to get involved with this, it could develop processes that differ according to the size of the landowner.

The case of the Bishop Estate is the harder one which, for better or worse, may have to get resolved in the courts. But there are some other activities that might help, especially given the estate's recent announcement that it will make a blanket one-time offer.

There has never been any continuous, constructive contact between Bishop Estate and its lessees. There is a need for estate representatives and a small group of their lessees to meet regularly to discuss these issues in a calm manner. What I have in mind is what people who work in alternative dispute resolution call roundtables, where people with something at stake meet regularly to clarify differences and strive for consensus.

During its 1993 session, the state legislature asked the state's Center for Alternative Dispute Resolution to get involved with the condo leasehold issue. A roundtable would be a good place for the Center to begin.

Fact 3 reminds us in yet another way that this is not simply a leasehold controversy. The conflict is part of, and is aggravated by, the overall housing problem in this state. There is an insufficient supply of low and moderately priced homes, and rents are so high it's virtually impossible for most people to save and struggle enough—the things that good Americans are supposed to do—to achieve the American Dream.

Trouble in paradise for condo leaseholders

Most of the 43,572 condo owners on Oahu will have their lease rent renegotiated within the next 15 years and their ownership interests terminated during the next 45 years, if they don't buy the fee interest.

Renegotiation schedule of leasehold agreements

Years	Number of units	Percent of total units
Before 1996	2,050	4.7%
1996-2000	5,887	13.5%
2001-2005	8,983	20.6%
2006-2010	10,690	24.5%
After 2010	15,962	36.6%
Total	**43,572**	**100%**

Termination of leasehold agreements

Years	Number of units	Percent of total units
Thru 2010	306	0.7%
2011-2015	1,495	3.4%
2016-2020	1,175	2.7%
2021-2025	2,192	5.0%
2026-2030	6,435	14.8%
2031-2035	7,691	17.7%
2036-2040	8,251	18.9%
2041-2045	7,556	17.3%
2046-2050	4,278	9.8%
After 2050	4,193	9.6%
Total	**43,572**	**100%**

Source: Honolulu Board of Realtors Research Department.

CHAPTER 35

INSURANCE

KIT SMITH
Financial Writer
Honolulu Advertiser

"Why is insurance so expensive and hard to get in Hawai'i?"

With regard to auto insurance, this has long been a fair question. State-by-state figures, compiled by the National Association of Insurance Commissioners, show that Hawai'i motorists paid an average of $999 in 1991 to insure one vehicle for one year. Only New Jersey ranked higher at $1,081. We'll get into why in a moment.

By contrast, Hawai'i residents have gotten a home insurance bargain for years. The last general movement in rates came in 1987, and that was a *decrease*.

Iniki's impact. Hurricane Iwa in 1982 caused a blip in insured losses—$175 million—but that was viewed as something of a freak. Otherwise, losses in Hawai'i have run low. But that changed on a frightening Friday in September 1992 when Hurricane Iniki devastated the island of Kaua'i. Iniki caused $1.6 billion of insured losses and forever changed how property insurers regard Hawai'i. When all accounting is done, companies will have ended up paying in claims more than they collected in premiums over the previous twenty years!

Before Iniki, a Hawai'i resident could obtain $300,000 of property insurance for a premium payment of about $953 a year. That compared with $1,634 for the same coverage in Chicago, $2,422 in Houston, and $2,477 in Miami. Insurance companies were making profits from homeowners in Hawai'i and actively sought new business here.

After Iniki, property insurers lump Hawai'i with the Gulf Coast and

Florida as high hurricane-risk locales. One company —the Hawaiian Insurance Group (HIG)—quit the business entirely, unable to cover more than a third of its $200 million losses from Iniki. Two other companies phased out their homeowners business, citing inability to line up reinsurance. Consequently, starting in late 1992, and for at least a matter of several months, homeowners insurance did indeed become difficult or impossible to get, primarily because of a reinsurance crisis.

Reinsurance crisis. Property insurers purchase reinsurance to bring in others, such as Lloyd's of London, to share risks of catastrophic loss. As the HIG case illustrates, lack of sufficient reinsurance can prove ruinous. By itself Iniki would have driven up the cost of reinsurance for companies doing business in Hawai'i. But coming in the same year as Miami's Hurricane Andrew, the Los Angeles riots, and winter storms in the Northeast, Iniki made reinsurers reluctant to extend coverage at any price.

In an attempt to fill the gap, and with support from the insurance companies, the 1993 state legislature created a hurricane insurance "pool," called the Hawai'i Hurricane Relief Fund. After the pool is up and running, it will cover losses from storms officially designated as hurricanes up to $750,000 per home. The collective liability of insurance companies will be capped at $500 million. Companies choosing to participate will continue to write homeowners policies as before, insuring for fire, sub-hurricane wind, theft, and comprehensive personal liability. All or at least most companies are expected to participate.

Despite the new pool, premiums for basic homeowners will rise. Data developed by the Hawai'i Insurance Bureau and submitted to the State Insurance Division clearly will support increases, in part because of the high cost of reinsurance.

Auto insurance. Can we simply blame Hawai'i's high cost of living for lofty auto insurance premiums? Not really. If it were that simple, why was homeowners insurance so reasonable here for so long?

Hawai'i's 20-year-old no-fault auto insurance law deserves much of the blame. In national comparisons, it is in many ways unusual, in some ways unique.

Here's how Hawai'i-style no-fault works. If you or your passengers are injured in an accident, your insurance company pays for medical, rehabilitation, loss of income, and certain other costs. Fault is irrelevant, but the ability to sue kicks in if an injured person dies or suffers serious disfigurement, or if medical and rehabilitation costs exceed a dollar limit (the "threshold"). The legislature intended that the threshold be set such that no more than 10 percent of all injury cases would end up in lawsuits.

As of mid-1993, the threshold had risen to $10,000 from the original $1,500. Observers believe many accident victims have deliberately run up medical and rehabilitative costs just to reach the threshold and thus be able to sue. Insurance companies are widely perceived as being willing to offer cash settlements well above threshold limits, just to avoid the ridiculously high cost of litigation.

High settlement costs. Indeed, insurance settlements in Hawai'i run much higher than national averages. According to a study by an industry-backed research group, the average bodily injury liability settlement in Hawai'i was $35,705 in 1990, about six times the national average.

To some extent that average was high because Hawaii's threshold is the highest for any state having a no-fault law, and that limits the number of lawsuits. But the same 1990 study showed that 28 percent of all bodily injury cases in Hawai'i that year were eligible for lawsuits, far above the 10 percent target. One reason: in 1985 the legislature, seeking administrative simplicity, tied increases in the threshold to an inflexible formula based on annual increases in the cost of living.

Now comes some hopeful news. In 1992, the legislature mandated a return to the concept of limiting lawsuit-eligible cases to 10 percent. Equally important, it also adopted a system of medical fee schedules for specific services, much like those long used in workers compensation insurance. As a result, a party injured in an auto accident will now find it more difficult to run up big medical bills. Any increase in the allowed number of chiropractic visits, for example, will require special approval through a peer review process.

The 1992 reform package also called for insurance companies to reduce their premiums by 15 percent in 1993. Few did so, however, invoking their rights to "fair and reasonable" rates of return. The State Insurance Division, with an eye to court decisions in California and Nevada, determined it couldn't enforce the 15 percent rollbacks.

Other factors. While high claims and settlement costs have been the primary villains in past years, other factors also help explain why auto insurance in Hawai'i is so costly.

• Hawai'i's law requires insurance companies to accept any applicant presenting a valid driver's license and the money to pay the premium. This "take all comers" rule bars a company from rejecting an applicant it feels poses an unacceptable risk. An example would be a young male driver with a record of tickets, an accident or two, and perhaps a drunk-driving conviction.

• In submitting premium schedules to the state for approval, a company can't charge different rates based on age, sex, or marital status. This means, assuming a clean driving record, that a 19-year-old unmarried male pays the same premium as a 45-year-old married female. That's so even though statistics show that the young male is far more apt to cause a loss for the insurer.

• Crowded highways produce more accidents, and in Hawai'i the ratio of miles driven to miles of highway runs almost four times the national average.

• In Hawai'i, every welfare recipient gets basic liability insurance for free, compliments of the insurance-buying public. As of early 1993, about 10,000 welfare recipients were enjoying this benefit, the cost of which adds to the cost of each auto insurance buyer's policy.

• As many as 20 percent of the more than 670,000 vehicles on Hawai'i's roads lack insurance, according to Insurance Division estimates. That's so even though coverage is mandatory. Also, drivers with low limits of coverage—$25,000 of bodily injury liability is the minimum written—may lack enough coverage to meet judgments against them. This is why insurance companies offer coverage for uninsured motorists and underinsured motorists. If every driver were adequately insured, there would be no need to buy either.

Reform. The 1993 legislature, in its regular session, repealed "take all comers" and went so far as to allow companies to drop up to 2 percent of their insured drivers from their books at renewal time. Governor John Waihee called the repeal "an idea whose time has come" but vetoed it anyway, citing technical flaws in how key provisions were drafted. But then in its special session later that year, the legislature passed reform again, having corrected the flaws.

Insurance regulators say that companies eyeing entry into the Hawai'i market have cited "take all comers" as a principal reason for balking. If more companies were to operate here, competition would rise and, if theory holds, premiums would become more reasonable.

Many believe the insurance companies should be allowed to charge different rates based on age, sex, and other criteria. This would bring Hawai'i more in line with most other states. It would also encourage into the market companies specializing in good or substandard risks. By specializing, a company is better able to control and plan for its risks—and thus lower its premiums.

Finally, if the legislature deems that welfare recipients and other low-income people should get free auto insurance, it—the state—should pay. Forcing the insurance-buying public to subsidize others is a hidden tax. If a tax is in order, it ought to be labeled a tax.

CHAPTER 36

ENVIRONMENT

KIRK R. SMITH
Senior Fellow, Environment
East-West Center

"Are we adequately protecting our environment?"

Hawai'i's natural environment is in great shape (relative to all other places inhabited by human beings), even in and around Honolulu, our only big city. But we really can't take much credit for that.

Honolulu is the most isolated big city in the world. Our water and air come across 2,500 miles of ocean, cleansed to the maximum extent possible by natural processes. We have no heavy industry, and what air pollution is produced by cars, power plants, Big Island volcanoes, and agricultural burning is usually swept out to sea by the trade winds. We have not done a great job in some areas (e.g., controlling pesticides), but the fact remains, compared to other contemporary cities, Honolulu is near or at the top of the "clean" list for all major environmental health hazards.

Hawai'i's moderate climate plays an important role in our environmental health. The demigod Maui chose the ideal spot on Earth to create his islands. We are farther from the continents than any other island group in human times. We are at the edge of the tropics, close enough for coconuts and coral, but still in the trade winds for ventilation. By comparison with other coastal areas, we seem to be at low risk from extreme storms, even hurricanes. Our latitude and winds combine with the temperature buffering of the world's largest ocean to produce the lowest maximum daily temperature and the highest minimum daily temperature of any in the United States. Even our volcanoes erupt moderately, although more often than any others on Earth today.

We're number one. Three recent national ratings found Honolulu to be number one among U.S. cities in "green conditions." Each rating was composed of a different mixture of dozens of environmental indicators, such as those for water and air pollution, toxic and other waste, auto fuel efficiency, facilities releasing chemical carcinogens, and community and worker health. Not only is Honolulu always first, there is sometimes a big gap between it and the next-cleanest city in the nation.

Honolulu also fares well in comparisons to cities around the world. In thousands of daily outdoor air pollution measurements taken here, not even one has exceeded World Health Organization recommendations in recent years, a rare boast in the world today. Some Scandinavian cities have equally clean air during summers, but they slip in quality during cold winters when fuel burning increases. Indoor air pollution, which is the largest source worldwide for exposures to some pollutants, is low here as well. This is because, unlike households in Japan, Europe, and the U.S. mainland, Honolulu's are well ventilated; and unlike other well-ventilated residences in the tropics, ours do not rely upon dirty fuels such as biomass, coal, charcoal, and kerosene.

The recently completed Hawai'i Environmental Risk Ranking Study concluded that our highest risks are of the same magnitude as the lowest risks on the mainland. In turn, the environmental health hazards in the United States as a whole are at the low end of the range when compared to the rest of the world.

Problems in paradise. It is ironic that the very factors that make Hawai'i so environmentally healthy also make it extremely vulnerable to another type of environmental damage: loss of our precious and unique natural heritage. This is the paradox of Hawai'i's geography: although extremely moderate in seasonal and daily changes, Hawai'i nurtures the most concentrated aggregation of different ecological zones in the world. Just ask any snorkeler who looks up from the fish off Kona to see the snowy summit of Mauna Kea. Between Hawai'i's offshore reefs and its peaks lie examples of nearly every major ecological zone, tropical to arctic.

Because the Hawaiian Islands have never been connected or even close to any large land mass, the few hundred animals and plants that did arrive during the first 70 million years were free to evolve rapidly to fit into the extensive range of ecosystem niches available here. Before humans arrived, only about one new species arrived every 100,000 years, but evolution has produced more than 10,000 species here that exist nowhere else on the planet.

Globally, therefore, Hawai'i has one of the largest and most important sets of endemic species (ones existing nowhere else). This is simply because the Islands are so remote from other lands. The factors that made the Galapagos Islands so well suited for Charles Darwin's deductions about natural selection have operated here to an even greater degree.

Another result of this isolation is that Hawai'i was one of the last places of any size on Earth to be inhabited by humans. Compared to Africa, Asia, and Europe, humans spread relatively recently to the Western Hemisphere and Australia. Still, these migrations occurred tens of thousands of years earlier than the A.D. 400 arrival of the first Polynesians in Hawai'i. By comparison, this arrival is so recent that Hawai'i's natural environment is still reeling from the first shocks that inevitably accompany human inhabitation.

This, then, is another aspect of Hawai'i's uniqueness. Our lands

Actually, Evolution is still going on...

have lived under the destructive yoke of humanity for a shorter time than almost any other. Hawai'i thus has much left to teach us about what it means to be "natural."

Our assigned stewardship. Communities on the mainland with typically long lists of environmental challenges may have difficulty choosing priorities, but our responsibility is quite clear. Our assigned stewardship is to assure that the world does not suffer further destruction of the special ecosystems and endemic species that make Hawai'i unique.

It is up to us to stop the ecosystem destruction, particularly to our reefs, occurring through soil erosion and poorly planned development. We could achieve much benefit just by enforcing the existing regulations. Very few projects would have to be stopped, if everyone simply followed the law.

It also is up to us to rid the Islands of foreign species brought by humans over the past 1,600 years which threaten our land's very soul. There are dozens of introduced animals and plants that destroy our precious natural heritage, but the worst is the large feral pig. What possible justification can there be for preserving a species dumped here by foreign ships only a short two hundred years back? What a mocking irony is the claim that the hunting of those destructive animals is somehow part of Hawaiian cultural heritage. The truth is just the opposite: only by eliminating them where we can, and excluding them from other important native ecosystems, can Hawaiian heritage be preserved.

Convince neighbors. The rate that new species are introduced into Hawai'i today is millions of times greater than in prehuman times. It is up to us to convince our neighbors that such introductions must be limited as much as possible. We must keep foreign species away from our shores, even if it means less-colorful gardens, duller pet shops, and tedious inspections. We must understand, for example, that those seed packets sent from the mainland by well-wishing friends and family are extremely hazardous to our heritage. Although most of those seeds are harmless and others are of plants already here, there is too high a risk that the packet will contain another banana poka or haole koa to spread and further degrade our environment.

We must support our state and federal government actions to set lands aside in Hawai'i so that the natural ecosystems can be preserved. We must encourage our politicians to give more support to the federal Fish and Wildlife Administration and the Hawai'i Department of Land and Natural Resources to enhance their ecosystem management capabilities. Private efforts through such organizations as the Nature Conservancy also deserve our support. We must enhance environmental education at all levels to make islanders of every age proud of our uniqueness and aware of ways to preserve it.

These are our duties and a small price indeed for being able to share life in paradise.

Hostage

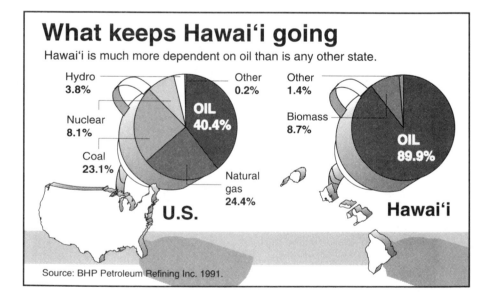

What keeps Hawai'i going

Hawai'i is much more dependent on oil than is any other state.

U.S.
- Hydro 3.8%
- Nuclear 8.1%
- Coal 23.1%
- OIL 40.4%
- Other 0.2%
- Natural gas 24.4%

Hawai'i
- Other 1.4%
- Biomass 8.7%
- OIL 89.9%

Source: BHP Petroleum Refining Inc. 1991.

CHAPTER 37

ENERGY SOURCES

RICHARD E. ROCHELEAU
Associate Researcher
Hawai'i Natural Energy Institute
University of Hawai'i

HEIDI K. WILD
BHP Petroleum Refining, Inc.

"Should we become less dependent on oil?"

Hawai'i is unique among states in its level of reliance on oil as an energy source. What Jedd Clampet and J. R. Ewing called "black gold" is used to produce 75 percent of our electricity and close to 100 percent of the transportation fuels used in our cars, boats, and airplanes. Our "lifeline" is uncomfortably long: the nearest supplier is thousands of miles away. And we are concerned about the threat oil poses to the environment. Some would say we are "over a barrel."

Most of us can remember when headlines in the 1970s warned that worldwide oil reserves might run out within fifty years. Industry experts now feel that there are significant domestic oil reserves yet to be discovered, and that foreign reserves won't run out for centuries. By then an inexpensive substitute will have taken its place . . . we hope. Meanwhile, we should have plenty of oil for all our energy needs. And it will probably continue to be relatively cheap.

Externalities. In some people's view, the price of oil should be higher—perhaps *much* higher. Why? Because the market price of oil, like all energy sources, doesn't include many environmental and social costs. If these costs, called "externalities," were fully factored into the price of fuel, energy derived from oil would be more expensive and alternative fuel sources might be economically competitive.

This is not as simple as it sounds. For example, it is difficult to calculate the cost of thermal waste, air pollution, and potential spills. Furthermore, other energy sources have their own externalities that are equally difficult to pin down. The really big question is, how do we balance our concerns for self-sufficiency and the environment with our expectation of convenience and affordability provided us by energy from oil? You, for example, may have personal concerns about drilling for oil in the untouched wilderness of Alaska, or about possible damage to our scenic shoreline should an oil spill occur here. But what would you pay to protect the planet in general and Hawai'i in particular? Everything you have, or something less than that? How much less?

The oil industry in Hawai'i has committed millions of dollars to preventative programs and response equipment to protect us from oil spills. During the 1993 legislative session, the state enacted a fee to build a local fund that can supplement any amounts available from a $1 billion federal cleanup fund. Most political observers expect more such regulations and therefore higher costs for oil and oil products. All these additional costs will be passed on to consumers, and it is already expensive living in paradise. Consequently, everyone—including the oil industry—is looking to use this resource as efficiently as possible and to find viable alternatives. As an example, synthetic natural gas and propane, both products from the refining process, offer efficient clean-burning fuel for homes, businesses, and vehicles.

Coal makes up almost 90 percent of all known fossil reserves, but like oil it would have to be imported. Surveys taken in 1992 indicate that coal is the public's least favorite alternative to oil, but new technology may eventually change that. The modern Barber's Point plant is currently generating electricity with coal using an advanced technology. Other technologies exist for conversion of coal to liquid fuels. But expanded use of coal would require expensive new boilers, processors, and handling facilities—and so a whole new array of environmental issues, including disposal of solid waste, would have to be addressed.

HPOWER is a good example of Hawai'i finding ways to solve both our energy and land use problems. The HPOWER plant has been burning our solid waste in a high-temperature furnace since 1989, producing enough electricity for over 50,000 homes. More than two hundred garbage trucks per day deliver fuel to HPOWER, reducing the volume of solid waste going to Oʻahu landfills by an amazing 90 percent.

Renewable energy sources. Hawaiʻi is blessed with an abundance of naturally occurring resources such as wind, sunlight, geothermal heat, flowing water, and ocean resources. But, as of 1993, only 9 percent of our total energy needs were being supplied by such renewable sources, and that was mostly in the form of electricity from biomass combustion.

The current decline of Hawaiʻi's sugar industry casts doubts on the future availability of bagasse (a remnant of sugar cane processing used for fuel), but we may be able to develop another biomass fuel source.

Ongoing studies are evaluating the potential of different energy crops—including algae from the ocean. The use of such an indigenous source could help free Hawai'i from some of its dependence on oil, and it might offer environmental advantages as well. For example, net carbon dioxide output (which has been associated with global warming) would be zero because the burning of this material would release no more carbon dioxide than had been utilized by the growing crop. Local environmental issues, however, aren't so clear. Air pollution, soil erosion, and nutrient depletion would also have to be considered, as well as the amount of water that might be required.

Twenty hydropower plants owned and operated by the sugar plantations have been providing about 1 percent of our electrical needs. The amount of electricity sold varies with rainfall in these run-of-the-river plants. New hydropower plants have been proposed, but many are encountering delays because of environmental concerns.

Today's windfarms can generate electricity efficiently, but there are problems. Wind systems work only when the wind blows, and connection to the electric grid can cause operating problems. Assuming the best, wind is likely to contribute only a small percentage of our total electric generation needs. Some people, especially close neighbors, complain that windmills are ugly and loud.

Solar technology is commercially available and environmentally friendly. Sunlight can generate electricity directly through devices called photovoltaic cells or it can heat a fluid for conventional electricity generation. Photovoltaics make sense for small systems removed from the utility grid, but the cost of this solar-generated electricity is higher than most are willing to pay. Utility-scale thermal generators like those deployed in the Mojave Desert aren't likely to be cost effective in Hawai'i because of our poorer solar resource (these systems can't use sunlight scattered by moisture in the air) and the smaller systems required for our islands. Even solar technology involves externalities (e.g., the manufacture of solar cells can involve toxic materials), and some people would complain about acres of solar collectors for aesthetic and environmental reasons. Although electricity generation from the sun seems too expensive at this time, solar-heated hot water makes sense.

Given one of the most active volcanoes in the world, one would expect large-scale attempts in Hawai'i to capture the benefits from geothermal conversion. The technologies are well developed and have proven successful in such countries as New Zealand and Iceland. A commercial plant on the Big Island using hot steam from wells is currently producing enough electricity to meet almost one-fourth of that island's needs. Even conservative studies estimate the capacity for significantly more development, but the costs here entail more than money. Social and spiritual beliefs must be addressed. As anyone who reads the newspaper knows, those costs are way too high for some.

A process called ocean thermal energy conversion (OTEC) uses the temperature difference between the warm surface waters and cold deep waters to drive a turbine to produce electricity. OTEC has been under development in Hawai'i for over a decade, and experiments on the Kona Coast of the Big Island are demonstrating its potential. If costs can be brought down, the potential to meet our electricity needs is great. But many people might be expected to resist the construction of large plants that may have impacts on the shoreline environment.

Special dilemma. Renewables versus oil for electric generation cannot be looked at in isolation: approximately 61 percent of Hawai'i's oil consumption is for liquid fuels to power our cars, buses, airplanes, and boats. Jet fuel alone accounts for over 37 percent of our consumption. It gets us to where we want to go, but more important it brings us our tourists. With perhaps half of Hawai'i's jobs tied to the visitor industry, the availability and affordability of jet fuel are essential to Hawai'i's economy. There is no substitute today for jet fuel derived from oil.

For gasoline and diesel fuels, there are a few alternatives. Biomass crops can be converted to methanol or ethanol, but the availability of the land to grow these crops depends on the future of the sugar industry and the land it now dominates. And it's likely that the cost of our fuel, already the highest in the nation, would be even higher. Electric vehicles might be ideal in the future for Hawai'i's limited driving needs, but they would reduce our dependence on oil only if we change the way we generate our electricity.

What can be done? The energy industry must find ways to be energy efficient, and it must be willing to consider alternatives. Government must work with industry to assure that policy roadblocks are torn down

"HERE IT IS—OH, SHUCKS. WE'RE OUT OF C-BATTERIES..."

and must provide incentives to find solutions. And consumers need to be aware of conservation efforts in their homes and places of work.

The state government is working on an energy policy that would lessen our energy dependence. It relies heavily on Hawai'i's utilities to evaluate alternative fuels and to consider energy conservation and efficiency (demand-side management). In the meantime, we must realize that oil does serve a large demand in the state in a cost-effective manner. We must use all our energy efficiently in order to give us the time needed to build the best technologies for the future. If we don't pursue the technology of the future today, will it be there when we need it?

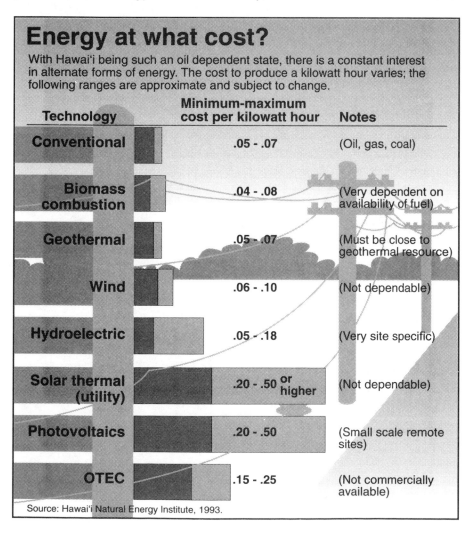

Energy at what cost?

With Hawai'i being such an oil dependent state, there is a constant interest in alternate forms of energy. The cost to produce a kilowatt hour varies; the following ranges are approximate and subject to change.

Technology	Minimum-maximum cost per kilowatt hour	Notes
Conventional	.05 - .07	(Oil, gas, coal)
Biomass combustion	.04 - .08	(Very dependent on availability of fuel)
Geothermal	.05 - .07	(Must be close to geothermal resource)
Wind	.06 - .10	(Not dependable)
Hydroelectric	.05 - .18	(Very site specific)
Solar thermal (utility)	.20 - .50 or higher	(Not dependable)
Photovoltaics	.20 - .50	(Small scale remote sites)
OTEC	.15 - .25	(Not commercially available)

Source: Hawai'i Natural Energy Institute, 1993.

"WE CAN CALL OFF THE EXERCISE, SIR—THE WHOLE TOWN OF WAHIAWA IS SURRENDERING..."

CHAPTER 38

MILITARY & ECONOMY

LEROY LANEY
Vice President and Chief Economist
First Hawaiian Bank

"Just how important is the military to Hawai'i's economy?"

The U.S. Defense Department budget has been targeted for massive cuts. The debate over where to cut and how much to cut has been, and will continue to be, an intensely political process. It will also be slow. Affected areas will feel the actual cuts when they occur, but even speculated cutbacks can be critical to regional economies.

Hawai'i's stake is hard to overestimate. A few other states are looking at larger numbers, but Hawai'i is at the top of the "vulnerability list" when the relevant criterion is share of state output.

Historical perspective. Hawai'i's economy grew dramatically during World War II. The annual rate of growth in personal income averaged 36 percent from 1940 to 1944. Predictably, Hawai'i's economy underwent an extreme contraction after the war, primarily because of reduced military spending. Personal income fell at an average annual rate of 15 percent from 1945 to 1949.

The military's percentage contribution to Hawai'i's economy has been shrinking steadily since then, but that has been due to growth elsewhere in our economy (i.e., tourism) rather than to a diminishing defense sector. Over the long haul, the military's contribution to our economy has been more stable than either tourism or agriculture.

The military in Hawai'i today. The military currently controls about 5 percent of land in the state—239,000 acres. By comparison, the State of Hawai'i controls 28 percent. About 10 percent of military land is owned in fee and 38 percent is leased from private owners. The remaining 52 percent is on loan from the state, which sets terms and compensation. Nine military properties have been conveyed to the state or sold since the 1970s, not including soon-to-be conveyed Kahoʻolawe and Barber's Point.

Hawaiʻi's military installations are concentrated on densely populated Oʻahu, where they occupy 23 percent of the land. Of that, 35 percent is owned in fee, 45 percent leased from private owners, and 20 percent on loan from the state.

Today, the total military expenditures in Hawaiʻi annually amount to about 12 percent of the annual gross state product. Despite the steady shrinkage of the military's economic role since World War II, the defense sector still ranks as Hawaiʻi's number-two export industry, after tourism.

The military's future in Hawaiʻi. Even if Hawaiʻi were untouched by cutbacks, the military's percentage contribution to our economy would continue to drift downward. This is because the rest of Hawaiʻi's

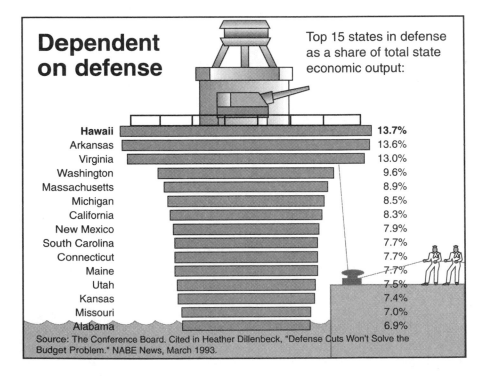

Dependent on defense

Top 15 states in defense as a share of total state economic output:

State	%
Hawaii	**13.7%**
Arkansas	13.6%
Virginia	13.0%
Washington	9.6%
Massachusetts	8.9%
Michigan	8.5%
California	8.3%
New Mexico	7.9%
South Carolina	7.7%
Connecticut	7.7%
Maine	7.7%
Utah	7.5%
Kansas	7.4%
Missouri	7.0%
Alabama	6.9%

Source: The Conference Board. Cited in Heather Dillenbeck, "Defense Cuts Won't Solve the Budget Problem." NABE News, March 1993.

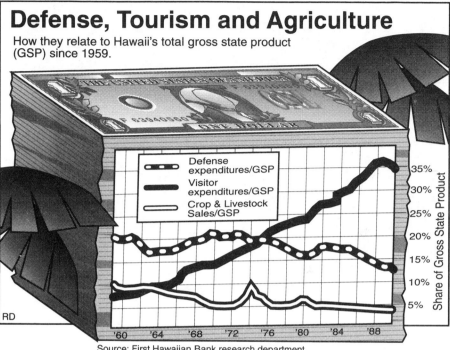

Defense, Tourism and Agriculture

How they relate to Hawaii's total gross state product (GSP) since 1959.

Defense expenditures/GSP

Visitor expenditures/GSP

Crop & Livestock Sales/GSP

Share of Gross State Product

35%
30%
25%
20%
15%
10%
5%

'60 '64 '68 '72 '76 '80 '84 '88

RD

Source: First Hawaiian Bank research department.

economy is expected to grow at some pace, while military expenditures are virtually certain not to increase. A realistic goal is to maintain that downward drift rather than lapse into a free fall. Sudden change would result in substantial hardship to many people in Hawai'i.

Hawai'i's vulnerability is more related to bases and personnel than to defense contracting firms. Thus, we will escape hits like those to California, where massive layoffs associated with a weakening defense industry have been particularly painful.

There has been much talk about programs that would facilitate the conversion of military technology to civilian applications. Hawai'i would not benefit significantly from this sort of thing because we have bases and personnel but very little else. Any "conversion funds" headed our way probably would take the form of direct subsidies, displaced worker training, or funding for new industry startup. Provision of any such funds is highly tentative in any case.

Hawai'i's advantages. Hawai'i's distinguishing characteristics include a strategic location and role as a command headquarters. Bases here are far forward, yet still in the United States. The global responsibility of the Hawai'i-based Commander-in-Chief Pacific (CINCPAC) extends from the U.S. west coast to the east coast of Africa, a geographic reach far larger than that of any other such command. It includes or at least serves logistically challenging spots such as North Korea, one border of the still volatile former Soviet Union, China and Southeast Asia, India/Pakistan, and the Middle East/Persian Gulf. Many of these areas are political hot spots that may get hotter.

In an atmosphere of federal budget reduction, combined with the collapse of the Soviet Union, some may forget that the world is still a dangerous place. The Cold War at least gave the world a certain predictable stability. Instead of a contest for global supremacy, the world now will likely see smaller regional conflicts that might be characterized as wars of interest, ethnicity, religion, culture, or conscience. The Gulf War, Somalia, and Bosnia stand as recent examples.

The fact that Hawai'i is in the middle of the Pacific Ocean and yet part of the United States is a critical advantage. Although we're only three to five hours closer than the mainland by air to any trouble spot in the CINCPAC area, airlift capacity and turnaround complications involved in massive deployments multiply that difference. And what is true for airlift is even truer for ships. In short, we have something the rest of the states will never have: location.

Obstacles to overcome. Despite Hawai'i's natural advantage, advocates of maintaining bases here must overcome several obstacles. The first is a certain Eurocentrism in global strategic affairs. Throughout the Cold War, it was the Soviet threat to Europe that was foremost in many minds. The Pacific has been viewed in some international circles more as an economy of force theater—one less likely to ever receive large increases in funding and resources.

Another obstacle is the fact that many people in Hawai'i fail to appreciate the military. Other places with a major military presence seem more aware of the military's contribution to their local economies and are willing to do more to retain it. In Hawai'i, this neglect is exacerbated by several factors: among them are scarce land and housing, native Hawaiian sovereignty issues, and environmental questions.

The greatest obstacle to maintaining military bases in Hawai'i is the same factor that discourages our economy's diversification into entirely new enterprises. Like so many other undertakings in Hawai'i, military installations are extremely expensive to operate. In the past, cost may not have been the overriding factor in Pentagon decisions, but it has kept Hawai'i's bases under constant scrutiny. The military, ever concerned about the welfare and quality of life of its personnel, does not look favorably on the economic hardships that must be endured by those stationed here as a result of our high cost of living.

Critical mass. There is a certain critical mass in maintaining military functions in Hawai'i. Reduction beyond some point is likely to mean relocation of an entire force. A good example is land now used for training. It may seem rational to convert some such properties to civilian use, but failure to provide training facilities locally may lead to the loss of the units that use them.

One specific example concerns the possible loss of the Pohakuloa Training Area (PTA) on the Big Island. This area has cultural significance and is home to several endangered species, so both Hawaiian

rights and environmental forces are working hard to "liberate" the PTA from military occupation. But if the PTA is lost, arguments for stationing ground troops in Hawai'i are weakened greatly. The 25th Light Infantry Division at Schofield Barracks and the Marine Expeditionary Brigade at Kane'ohe Marine Corps Air Station might then be withdrawn.

Conclusion. In land-short Hawai'i, any conversion of military real estate to civilian use is tempting. But, when one balances the known economic contributions from military use against the possible benefits of any proposed civilian use, it is far from clear that the latter is more desirable. This is particularly true in that the military use qualifies unambiguously as a true "export" industry—one that brings money to the state rather than simply recirculating what's already here. Civilian use—a housing project, for example—might provide a temporary injection to the construction industry, but it would not continue to inject external funds into the economy year after year as the military does.

It is often overlooked that many businesses in Hawai'i that give the economy a diversified appearance owe their existence to secondary spending out of the military's primary export stream. As tourism slows, agriculture fades, and diversification into new export industries eludes the state, keeping the military is all the more important.

The force of the Armed Forces

Since statehood, the military's share of total residents in Hawaii has declined.

10%

Military share of total residents

5%

0%

'60   '65   '70   '75   '80   '85   '90

Source: State of Hawai'i, Department of Business, Economic
Development and Tourism, Data Book 1992, table 3.

'A gusher! From number one well...'

CHAPTER 39

CONGRESSIONAL REPRESENTATION

PETER ROSEGG
Journalist
Honolulu Advertiser

"How well are we being represented in Washington D.C.?"

One answer to this question can be found in *Roll Call*, an independent newspaper of politics and personalities widely read on Capitol Hill. One of its annual studies, "Clout on the Hill," notes the power of each state's congressional delegation according to a complicated list of factors, like members' seniority and the posts they hold.

For the 103rd Congress (1993/94), Hawai'i ranks thirty-third in "clout," even though our population, according to the 1990 census, places us fortieth of fifty states. Not bad for a small, isolated state far from Washington.

"Bringing home the bacon." One of the factors that *Roll Call* and many others consider in ranking clout is how much each state receives in federal funds. It's fashionable these days to stick one's nose up at old-style pork-barrel politics, but looking after the home front is taken for granted in Washington. All members do it, and failure to do so is seen as the way to lose elections.

It's been estimated that Hawai'i received one dollar in federal spending for every 92 cents paid in federal taxes for 1992. But then, numbers don't tell the whole story. How is the money spent? The answer is not entirely satisfying. Per capita defense spending in Hawai'i was fourth *highest* in the nation in 1990. But for all nondefense spending, Hawai'i was fifth *lowest*. Not so hot.

Beyond the numbers. *Roll Call's* clout survey is purely quantitative calculation. It tells nothing about such subjective topics as what members of Congress have accomplished or what reputations they have.

Few major bills or programs carry the name of a Hawai'i lawmaker, with the possible exception of the late Senator Spark Matsunaga's work, most notably the apology and reparations for Japanese Americans wrongfully interned during World War II. Nor are Hawai'i legislators big players in national debates on budgets, taxes, and war or the reorganization of Congress and reform of campaign spending laws.

One political science professor in Washington who follows Congress closely had this to say about the Hawai'i delegation: "Overall, my impression is they are a poor bunch. They are better known for constituent services and protecting major industries like defense, tourism and, to a lesser extent, agriculture." That sounds critical, but it would be taken as a compliment by many in Congress; there are worse "sins" than taking good care of constituents.

Senator Daniel Inouye

Senator Daniel Inouye. In Washington, Senator Inouye is regarded with respect and even an awe that in some quarters borders on dread. He is acknowledged as an inside player of consummate skill and long experience, extremely knowledgeable in such areas as military spending and foreign aid, and a hard bargainer for causes he believes in. He is a very private man, reserved, and aloof to the point of seeming arrogant.

Inouye is legendary for his loyalty to the institution of the Senate and to his colleagues there. His key role in the two most important ethics cases since World War II (Watergate and Iran-contra) put him in a position to defend other senators, including the notorious "Keating Five" of the savings-and-loan scandals. That won him no points at home, but he did earn the gratitude of fellow senators, adding to his influence.

Inouye, who has sat on the powerful Appropriations Committee since 1971, now also chairs its subcommittee on defense, making him one of the so-called cardinals in Congress.

Is Inouye's hand on the defense purse strings all that crucial? Most defense dollars for Hawai'i would probably be spent here anyway at the behest of Pentagon brass. As evidence of Hawai'i's strategic value in the Pacific, in two rounds of base closings by an impartial, independent commission immune to congressional meddling, the state fared better than many others. It lost only one major—but not critical—base.

But Inouye's position does more than give him a huge say in *how* defense dollars are spent in Hawai'i; just as important, it enables him to take care of the wishes of other senators who control other federal spending Hawai'i may need. That's how the Washington game of trade-offs is played, and Inouye is Hawai'i's heaviest hitter.

Inouye also chairs the Senate Committee on Indian Affairs, a politically thankless task, though its jurisdiction includes native Hawaiians. But some people (and not just Hawaiian activists) ask if Inouye is happier spending time on mainland Indian reservations than laboring at the difficult task of gaining federal recognition for Hawaiians, like that of other native Americans, to say nothing of some form of sovereignty.

Inouye has long been a jealous guardian of his good reputation for the highest personal integrity. But he has had his well-publicized embarrassments. In 1987, he inserted into the foreign aid budget $8 million to build religious schools for North African Jews living in France. In 1990, he sought to provide $50 million in federal funds to expand the hospital at private George Washington University in Washington, where he graduated and served as a trustee. Both appropriations were withdrawn or blocked when they drew public attention. But such actions led one Honolulu columnist to label Inouye the "prince of pork." Unlike most "pork," these monies did nothing for Hawai'i.

Senator Daniel Akaka

Senator Daniel Akaka. Senator Akaka is still too junior in the Senate to aspire to any substantial leadership or committee post, even if he would be comfortable in that sort of limelight. His assignments, like Veterans Affairs and Governmental Operations, have some value to Hawai'i, but they are not the choicest to be had.

Akaka was seen as a Democratic party stalwart but something of a nonentity while he served fourteen years in the House. Being in the much smaller Senate has barely given him a higher profile, although he chairs a minor subcommittee of the Energy and Natural Resources Committee. Asked about his major goals, he expounds on his efforts at educating fellow senators about Hawai'i rather than discuss particulars of Hawai'i's needs, much less controversial national issues.

But, like Senator Matsunaga before him, Akaka is extremely amiable. He is seen as a fellow who looks after Hawai'i's interests first, foremost, and finally. With his genial personality and gentle manner, when he asks for something important to Hawai'i in his heartfelt way, he must be hard to turn down.

Akaka, the first senator of Hawaiian ancestry, also sits on Inouye's Indian Affairs Committee. He got the Senate to agree to a resolution of apology for the overthrow of the Hawaiian kingdom in time for the centennial commemoration in January 1993, but he was deeply disappointed when the House refused to act.

Akaka may not have the intellect or breadth of esoteric interests that Matsunaga brought to the Senate, but many who deal with him often come away with the sense that Akaka is almost certainly a lot smarter than he lets on.

"YOU HAVE MY APOLOGY..."

Representative
Neil Abercrombie

Representative
Patsy Mink

Representatives Neil Abercrombie and Patsy Mink. Hawai'i's
two House representatives, Neil Abercrombie and Patsy Mink, have
similar liberal voting records and both are described as feisty, opinion-
ated, and outspoken. But in many other ways they are a study in
contrasts. He is haole flashy, she AJA reserved. He is easygoing with
staff, taking their friendly criticism in stride; she prides herself as a
taskmaster, working herself even longer hours than her staff. His
committee choices reflect parochial Hawai'i's needs; hers deal with
broader national issues.

Abercrombie's committees parallel Inouye's. On the House Armed
Services Committee, says *The Almanac of American Politics*, "he can
vote against defense spending generally but for spending to help
Honolulu area service families." On the Natural Resources Committee,
which controls national parks and other federal lands, Abercrombie sits
on the Indian Affairs subcommittee, counterpart of the full committee
chaired by Inouye.

Though still best known for his beard, ponytail, and a hip reputation, Abercrombie's combative, sometimes abrasive, '60s radical image
has mellowed, politically and personally. He surprised many by leading

286

a spirited fight for the "three-martini lunch," more soberly known as the tax deduction for business travel and entertainment expenses, in the name of saving tourism and restaurant industry jobs. And he goes out of his way to be a more convivial, sympathetic listener to other members.

Patsy Mink, returning after a thirteen-year absence, lost the seniority from her previous six terms in Congress. But she can draw on her acquaintance with senior members now risen to positions of power. She took up where she left off, with reassignment to the Committee on Education and Labor, lifelong interests to her. She also serves again on Natural Resources and on the Budget Committee, which brings prestige if not great power.

As a trail-blazing Japanese American woman lawyer, Mink has also dealt with women's equity issues all her life and remains a very active leader in the Congressional Women's Caucus. Caucus leaders pushed her for an important leadership position in 1992 and, though not chosen, she was elected to the influential Democratic party panel that assigns members to committees.

Mink is seen as an extremely serious, principled legislator, dependably liberal but not afraid to go against the party leadership on matters of importance, as can be seen by her strong opposition to NAFTA—the free trade agreement with Canada and Mexico—which would be harmful to the Hawaiian sugar industry.

Ultimate standard. In Washington, members of Congress are judged by many standards: ability to legislate, skill at communication, political agility, even honesty and integrity. Power is accumulated by longevity and gaining positions of influence in the leadership and on major committees. But, ultimately, power within the institution and the esteem of other lawmakers mean nothing unless members get reelected. So, as a practical matter, it counts little what Washington thinks. The opinion about the job being done by Hawai'i's congressional delegation that counts is the opinion of the majority of those at home who bother to vote.

By that standard, Hawai'i lawmakers have been very successful. Only ambition for higher office, retirement, or death has ever removed a Hawai'i legislator. No member of Congress from Hawai'i has ever been voted out of office by the people.

"RELAX—YOU AND I KNOW A LI'L GOLF GAME DIDN'T INFLUENCE YOUR DECISION OR YOUR VOTE..."

CHAPTER 40

CRONYISM

JERRY BURRIS
Editorial Page Editor
Honolulu Advertiser

"Has Hawai'i been hurt by cronyism in government?"

A lot of folks believe so. They see Island politics (which means, mostly, Democratic politics) as an inbred playground for cronies, who only talk to and care about fellow insiders. Fresh blood and new ideas are kept out; goodies and the spoils of political domination are hoarded among themselves. Consider, for example, a few recent stories:

• A rogue head of the Office of Environmental Quality Control hands out contract after contract to friends without regard to bidding and apparently even without much concern about whether the work had any value.

• A former legislator and deputy comptroller sidesteps the competitive bidding process by parceling government purchases to friends.

• A rush order for new computers is handed to the budget director's golf buddy on orders from the budget director himself.

• The governor nominates a close political associate (and, incidentally, wife of the outgoing attorney general) for a seat on the Hawai'i Supreme Court.

Public gags. The public truly howled on the last one, and even the normally docile State Senate revolted, surprising itself by rejecting the nomination of youthful attorney Sharon Himeno. The rejection was not centered on Himeno's political philosophy, legal qualifications, or even allegations of conflicts of interest. It was a gag reflex by voters and lawmakers who had simply had it up to here with what they perceived to be arrogant cronyism by an entrenched political elite.

If the fuss had been made simply by the traditional complainers (Republicans, newcomers, and so forth), it might have been dismissed as business as usual. But it wasn't. A well-attended town meeting in Manoa, for example, erupted into a long, loud, and 100 percent negative discussion when the Himeno nomination was raised. "Real people" of all races, many of whom had been born and raised in Hawai'i and had thought they had "seen it all," were outraged.

Insiders complain. State Senator Mike McCartney talks about a "Mega Club," a nexus involving the political parties, powerful unions, big banks, land trusts, and major downtown firms that cough up the money to keep the Club in political tune. The Mega Club runs things nowadays, McCartney says. It's another way to describe "the old boy network" in which it no longer matters what you know—"it's who you know." In short, cronyism.

McCartney's plaint is striking. Yet look at *his* background: teacher, negotiator for the teachers union, and now lawmaker. His mentor, Charles Toguchi, had gone from teaching to the union to the legislature on his way to being superintendent of the State Department of Education. Interestingly, understudy McCartney has followed the same route, including service as chairman of the Senate Education Committee. In short, the politically privileged McCartney looks as much a product of the crony system as he is a frustrated victim. Interesting.

Beyond politics. What we call cronyism actually goes beyond politics. People in Hawai'i (like people in other insular places) tend to deal with each other based on past associations, kinship, and shared experience. To an outsider, this looks like cronyism and it's bad. To an insider, it's ohana and it's perfectly natural. Why wouldn't you tend to favor old buddies from school or the war years? What, you're going to treat your auntie's son-in-law like a stranger?

Imagine the frustration of a newcomer to the Islands trying to get his car fixed at the local garage. He's impatient, anxious, and not even sure what kind of communication he has established with the local service station owner. Then in drives the owner's high school buddy. "Howzits" are exchanged and immediately they're cooking on the same wave length. The newcomer, not even sure what is being said, drives off steaming. You can't get anything done around here unless you went to high school with someone and speak pidgin, he mutters to himself.

Not true. But it helps, whether it involves getting a car repaired, successfully arguing a case before a local jury, or getting an important piece of business rushed through government bureaucracy. In each case our newcomer is likely to experience, not hostility toward himself or even his impatient ways, but a level of comfort and understanding between people who may have known each other a long time and who, in any event, share a common culture, a common experience. Right on, bruddah.

But should government work this way?

Unequal opportunities. We all pay our taxes and are entitled to equal opportunities, equal treatment. That's why Gavan Daws and George Cooper's *Land and Power in Hawai'i* created such a stir. That book documented how the Democratic powers who came to run politics in Hawai'i during the post-statehood years also became prime winners in the land boom that followed. Time and again, those who had political connections were shown to benefit from the development that government encouraged and controlled. The closer one was to the system, the better one did at all this. It was a crony network that paid off handsomely to its members.

It was also a crony system that "worked," politically, because for a rare moment the interests of the "good old boys" (economic growth, broadened social opportunities, development) coincided with the interests of a broad majority of the people. And the dominant Democrats were able to articulate those interests in a way that appealed to the voters.

In the late 1970s, a group attempted to forge a new coalition of idealistic "local" activists who would see to it that the social gains and special nature of Hawaiian society would not be lost to haole or outside influences: "Let's accept what's good from the rest of the United States (and indeed the Pacific Rim) but not apologize for, or lose, what is special about our own way of doing things." It was called Palaka Power, and its credo *sounds* pretty good, even today. But most observers believe Palaka Power became just another wheel of cronies, in power and in politics, to serve themselves and each other.

A related network developed out of the first few graduating classes of the UH Law School and, to a degree, the 1978 Constitutional

Convention. Both institutions produced people who considered themselves heirs to the power and influence held at that time by the postwar generation of Democrats. And they did indeed rise to power, much more quickly and completely than many had expected. Unfortunately, this group has generated more complaints of cronyism than any other. And as idealistic as the first UH Law School graduates and Con Con delegates were, it's tough to point to a political philosophy (or group goal) that holds them together today. There are strains of the proud localism found in Palaka Power, an environmental awareness that didn't exist in earlier groups, and a grudging acknowledgment that the needs of native Hawaiians must be redressed. But that's about it— hardly enough to define a political movement.

In both cases —Palaka Power and the law school group—there was a conscious effort to recreate the somewhat idealized sense of political mission associated with earlier Democrats. Unfortunately, today's generation doesn't have the crucible of World War II or the symbolic power of the statehood drive to bind them.

Need vision. The challenge for such groups, then, is to define their goals, philosophy, and hopes for Hawai'i in ways that go beyond their own individual political and economic survival. If they do that, the public will decide for itself whether Hawai'i is being led in the proper direction. Cronyism will become a moot issue.

If they fail, if they lack vision (or fail to articulate it), the public will be forced to conclude that those who make up this emerging generation of politicians have little going for themselves other than the fact that they know each other, share a few common experiences, are comfortable with each other—and that they are cronies.

AT A CROSSROAD ...

CHAPTER 41

SOVEREIGNTY

MAHEALANI KAMAU'U
Executive Director
Native Hawaiian Legal Corporation

H. K. BRUSS KEPPELER
Attorney at Law
Lyons Brandt Cook & Hiramatsu

"What might sovereignty look like?"

In less than a decade, the subject of Hawaiian sovereignty has evolved from a misunderstood and feared underground radicalism to a mainstream object of enlightened debate, the stuff of dinner table conversation. Has sovereignty changed or have we?

Proponents of Hawaiian sovereignty have deep philosophical differences among themselves, but one can more or less align them into three groupings: (1) those propounding complete *separation* from the United States and a return to status as an independent, internationally recognized Hawaiian nation; (2) those advocating *nation-within-a-nation* status with federal recognition as a new native American nation; and (3) those desirous of maintaining the *political status quo* while pressing for redress, reparations, and full control of Hawaiian trust assets by Hawaiians. All three views may prove important to the debate's outcome.

The separatists. The earliest, still-active advocate of separation is Poka Laenui, also known as Hayden Burgess, director of the Institute for the Advancement of Hawaiian Affairs.

Burgess's dream is for a decolonized Hawai'i, formed into an independent nation, in which citizenship is available to those who pledge their allegiance to Hawai'i and to no other nation: "We cannot build a Hawaiian Nation on racism," says Burgess. "The Nation of Hawai'i in 1893 was composed of citizens of the indigenous Hawaiian race as well as people of many other races and cultures. The crucial determination for citizenship was not race but relationship to Hawai'i."

He warns, though, that the national history and indigenous cultural roots must continue to form the foundation of the Hawaiian nation. He urges that policies be changed with respect to foreign ownership of land (including American ownership), collective rights of ownership or use, and special uses by Hawaiians. He suggests that strong steps be taken to prevent further degradation of nonrenewable resources and he promotes self-sufficiency for Hawai'i. The Hawaiian nation would lessen its foreign dependence by increasing the number and diversity of its trade partners. As a nation, it would be able to do what the State of Hawai'i could never do: place limitations on immigration. "We cannot continue a policy of unlimited foreign infiltration into Hawai'i. We are islands with finite land resources."

The governmental form would be a matter for its citizens to decide. As with any nation, Hawai'i would control its own international relations, establish diplomatic posts around the world, and join regional and international forums. U.S. control of military bases in Hawai'i would end.

The territory of the reemerged Hawaiian nation would include all the lands and waters that form the present state, plus Kalama (Johnston), Midway, and Palmyra Islands. When asked if he'd be willing to settle for Kaho'olawe, plus the Hawaiian Homestead lands and the ceded lands, Burgess replied, "If someone stole eight of your children, would you be satisfied if he returned only one and bits and pieces of the other seven?"

Another separatist. Like the Institute for the Advancement of Hawaiian Affairs, Ka Pākaukau seeks ultimate independence and the reestablishment of the Hawaiian nation with complete U.S. withdrawal. Kekuni Blaisdell, spokesman for Ka Pākaukau, differs with Burgess, however, in that he suggests that nation-within-a-nation status could be a step along the path to complete independence:

To begin the transition toward the goal of kū'oko'a (independence), Ka Pākaukau proposes a series of treaties to be negotiated by representatives of the two nations as equals. . . .

The first treaty will clearly declare the long-range goal of *complete* kanaka maoli independence, with U.S. *withdrawal.* Meanwhile, as an initial, interim step, the first treaty will provide for us kanaka maoli, *all* of the measures now theoretically recognized by the U.S. for American Indian and Alaskan Native tribes and nations, namely, *return of our lands and recognition of our government, separate from the U.S. and state.*

Ka Pākaukau asserts that *all* acts that brought Hawai'i into its present status were illegal under both international law and the U.S. Constitution, and that the truth of this fact has been intentionally hidden or distorted as part of an official U.S. policy of colonialism, exploitation, coercive assimilation, and aggression. The *only* remedy is U.S. withdrawal and Hawai'i's complete independence.

Ka Pākaukau demands respect for the dignity and diversity of all people, including indigenous people, "rather than dominant Western homogenization and arrogant supremacy." It seeks reason, justice, peace, and nonviolence "in place of authoritarianism, racism, militarism and cynical legalism." It pledges itself to self-determination and independence with "taro roots, community-based, consensus democracy."

More separatists. A new proposal for independence surfaced at a Hawaiian Sovereignty Economic Symposium held on June 5, 1993. Michael Kioni Dudley, of Na Kane O Ka Malo, presented a model he called "Some Islands, Hawaiian Nation—Some Islands, State." This model calls for a dividing up of Hawai'i into three separate, temporary jurisdictions: a new Hawaiian nation, a U.S. state jurisdiction, and the Cooperative Zone in the Honolulu area. "The continuing existence of the State and the establishment of a Cooperative Zone both allow for a more gradual evolution to full nationhood for the entire island chain. But the ultimate goal is full decolonization."

Another goal of this model is to curtail immigration, with the expectation that the percentage of people with Hawaiian blood would steadily increase as a result of intermarriage.

There are other proponents of separation from the United States, notably the ʻOhana Council of the Hawaiian Kingdom. The ʻOhana Council adheres strongly to the precept that "those who maintain and assert their self-government, their freedom from outside domination, and their own economic, social and cultural development are most likely to eventually gain international recognition as people who have the right to self-determination, regardless of formal rules." Thus, the ʻOhana Council has taken steps to manifest its inherent right to self-governance by occupying and utilizing Hawaiian trust lands.

Other groups agree substantially with the main concepts embodied in the models proposed by Mr. Burgess's group, Ka Pākaukau, and the ʻOhana Council.

Nation-within-a-nation. The oldest group espousing the "nation-within-a-nation" model of Hawaiian sovereignty is Ka Lāhui Hawaiʻi. Headed by Kiaʻāina (Governor) Mililani Trask, Ka Lāhui was established in 1987 by 250 delegates who attended its first constitutional convention held in Keaukaha, Hawaiʻi. Ka Lāhui has had two additional constitutional conventions since then. Its approach is simple and direct:

> Ka Lāhui seeks inclusion of the Hawaiian People in the existing U.S. federal policy which affords all Native Americans the right to self-government and provides access to federal courts for judicial review. . . . Precedents for America's native people to be self-determining and self-governing has already been set—hundreds of times; Hawaiians are a native people and are entitled to self-governance just as other native groups have been afforded.

To accomplish these objectives, Ka Lāhui has enacted a detailed constitution which establishes four branches of government, including legislative, executive, and judicial branches as well as an Aliʻi Nui branch which is responsible for all matters relating to culture, traditions, and protocol.

Ka Lāhui boasts a citizenship of about 18,000 members, or approximately 7 percent of the total Hawaiian populace. Anyone of Hawaiian ancestry may enroll as a citizen of Ka Lāhui. Citizens 18 years or older gain the right to vote in all elections after one year's enrollment. Non-Hawaiians can be granted honorary citizenship but are not entitled to vote.

Despite the rhetoric of some of its leaders, the approach Ka Lāhui has taken toward sovereignty is actually quite conservative. Under its model, Hawaiians will generally continue to live, work, and worship as they do today. Jobs, social security, retirement, or pension from the United States or the State of Hawai'i will not be affected. The primary change is that Hawaiian lands and assets will be managed and controlled by laws passed by a Hawaiian legislature. "Hawaiians would elect Hawaiians to represent Hawaiian interests and concerns."

Perhaps the largest group (30,000 members) formulating a plan for Hawaiian sovereignty is the State Council of Hawaiian Homestead Associations (SCHHA). Although established primarily to address the concerns of homesteaders and would-be homesteaders, SCHHA has turned its attention to the issue of sovereignty. This organization points out that its membership, already living on lands that in many ways resemble trust lands reserved for native Americans on the mainland, can bring a special insight into the battle for sovereignty. Many of its

"HAWAIIAN HOMESTEAD ? OH, IT'S SOMETHING LIKE A LOTTERY MY FATHER KEPT BETTING ON..."

members believe, as do citizens of Ka Lāhui, that they have already achieved sovereignty, with the organization and structure in place to run it, and simply need federal recognition of these facts.

Political status quo. This approach to the redress of Hawaiian claims is not a sovereignty movement, but it must be discussed if we are to see a full landscape of the issues.

Many Hawaiians are reasonably happy with the existing forms of government but irate over past wrongs (see Chapter 30 of *The Price of Paradise*, Volume I). They stand forthright behind initiatives that would give Hawaiians as a class the right to sue the United States for reparations and redress. They believe it's high time that a formal and official apology be given by the U.S. government to the Hawaiian people for the wrongs committed. And they are watching eagerly to see the result of ongoing efforts to win further redress from the state for its breaches of trust as well as those of the predecessor territorial government.

These Hawaiians are keenly aware of the loss of water rights, the erosion of the Hawaiian private trust assets, and the sad health and social statistics of Hawaiians. And they want something done about it *now*. But they enjoy federal, state, and county services. They get federal, state, or county paychecks or pension checks. They are intrigued by all the talk and commotion and proud that Hawaiians are speaking out. But, when the cards are down, they can't see themselves taking that final step to sovereignty.

Moving ahead. A long and challenging path lies ahead for the Hawaiian sovereignty movement. There will be strenuous debate and pervasive disagreement. To comment on this process, one cannot improve on the following, which appeared in a Ka Lāhui publication:

> The advantage of living in a democratic society is that people can embrace their own ideals. The Hawaiian community is moving ahead with sovereignty through its discussions and even through its differences. Some might call this "infighting," but remember that disagreement occurs only when you have commitment to an issue—people fight for things worth fighting for. No ethnic group agrees on everything— Hawaiians are no different.

"AUWE, I THOUGHT IT WOULD BE A NICE FAMILY THING TO DISCUSS SOVEREIGNTY..."

BIOGRAPHICAL SKETCHES

Peter S. Adler Executive Director, Hawai'i Bar Foundation. Ph.D. in sociology, Union Graduate School. Helped establish the Neighborhood Justice Center of Honolulu and the Judiciary's Center for Alternative Dispute Resolution; has taught, consulted, and written in the field of mediation and alternative dispute resolution and is the author of *Beyond Paradise: Encounters in Hawai'i Where the Tour Bus Never Runs*.

Jerry Burris Editorial Page Editor, *Honolulu Advertiser*. Former *Advertiser* City Editor and for nearly twenty years the *Advertiser*'s chief political reporter and columnist. Former Jefferson Fellow and Fulbright-Hays grantee in Southeast Asia.

Desmond J. Byrne Owner of Honolulu Information Service, performing business and government research and tracking large estates in Hawai'i. Chartered accountant (England). M.B.A., University of Hawai'i. Administrative and financial officer of companies in Hong Kong, Bahamas, and Hawai'i (since 1960).

George Darby J.D., M.B.A., Chair of the Hawai'i Bar Association Technology Committee. Twenty-three years' experience consulting on information technology and intellectual property; law practice concentrates in technology law, and clients include several companies with plans to introduce new telecommunications services in Hawai'i.

James Dooley Staff writer for the *Honolulu Advertiser* since 1974; broke the Kukui Plaza scandal at City Hall in 1975; full-time investigative reporter since 1978; has written extensively on subjects including Japanese organized crime activities in the United States and corruption and abuse in federal, state, and local government in Hawai'i.

Dolores Foley Assistant Professor of Public Administration, University of Hawai'i. Ph.D. in public administration, University of Southern California. Research focuses on international and local nongovernmental organizations and on collaboration between the public, private, and nonprofit sectors.

Chuck Freedman Vice President of Corporate Relations, Hawaiian Electric Company. Former Director of Communications in the cabinet of Governor John Waihee; chief planner for community action agencies on the Big Island and in Micronesia; starred as the monster created from nuclear waste in the classic film *Horror of Party Beach*.

Peter V. Garrod Professor of Agricultural and Resource Economics, University of Hawai'i. Ph.D. in agricultural economics, University of California. Member of the University of Hawai'i faculty for twenty-one years; publishes extensively in the areas of marketing, transportation, and agriculture in Hawai'i.

Thomas P. Gill Attorney at law. J.D., University of California. Former state legislator, U.S. congressman, lieutenant governor. Democratic County chairman, 1954–58; Board member, ACLU Hawai'i; part-time curmudgeon.

John Griffin Editorial Page Editor of the *Honolulu Advertiser*, recently retired to freelance writing. Former Asia correspondent for the Associated Press and program evaluator for the Peace Corps. Pursued graduate study at Bristol University in England.

Meheroo Jussawalla Senior Fellow, East-West Center. Ph.D. in economics. International authority and author of five recent books and scores of journal articles in the field of telecommunications economics; editorial board member of the journal *Information Economics and Policy*.

Lowell L. Kalapa President, Tax Foundation of Hawai'i. M.A. in journalism, Northwestern University. The Tax Foundation, a nonprofit research group, works with elected officials, community groups, and the public at large to bring about a better understanding of state and local government finances.

Mahealani Kamau'u Executive Director, Native Hawaiian Legal Corporation. Board member of the Native American Rights Fund. Actively involved in a variety of civic and Hawaiian organizations, including the Judiciary's Center for Alternative Dispute Resolution; Hui Na'auao, a sovereignty education consortium; and the Hawaiian Sovereignty Advisory Commission. 1990 State Bar Association Liberty Bell Award winner.

Kent M. Keith President, Chaminade University. Former Coordinator, Deputy Director, and Director, State of Hawai'i Department of Planning and Economic Development; Chair, State Plan Policy Council; Project Manager, Mililani Technology Park; and Vice President for Public Relations and New Business Development, Oceanic Properties, Inc.

H. K. Bruss Keppeler J.D., University of Washington. Of counsel, Lyons Brandt Cook & Hiramatsu, concentrating in real estate, corporate, and estate-planning law; President of the Association of Hawaiian Civic Clubs and advocate for the preservation of Hawaiian culture and the betterment of conditions for Hawaiians.

Leroy O. Laney Vice President and Chief Economist, First Hawaiian Bank, since 1990; Ph.D. in economics, University of Colorado; M.B.A., Emory University. Served in the Federal Reserve System, the U.S. Treasury, and the President's Council of Economic Advisers, as well as in academia.

Cori Lau Executive Director, Hawai'i Institute for Continuing Legal Education. J.D., Lewis and Clark Northwestern School of Law. 1993 President of Hawai'i Women Lawyers; member of the Board of Directors of the Hawai'i Women's Legal Foundation; past co-chair of the Gender and Other Fairness Committee of HSBA. Previous law practice in maritime, personal injury defense, and employment law.

Carol Mon Lee Attorney in private practice; formerly Senior Vice President of American Financial Services of Hawai'i; staff attorney for the 1978 Hawai'i Constitutional Convention; former faculty member of the Richardson School of Law, University of Hawai'i.

James Mak Professor of Economics, University of Hawai'i. Ph.D. in economics, Purdue University. Authority on Hawaiian economics and the tourist industry; publishes extensively in the area of tourism and is on the editorial board of the *Journal of Travel Research*.

George Mason Editorial Page Editor and Publisher Emeritus, *Pacific Business News*. Founded Crossroads Press in 1963 to publish *Pacific Business News* after eight years as Territorial and State Director of Economic Development; numerous leadership positions in nonprofit organizations in Hawai'i, including Chair of the Chamber of Commerce of Hawai'i, Better Business Bureau, and Junior Achievement.

David McClain Henry A. Walker, Jr., Distinguished Professor of Business Enterprise and Financial Economics and Institutions, College of Business Administration, University of Hawai'i. Ph.D. in economics, M.I.T. Taught at M.I.T., Boston University, and Keio University, Tokyo; senior staff economist on the Council of Economic Advisers under President Jimmy Carter; author of *Apocalypse on Wall Street*.

John C. McLaren Associate Attorney in the Law Office of Dennis W. S. Chang. Former legislative aide to U.S. Representative and Senator Spark Matsunaga (1975–80), community activist, and Neighborhood Board member.

Roderick F. McPhee President, Punahou School, since 1968. Ph.D. in educational administration, University of Chicago. Educator since 1950. Former Director, Advanced Administrative Institute, Harvard Graduate School of Education; and Superintendent of Schools, Glencoe, Illinois. Coauthor of *The Organization and Control of American Schools*.

Walter Miklius Professor of Economics and Agricultural Economics, University of Hawai'i, since 1967. Ph.D. in economics, University of California at Los Angeles; taught at the University of California at Davis; economist with the U.S. Department of Agriculture in Washington, D.C.

Neal Milner Professor of Political Science, University of Hawai'i. Member and Director (1989–93) of the University of Hawai'i Program on Conflict Resolution; mediator and meeting facilitator for the Center for Alternative Dispute Resolution. Author of works on the politics of rights, mental health policy, and leasehold land; coauthor with Sally Merry of *The Possibilities of Popular Justice*. Owns a leasehold condo.

Seiji Naya Chairman, Department of Economics, and Professor of Economics, University of Hawai'i. Ph.D., University of Wisconsin. Former Director, Resource Systems Institute, and Vice President, East-West Center. Activities focused on Asia-Pacific economic problems and possibilities for economic cooperation. Past advisor to several UN organizations and author of books including *A Free Trade Area: Implications for ASEAN* and *Economic Success and Policy Lessons*.

Francis S. Oda AIA, AICP. Chairman and Chief Executive Officer, Group 70 International. Architect and planner for projects in Hawai'i, Australia, China, Japan, other Pacific nations, including the City of Kapolei, Lodge at Koele, and Manele Bay Hotel. Past President of the Hawai'i Society, American Institute of Architects; board member of the Hawai'i Visitors Bureau and Historic Hawai'i.

Franklin Odo Director, Ethnic Studies Program, University of Hawai'i. Research and teaching on topics related to Asians in America, with particular emphasis on Japanese Americans. Former faculty member at UCLA, Long Beach State College, the University of Pennsylvania, and Kansei Gakuin University.

Norman H. Okamura Associate Specialist, Social Science Research Institute. Specialist in telecommunications and information technology policy, planning, and systems management. Former Senior Manager, KPMG Peat Marwick; Administrator, Information and Communication Services Division, State Department of Budget and Finance; Assistant Professor and Projects Administrator, Department of Urban and Regional Planning, University of Hawai'i.

Michael J. O'Malley J.D., Harvard Law School. Partner, Goodsill Anderson Quinn & Stifel. Tax attorney engaged in tax transactional and planning matters; Chair of the Hawai'i State Bar Association, Tax Section; pro bono legal counsel to Hawai'i State Foster Parents Association and other nonprofit organizations; foster/adoptive parent to twelve children in six years.

Nancy J. O'Malley M.A in public administration, Columbia University. Board member, Windward Coalition of Churches. Former Officer and Director, Hawai'i State Foster Parents Association; foster/adoptive parent to twelve children in six years.

Nicholas Ordway Professor and Chairholder, Hawai'i Chair of Real Estate, College of Business Administration, University of Hawai'i. Director of the Hawai'i Real Estate Research and Education Center and author of *Income Property Appraisal and Analysis* and *International Real Estate Investments*. Former National President, Real Estate Center Directors and Chairholders Association; and President, Honolulu Chapter of the American Society of Appraisers.

Noralynne K. Pinao J.D., Richardson School of Law, University of Hawai'i. Director of the Hawai'i Bar Foundation. Attorney in private practice, in the Law Offices of Amano & Pinao, concentrating on workers' compensation defense. Former prosecutor and deputy attorney general in Honolulu.

Bruce S. Plasch President, Decision Analysts Hawaii, Inc., specializing in economic development, public policy analysis, land and housing economics, market assessments, project feasibility, valuations, and economic impact analyses. Ph.D. in engineering-economic systems, Stanford University. Economic and financial consultant in Hawai'i since 1971.

Richard C. Pratt Director, Public Administration Program, and Associate Professor of Political Science, University of Hawai'i. Co-editor with Zach Smith of the recent volume *Politics and Public Policy in Hawai'i*, an anthology of essays about issues important to the future of Hawai'i.

Joanne K. Punu Assistant Dean, Richardson School of Law, University of Hawai'i. M.A. and M.B.A., University of Hawai'i. Three decades administering student services in higher education in Hawai'i, and editorial assistance on both volumes of *The Price of Paradise*.

Robert M. Rees Producer and Host of KFVE's "Island Issues," and Lecturer in Marketing and American Studies at the University of Hawai'i. M.A. in political science, University of California, and M.B.A., Columbia University. Former President, DDB Needham Worldwide Advertising, Detroit. Currently at work on a book about individualism in America.

Richard E. Rocheleau Associate Researcher, Hawai'i Natural Energy Institute, University of Hawai'i. Ph.D. in chemical engineering, University of Delaware, and M.S. in ocean engineering, University of Hawai'i; twenty years' involvement in development and commercialization of renewable energy technologies, specializing in photovoltaics and hydrogen energy systems.

Louis A. Rose Professor of Economics, University of Hawai'i. Has taught applied microeconomics and researched land and housing economics, with a focus on behavior at the interface of market and government, for more than twenty years; scholarly studies include articles in such professional journals as *Economic Inquiry*, the *Journal of Urban Economics*, and *Land Economics*.

Peter L. Rosegg Long-time editorial writer, reporter, and reviewer for the *Honolulu Advertiser*. Graduate of Columbia University, the University of Hawai'i, and the East-West Center. 1992–93 American Political Science Association Congressional Fellow.

Randall W. Roth Professor of Law, Richardson School of Law, University of Hawai'i, since 1982. Tax counsel to the Honolulu law firm Goodsill Anderson Quinn & Stifel since 1985; nationally recognized author on taxation and estate planning; former member of the Hawai'i State Tax Review Commission.

Kirk R. Smith Senior Fellow and Program Area Coordinator in Environmental Risk and Development, a World Health Organization Collaborating Centre, East-West Center. Ph.D. in biomedical and environmental health sciences, University of California. Research focuses on the changes to and management of environmental risk during economic development in Asia.

Kit Smith Financial writer for the *Honolulu Advertiser* for the past twenty-two years. Previously a business writer with *Business Week* magazine's Los Angeles bureau and with the *San Diego Union*.

A. A. "Bud" Smyser Writer and editor with the *Honolulu Star-Bulletin* since 1946. Born and educated in Pennsylvania and first came to Hawai'i as a naval officer during World War II.

Jack P. Suyderhoud Professor of Business Administration, University of Hawai'i, since 1978. Ph.D. in Economics, Purdue University. Former Executive Director, Hawai'i Tax Review Commission. Has published papers on state and local tax policy.

Ken Tucker Matson Distinguished Professor of Travel Industry Management, University of Hawai'i. Ph.D. in economics, London School of Economics. On leave from Graduate School of Management, University of Queensland. Professor of International Business and Director of Australian International Business Centre since 1987. Former Dean, David Syme Business School, Melbourne.

Charles H. Turner Freelance writer, covering Hawai'i since 1951 as wire service correspondent, labor writer, and stringer for the *New York Times* and other publications. Former mainland union officer. Charter officer, Hawai'i Newspaper Guild.

Bruce Voss Freelance journalist. Former television news reporter, covering business and labor, for KHON-TV in Honolulu; writer/assistant editor, *Hawaii Investor* magazine; financial writer, *Pacific Business News*. Currently pursuing a law degree at Richardson School of Law, University of Hawai'i.

Heidi K. Wild Director of Marketing, BHP Petroleum Refining, Inc. M.B.A, University of Hawai'i. Currently leading the Transportation Subcommittee of the State Legislature's Energy and Environmental Summit. With BHP (formerly Pacific Resources, Inc.) since 1976, predominantly in petroleum products supply and demand-balancing roles, and in marketing since 1991.

Bill Wood Former editor of *Hawaii Investor* and *Hawaii Business* magazines. Business writer for thirty-five years, the last twenty based in Hawai'i; has written for the *Wall Street Journal, Far Eastern Economic Review, The Economist, Forbes, Newsweek*, and other publications in the United States, Europe, and the Far East.

Eric Yamamoto Professor of Law, Richardson School of Law, University of Hawai'i since 1985. Has served on the Board of Directors of the Native Hawaiian Legal Corporation, the Legal Aid Society of Hawaii, and Advocates of Public Interest Law. Advisor to the Native American Advisory Council and Japanese American Citizens League, and recipient of the University of Hawai'i Presidential Citation for Excellence in Teaching (1990).

Susan Yim Freelance journalist, has spent close to twenty years working for newspapers in Hawai'i, most recently as Managing Editor for features and design with the *Honolulu Advertiser*. In her youth, she pursued graduate studies in the history and culture of China and Southeast Asia.

Corky Trinidad
Political Cartoonist
Honolulu Star-Bulletin
Award winning, nationally syndicated political cartoonist with the *Honolulu Star-Bulletin* since 1969; first cartoonist of Asian descent to break into the American cartoon journalism field; his works have appeared in newspapers nationally, including the *Washington Post*, *New York Times*, *Los Angeles Times*, *Miami Herald*, and *Philadelphia Inquirer*, as well as *Time* and *Newsweek*.

Dick Adair
Editorial Cartoonist
The Honolulu Advertiser
Winner of numerous local and national awards including the Freedoms Foundation Medal and Honor Certificate and first place 1988 "Best of the West" for editorial cartooning; author and illustrator of best-selling children's books *The Story of Aloha Bear* and *Aloha Bear and the Meaning of Aloha*; his works have appeared in *New York Times*, *Newsweek*, *Readers' Digest*, and the *Washington Post*.

309

Jim Abts
Freelance Political Cartoonist
U.S. General Accounting Office international military affairs analyst turned cartoonist/caricaturist with work appearing in *MidWeek*, *Sun Press*, *Mauian Magazine*, and *Hawai'i Business Magazine* as well as in several mainland newspapers.

John S. Pritchett
Political Cartoonist, *Honolulu Weekly*
Renegade advertising artist turned cartoonist. Coauthor of *Drawn & Quartered: Hawai'i Politics Rendered*, and author of *Pritchett: A Collection of Hawai'i Political Cartoons*; his works have appeared in national newspapers such as the *Los Angeles Times*, *Boston Globe*, *Philadelphia Inquirer*, and *Seattle Times*.

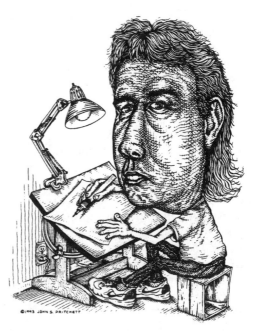

Roy Chang
Freelance Cartoonist
A featured editorial cartoonist in the *Honolulu Star-Bulletin*'s "Ribs" and an editorial cartoonist for the University of Hawai'i newspaper, *Ka Leo O Hawai'i*. Doctoral student in art education at the University of Hawai'i.

Sandy Ritz
Cartoonist
Regular cartoon contributor to Kaua'i's *Garden Island*. Her works have appeared in the *Hawaii Bar News*, the *National Nurses in Business Association Newsletter*, and the *Journal of Nursing Jocularity*. Doctoral student in public health at the University of Hawai'i.

GRAPHIC ARTISTS

Bryant Fukutomi
Honolulu Star-Bulletin

Rob Dudley
Honolulu Advertiser

Kevin Hand
Honolulu Star-Bulletin

ACKNOWLEDGMENTS

This volume is a reality because of a talented and dedicated editorial board who met every Saturday from late March through mid-August to establish guidelines, select topics and authors, evaluate and help edit drafts, plan and coordinate the graphics, and inspire others to stay on schedule. They had a wonderful knack for having fun while working hard. Their energy, wisdom, and spirit can be seen in all that is good about this book. Any weakness is likely the result of one of those rare occasions when I would deviate from their recommendations. Thank you Peter Adler, Carol Mon Lee, David McClain, Dick Pratt, Joanne Punu, Bob Rees, Jack Suyderhoud, Bill Wood, and Sue Yim. Working with you was an honor and a joy.

The authors had other important matters competing for their valuable time, yet each managed to meet every deadline. Several contended that I had raised nagging to an art form, and one labeled me the editor-from-hell, but they were just kidding . . . I think.

In our first volume, I referred to Helen Shikina as "the world's best secretary." She's that, and more. I would not have undertaken this project had Helen not been willing to help. She did the work of many, and she at least pretended to enjoy every minute of it. Helen, you're one in a million.

Our cartoonists were a delight. Once again, we had Hawai'i's longtime pros, the *Advertiser*'s Dick Adair and *Star-Bulletin*'s Corky Trinidad. Joining them in this volume are four other local talents from various rungs of the professional ladder: Jim Abts, John Pritchett, Roy Chang, and Sandy Ritz. I'm sure no editor has ever assembled a more likable or talented group.

Other graphics were created by the *Star-Bulletin*'s Kevin Hand and Bryant Fukutomi and the *Advertiser*'s Rob Dudley. I could watch those guys do their computer magic for hours on end. They are true magicians.

Jill Center is our communications adviser and the producer of public radio's "Price of Paradise" talk show. Thanks to her, just about everyone in Hawai'i knows about our efforts and a growing number tune us in each week.

Media law expert Jeff Portnoy provided wisdom as well as legal counsel. Lawyers Jim Bickerton and Greg Sato also provided sage advice and helpful background information.

Communications expert Claudia Schmidt and Department of Education educational specialist Sharon Kaohi did a super job arranging and presenting a series of workshops for DOE teachers on how best to utilize *The Price of Paradise* in their classes.

Former state statistician Bob Schmitt was his usual amazing self, providing the information we wanted, usually the day before we knew we wanted it.

Beverly Ashford, Clint Ashford, John Barkai, Henry Clark, Herb Cornuelle, Karen Gebbia, Laura Harrison, Virginia Hench, Lowell Kalapa, Kem Lowry, Norman Okamura, Miki Okumura, Cassie Roth, Susie Roth, Walter Roth, Marcia Sakai, Jane Smith, Keith Steiner, Carroll Taylor, and Eric Yamamoto provided invaluable comments and suggestions about an early version of the manuscript.

John Thomas did outstanding work copyediting the manuscript; Stuart Lillico refused to let a little thing like chemotherapy prevent him from helping me do my job; Michael Horton performed his usual wizardry turning our manuscript into an attractive, easy-to-read book; Frieda Honda, Jane Takata, and Jan Yamada went above and beyond the call of duty helping at crucial stages of the book's creation; Doc Berry's encouragement and suggestions meant more than he probably realizes; Frank Abou-Sayf came to the rescue whenever data needed to be summarized and explained; the *Star-Bulletin's* Diane Chang and the *Advertiser's* Ann Harpham were more than generous with their time and expertise; John Roth gave us a cover layout rivaling the nifty one he did last time; Tom Roth licked a zillion stamps and never complained; and many others helped in countless ways. It would take another book to give all of them the credit due.

Special mention does have to be made of publisher and now friend, Bennett Hymer. Others in the business don't believe me when I tell them about the demands I made and how he met every one. The guy is really something.

Finally, a wink and a smile for my best friend, Susie, and our wonderful crew: Cassie, Wally, John, and Tom. Aloha.

Randy Roth

INVITATION

The consensus within our ranks is that an annual *Price of Paradise* volume is in order, but only if new recruits—including an editor—can be found. Readers who believe in the guiding principles listed in the Introduction might want to send in a completed copy of this page. Those who don't agree with these particular principles should form their own group with its own guiding principles and write a book. Such a book, especially if it disagrees with positions taken in *The Price of Paradise* books, would help generate the kind of informed dialogue so essential to a functional democracy.

☐ I might be interested in contributing to the production of a future *Price of Paradise* volume in the following way(s):

_____

_____

_____

☐ I want to take issue with something I read in this book. My comments are attached. [We will do our best to respond.]

☐ I am interested in making a tax-deductible contribution toward putting copies of this book into the hands of high school seniors.

Mail to: The Price of Paradise Gang
Randall W. Roth, Editor Emeritus
2515 Dole Street
Honolulu, Hawai'i 96822

Name: _____

Address: _____

City, Zip: _____

Phone: _____